MATHEMATICS
FOR
ACTUARIAL STUDENTS

MATHEMATICS
FOR
ACTUARIAL STUDENTS

by

HARRY FREEMAN, M.A., F.I.A.

PART I
Elementary Differential & Integral Calculus

CAMBRIDGE

Published for the Institute of Actuaries

AT THE UNIVERSITY PRESS

1939

CAMBRIDGE
UNIVERSITY PRESS

University Printing House, Cambridge CB2 8BS, United Kingdom

Cambridge University Press is part of the University of Cambridge.

It furthers the University's mission by disseminating knowledge in the pursuit of education, learning and research at the highest international levels of excellence.

www.cambridge.org
Information on this title: www.cambridge.org/9781316606988

© Cambridge University Press 1939

First published 1939
First paperback edition 2016

A catalogue record for this publication is available from the British Library

ISBN 978-1-316-60698-8 Paperback

CONTENTS

DIFFERENTIAL CALCULUS

CHAPTER III
DEFINITIONS; STANDARD FORMS; SUCCESSIVE DIFFERENTIATION

CHAPTER IV
EXPANSIONS

CHAPTER V
MAXIMA AND MINIMA

CHAPTER VI
MISCELLANEOUS THEOREMS

INTEGRAL CALCULUS

CHAPTER VII
DEFINITIONS AND STANDARD FORMS

CHAPTER VIII
MORE DIFFICULT INTEGRALS: INTEGRATION BY PARTS

CHAPTER IX
DEFINITE INTEGRALS: AREAS: MISCELLANEOUS THEOREMS

INTRODUCTION

SINCE the publication in 1931 of *An Elementary Treatise on Actuarial Mathematics*, important changes have taken place in the syllabus for the examinations of the Institute of Actuaries. Algebra, Differential and Integral Calculus have been removed from Part I of the examinations and these subjects now form the mathematical section of the syllabus for the Preliminary Examination. Before a student can become a member of the Institute he must pass this examination and not until then can he become a candidate for Part I.

In the circumstances it is apparent that *An Elementary Treatise on Actuarial Mathematics* does not now satisfy present needs. The larger portion of the book is unnecessary for the Preliminary Examination and the Part I student does not require the chapters on Trigonometry and Differential and Integral Calculus.

Accordingly, the book has now been divided into two parts under the title of *Mathematics for Actuarial Students*. Part I of the book consists of the chapter on Trigonometry and the chapters on Elementary Calculus, taken with the minimum of alteration from *Actuarial Mathematics*. Part II, which is being almost entirely rewritten, will contain Finite Differences, Probability and Elementary Statistics.

H. F.

Dec. 1938

CHAPTER I

ELEMENTARY TRIGONOMETRY

1. A knowledge of trigonometrical functions is essential for the proper understanding of various formulae of the differential and integral calculus. The present chapter is therefore devoted to the development of the elementary functions and their properties. The account is short, and for the purpose of studying the functions generally recourse should be had to a recognized textbook. The chapter has been included only with the object of enabling those who have not studied trigonometry to obtain sufficient knowledge to follow the remainder of the book.

2. Definitions.

Consider a straight line X_1OX of indefinite length fixed in a plane. At a point O in the straight line is hinged another straight line OA, also of indefinite length, capable of being revolved about the hinge at O, but only in an anti-clockwise direction. Then, as OA revolves, it sweeps out an angle XOA.

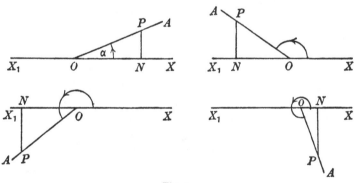

Fig. 1.

Take any point P on the moving line OA and drop a perpendicular PN on to the fixed line X_1OX. Then, by the properties of similar triangles, the ratios between the sides of the right-angled triangle PON will be the same for all positions of P, for any one

position of the line OA. These constant ratios are the trigonometrical ratios of the angle XOA, and are defined thus, where α
stands for the angle XOA:

$\dfrac{NP}{OP}$ is the sine of the angle XOA and is written sin α,

$\dfrac{ON}{OP}$ „ cosine „ „ XOA „   „   cos α,

$\dfrac{NP}{ON}$ „ tangent „ „ XOA „   „   tan α.

These are the principal ratios, and most trigonometrical problems
can be solved by the use of these three ratios only. It is often
convenient, however, to use the reciprocals of the ratios: the
respective reciprocals are

$\dfrac{OP}{NP}$, the cosecant of the angle XOA, written as cosec α,

$\dfrac{OP}{ON}$, the secant „ „ XOA, „ „ sec α,

$\dfrac{ON}{NP}$, the cotangent „ „ XOA, „ „ cot α.

3. It is important to note that, even if the two triangles PON in
the first two diagrams of Fig. 1 are geometrically equal, it does not
follow that the trigonometrical ratios of the two angles given by the
positions of OP are the same. In elementary plane geometry, the
straight line joining any two points L and M may be indifferently
denoted by LM or ML. On the other hand, the straight lines which
enter into the definitions of the trigonometrical ratios have *sign* as
well as magnitude, and the direction of the straight line determines
the sign. To ascertain the correct sign to be given to a straight line,
we proceed in the following manner. Imagine the plane in which
the fixed line has been drawn to be divided into four sections by the
straight line X_1OX and a straight line YOY_1 through O perpendicular to X_1OX.

If OP be any position of the revolving line, we can arrive at the
point P from O either by proceeding along OP or by the double
journey ON, NP. In order to develop a logical system we must
adopt a convention based on the direction to be taken to arrive at

P from O, and on the particular quadrant in which the point P lies. The convention is that lines drawn from O in the directions OX or OY are positive and that those drawn from O in the directions

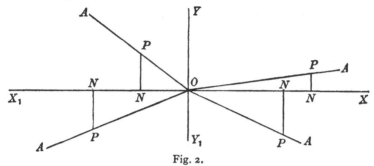

Fig. 2.

OX_1 and OY_1 are negative. The line OA is called the radius and is always to be considered as positive. The perpendicular line NP is to be regarded as drawn in the direction $N \rightarrow P$, i.e. from the line OX to the radius OA, and not from P to N.

In Fig. 2, therefore, we have

1. Quadrant XOY: ON positive and NP positive;
2. ,, X_1OY: ON negative and NP positive;
3. ,, X_1OY_1: ON negative and NP negative;
4. ,, XOY_1: ON positive and NP negative.

These quadrants are called the first, second, third and fourth quadrants respectively.

4. It is evident that the trigonometrical ratios, being derived from the ratios between ON, NP, OP, will have sign as well as magni-

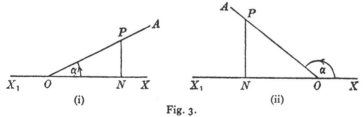

Fig. 3.

tude. For example, for the angle α in Fig. 3 (i) all the sides of the triangle ONP are positive in direction and as a result all the trigonometrical ratios of the angle will be positive.

On the other hand, in Fig. 3 (ii) we shall have

$$\sin \alpha = NP/OP \qquad \text{(positive)/(positive)} \qquad i.e. \; positive,$$
$$\cos \alpha = ON/OP \qquad \text{(negative)/(positive)} \qquad i.e. \; negative,$$
$$\tan \alpha = NP/ON \qquad \text{(positive)/(negative)} \qquad i.e. \; negative,$$

and similarly for the reciprocal ratios.

5. Negative angles.

If the revolving line be constrained to move in a *clockwise* direction, it is said to trace out a negative angle. For example, let the straight line OA_1 take up the position indicated, not by a

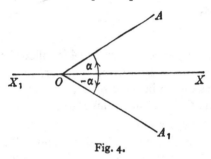

Fig. 4.

revolution passing first through the position OA, but by passing in the opposite direction direct to OA_1; then the angle XOA_1 is a negative angle.

In the figure the angle XOA is α, and the angle XOA_1 is $-\alpha$.

6. Relations between the ratios.

From the definitions of the ratios we have at once

$$\tan \alpha = NP/ON = \frac{\dfrac{NP}{OP}}{\dfrac{ON}{OP}} = \frac{\sin \alpha}{\cos \alpha} \qquad \text{......(i)}.$$

Similarly,
$$\cot \alpha = \frac{\cos \alpha}{\sin \alpha} \qquad \text{......(ii)}.$$

Again, from any of the diagrams in Fig. 1,

$$NP^2 + ON^2 = OP^2.$$
$$\therefore \; (NP/OP)^2 + (ON/OP)^2 = 1,$$

i.e.
$$(\sin \alpha)^2 \quad + (\cos \alpha)^2 \quad = 1.$$

A more convenient method of writing $(\sin \alpha)^2$, $(\cos \alpha)^2$, etc. is by omitting the brackets and denoting the squares of the ratios by $\sin^2 \alpha$, $\cos^2 \alpha$, etc. The above relation is therefore

$$\sin^2 \alpha + \cos^2 \alpha = 1 \qquad \ldots\ldots\text{(iii)}.$$

Similarly, by dividing both sides of the identity

$$ON^2 + NP^2 = OP^2$$

by ON^2 we shall have

$$1 + (NP/ON)^2 = (OP/ON)^2$$

or $\qquad 1 + \tan^2 \alpha \qquad = \sec^2 \alpha \qquad \ldots\ldots\text{(iv)}.$

Again, dividing by NP^2, we shall obtain

$$1 + \cot^2 \alpha \qquad = \operatorname{cosec}^2 \alpha \qquad \ldots\ldots\text{(v)}.$$

7. Identities.

Just as algebraic identities can be proved by the application of various fundamental rules, so the relations between the trigonometrical ratios can be applied to the proof of trigonometrical identities.

Example 1.

Prove that $\tan a + \cot a = \sec a \operatorname{cosec} a$.

$$\begin{aligned}
\tan a + \cot a &= \sin a/\cos a + \cos a/\sin a \\
&= (\sin^2 a + \cos^2 a)/\cos a \sin a \\
&= 1/\cos a \sin a \\
&= (1/\cos a)(1/\sin a) \\
&= \sec a \operatorname{cosec} a.
\end{aligned}$$

Example 2.

Prove that $\sec^2 a - \operatorname{cosec}^2 a = \tan^2 a - \cot^2 a$.

$$\begin{aligned}
\sec^2 a - \operatorname{cosec}^2 a &= (\tan^2 a + 1) - (\cot^2 a + 1) \\
&= \tan^2 a - \cot^2 a.
\end{aligned}$$

Example 3.

Prove that $\qquad \dfrac{\tan a - \tan \beta}{\cot a - \cot \beta} + \tan a \tan \beta = 0$.

Multiply through by $\cot a - \cot \beta$ and the expression becomes

$$\tan a - \tan \beta + \cot a \tan a \tan \beta - \tan a \tan \beta \cot \beta$$

or $\qquad \tan a - \tan \beta + \tan \beta - \tan a$, which is zero.

Alternatively:

$$\cot \alpha - \cot \beta = \frac{1}{\tan \alpha} - \frac{1}{\tan \beta} = -\frac{\tan \alpha - \tan \beta}{\tan \alpha \tan \beta}.$$

$$\therefore \frac{\tan \alpha - \tan \beta}{\cot \alpha - \cot \beta} = -\tan \alpha \tan \beta.$$

8. Magnitude of angles. Degrees.

The unit angle in elementary geometry is the *degree*. An angle of x degrees is denoted by $x°$. The degree is defined as the angle subtended at the centre of a circle by an arc equal in length to $1/360$ of the circumference. For arithmetical calculation the degree is a convenient unit, and we can obtain the values of the trigonometrical ratios of many angles by reference to simple geometrical figures.

Example 4.

Find the sine, cosine and tangent of (i) $45°$, (ii) $30°$, (iii) $60°$.

(i) Let ONP be an isosceles triangle, right-angled at N, so that $ON = NP$. Then, if ON be of unit length,

$$OP^2 = ON^2 + NP^2 = 1 + 1 = 2,$$

so that $OP = \sqrt{2}$.

Therefore, easily,

$$\sin 45° = 1/\sqrt{2}, \quad \cos 45° = 1/\sqrt{2}, \quad \tan 45° = 1.$$

(ii) Take the angle XOA to be $30°$. Then the angle NPO is $60°$ and the figure ONP is one-half of an equilateral triangle of side equal in length to OP.

If, therefore, NP be of unit length, $OP = 2$ and $ON = \sqrt{3}$, so that

$$\sin 30° = \tfrac{1}{2}, \quad \cos 30° = \sqrt{3}/2,$$

$$\tan 30° = 1/\sqrt{3}.$$

(iii) From a consideration of the above figure it is evident that

$$\sin 60° = \sqrt{3}/2, \quad \cos 60° = \tfrac{1}{2}, \quad \tan 60° = \sqrt{3}.$$

9. Magnitude of angles. Radians.

A more convenient unit for analytical purposes is the angle subtended at the centre of a circle by an arc equal in length to the radius: this angle is called a *radian*. Since the ratio between the angle at the centre and the arc on which it stands is constant for all circles, it follows that the radian is the same whatever the radius of the circle: the radian may therefore be taken as a unit of measurement.

To obtain the number of radians corresponding to the number of degrees in an angle, all that is necessary is to multiply the number of degrees by $\frac{\pi}{180}$. This is easily seen to be so, for if x be the number of degrees corresponding to a radian, we have

$$\frac{\text{angle subtended by the arc equal in length to the radius}}{\text{angle subtended by half the circumference}} = \frac{\text{radian}}{180°}$$

i.e. $\qquad r/\pi r = x/180$,

so that $\qquad x = 180/\pi$, or π radians $= 180°$.

In applying the calculus to trigonometrical functions it is essential that angles should be expressed in terms of an absolute unit of measurement. Consequently, in all the work that follows, unless otherwise stated, angles must be taken to be measured in radians.

10. Periodicity of the trigonometrical ratios.

If we consider the definitions of the ratios, taking into account the signs as well as the magnitudes, it can easily be shown that there will be more than one angle having the same particular ratio. To take a simple example: in the following figure, let the radius

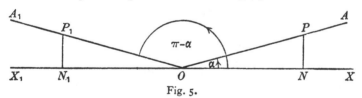

Fig. 5.

take up the positions OA and OA_1, where the angle XOA is the angle α and the angle XOA_1 is the supplement of XOA, i.e. $\pi - \alpha$.

Then, attending to the directions of the lines involved, we shall have

$$\sin \alpha = NP/OP = N_1P_1/OP_1 \quad = + \sin (\pi - \alpha),$$
$$\cos \alpha = ON/OP = - ON_1/OP_1 = - \cos (\pi - \alpha),$$
and $\qquad \tan \alpha = NP/ON = N_1P_1/- ON_1 = - \tan (\pi - \alpha).$

Again, from the figure it can be shown similarly that

$$\sin \alpha = -\sin (\pi + \alpha) = -\sin (2\pi - \alpha),$$
$$\cos \alpha = -\cos (\pi + \alpha) = +\cos (2\pi - \alpha),$$
$$\tan \alpha = +\tan (\pi + \alpha) = -\tan (2\pi - \alpha).$$

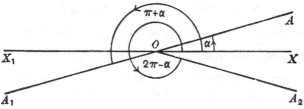

Fig. 6.

If now the radius make a complete revolution, so that, starting from the position OX it takes up the position OA after first tracing out the angle 2π, then it is evident that $\sin \alpha = \sin (2\pi + \alpha)$; $\cos \alpha = \cos (2\pi + \alpha)$; $\tan \alpha = \tan (2\pi + \alpha)$.

We have, therefore, that

$$\sin \alpha = \sin (\pi - \alpha) = \sin (2\pi + \alpha) = \sin (3\pi - \alpha) = \ldots\ldots,$$
$$\cos \alpha = \cos (2\pi - \alpha) = \cos (2\pi + \alpha) = \cos (4\pi - \alpha) = \ldots\ldots,$$
$$\tan \alpha = \tan (\pi + \alpha) = \tan (2\pi + \alpha) = \tan (3\pi + \alpha) = \ldots\ldots$$

These relations may be generalised in the forms:
all angles having the same sine as α are the values of $n\pi + (-1)^n \alpha$,

,,	,,	cosine	,,	,,	$2n\pi \pm \alpha$,
,,	,,	tangent	,,	,,	$n\pi + \alpha$,

where n is a positive integer.

For example, it has been proved above that $\sin 30° = \frac{1}{2}$. In absolute measure this is $\sin \pi/6 = \frac{1}{2}$, so that all angles whose sine is $\frac{1}{2}$ are the successive values of $\{n\pi + (-1)^n \pi/6\}$, i.e. $\pi/6$, $5\pi/6$, $13\pi/6$, $17\pi/6$, and so on.

It will be seen that if we replace n by $2m$, so that only even values of the positive integers are taken into account, the general angle for $\sin \alpha$ is $2m\pi + \alpha$; this brings the property of the sine into line with those of the other ratios. For all the trigonometrical functions, therefore, we may say that

$$f(x + 2m\pi) = f(x).$$

If a function have this property it is said to be a *periodic function* with period 2π.

A graphical representation (Fig. 7) shows quite clearly the periodic property of the sine, cosine and tangent.

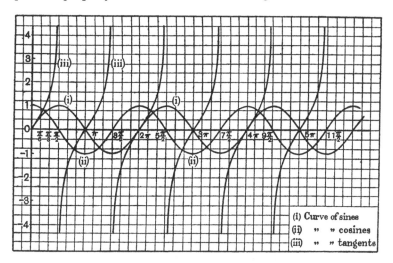

Fig. 7.

Notes: (i) The tangent and cotangent are periodic with period π.

(ii) It can be shown quite easily by the consideration of a diagram similar to Fig. 6 that the generalised forms hold equally for negative integral values of n.

11. Ratios of ($\tfrac{1}{2}\pi \pm a$).

(i) If in Fig. 8 the angles XOP and XOP_1 are a and $\tfrac{1}{2}\pi - a$ respectively, and we make $OP_1 = OP$, then by considering the geometry of the two triangles ONP and ON_1P_1 it is easily seen that

$$ON/OP = N_1P_1/OP_1,$$
$$NP/OP = ON_1/OP_1,$$
$$NP/ON = ON_1/N_1P_1;$$

so that

$$\cos a = \sin (\tfrac{1}{2}\pi - a),$$
$$\sin a = \cos (\tfrac{1}{2}\pi - a),$$
$$\tan a = \cot (\tfrac{1}{2}\pi - a).$$

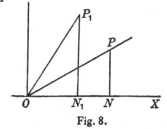

Fig. 8.

Similarly, $\cot \alpha = \tan \left(\tfrac{1}{2}\pi - \alpha\right)$ and $\operatorname{cosec} \alpha = \sec \left(\tfrac{1}{2}\pi - \alpha\right)$.

The angles α and $\tfrac{1}{2}\pi - \alpha$ are called *complementary* angles, the "co" in cosine, cotangent and cosecant corresponding to the *complementary* angle.

(ii) If the angle $XOP_1 = \tfrac{1}{2}\pi + \alpha$ as in Fig. 9

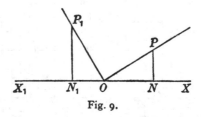

Fig. 9.

we shall have $ON/OP = N_1P_1/OP_1$, $\therefore \cos \alpha = \sin \left(\tfrac{1}{2}\pi + \alpha\right)$;

also $NP/OP = -ON_1/OP_1$, $\therefore \sin \alpha = -\cos \left(\tfrac{1}{2}\pi + \alpha\right)$;

and $\tan \alpha = -\cot \left(\tfrac{1}{2}\pi + \alpha\right)$.

(iii) When the angle XOP is so small that ON and OP coincide,

$$\sin 0 = 0,\ \cos 0 = 1,\ \tan 0 = 0;$$

and from the above

$$\sin \tfrac{1}{2}\pi = \cos 0 = 1,\ \cos \tfrac{1}{2}\pi = \sin 0 = 0,\ \tan \tfrac{1}{2}\pi = \infty.$$

12. Inverse functions.

From the identity $\sin \pi/6 = \tfrac{1}{2}$ we can obtain the inverse relation, namely, that $\pi/6$ is the angle whose sine is $\tfrac{1}{2}$. The notation adopted for this is

$$\sin^{-1} \tfrac{1}{2} = \pi/6.$$

This inverse notation is not to be confused with the algebraic notation for negative indices. Although a^{-1} is equivalent to $1/a$, $\sin^{-1} x$ is not $1/\sin x$, but the angle whose sine is x. We have generally from the above, that if $\sin \alpha = x$, then

$$\sin^{-1} x = n\pi + (-1)^n \alpha.$$

As a general rule it is convenient to take the inverse function as the numerically smallest angle (with the proper sign) giving the required value of the direct function.

Example 5.

Write down (i) the smallest positive angle, (ii) the general formula for the angle x, given that $x = \cos^{-1} o + \cos^{-1} \sqrt{3}/2 + \cos^{-1} 1/\sqrt{2}$.

$$\cos \tfrac{1}{2}\pi = o, \qquad \therefore \cos^{-1} o = \tfrac{1}{2}\pi;$$
$$\cos \pi/6 = \sqrt{3}/2, \quad \therefore \cos^{-1} \sqrt{3}/2 = \pi/6;$$
$$\cos \pi/4 = 1/\sqrt{2}, \quad \therefore \cos^{-1} 1/\sqrt{2} = \pi/4.$$

Therefore $x = \tfrac{1}{2}\pi + \pi/6 + \pi/4 = 11\,\pi/12$, which is the smallest positive angle. The general angle is $2n\pi \pm 11\pi/12$.

13. Projection.

If from the extremities of a straight line AB perpendiculars be dropped on to another straight line LM, produced if necessary,

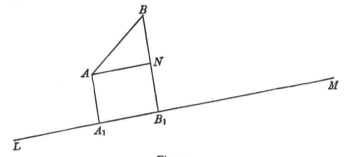

Fig. 10.

the part intercepted on LM by the feet of the perpendiculars is called the *projection* of AB on LM.

In Fig. 10 A_1B_1 is the projection of AB and B_1A_1 is the projection of BA. If AN be drawn through A parallel to LM, then $A_1B_1 = AN$. Call the angle NAB β; then $AN/AB = \cos \beta$, so that

$$A_1B_1 = AN = AB \cos \beta.$$

In other words, the projection of the line AB on the line LM is $AB \cos \beta$, where β is the angle between the lines AB and LM, both produced if necessary. As in para. 3, the lines are supposed to have signs according to the direction in which they are drawn: thus $BA = -AB$ and so on.

The following proposition is important.

The sum of the projections of the sides of a triangle XYZ, taken in order, on any straight line in the same plane, is zero.

The projection of XY is LM,

              ,, YZ is MN,

              ,, ZX is NL,

so that the sum of the projections of XY, YZ, ZX is

$$LM + MN + NL = 0.$$

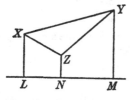 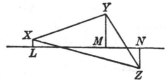

Fig. 11.

As a corollary to this, we have at once that the sum of the projections of XY and YZ = the projection of XZ. For, denoting the projection of XY by (XY), etc.,

$$(XY) + (YZ) + (ZX) = 0,$$

i.e. $(XY) + (YZ) \qquad = -(ZX) = (XZ).$

It is easily seen that if $ABCD...K$ be any closed figure, the sum of the projections of the sides AB, BC, CD, ... taken in order on any straight line in the same plane is zero.

14. The addition theorems.

Let the revolving line sweep out the angle α by taking up the position OA, and subsequently the angle β by the new position OB.

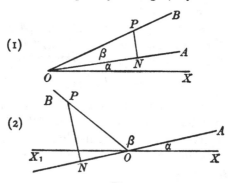

Fig. 12.

Drop a perpendicular PN from any point P in OB on to OA. Project the sides of the triangle ONP on to OX.

$(1)\ (OP) = (ON) + (NP)$

$\qquad = ON \cos \alpha + NP \cos (\tfrac{1}{2}\pi + \alpha)$

$\qquad = ON \cos \alpha - NP \sin \alpha.$

$\therefore OP \cos (\alpha + \beta) = OP \cos \beta \cos \alpha - OP \sin \beta \sin \alpha.$

$(2)\ (OP) = (ON) + (NP)$

$\qquad = ON \cos (\pi + \alpha) + NP \cos (\tfrac{1}{2}\pi + \alpha)$

$\qquad = ON (- \cos \alpha) - NP \sin \alpha.$

$\therefore OP \cos (\alpha + \beta) = OP \cos (\pi - \beta) (- \cos \alpha) - OP \sin (\pi - \beta) \sin \alpha$

$\qquad = OP \cos \beta \cos \alpha - OP \sin \beta \sin \alpha.$

Therefore in both cases we have that

$$\cos (\alpha + \beta) = \cos \alpha \cos \beta - \sin \alpha \sin \beta \qquad \ldots\ldots\text{(vi)}.$$

By changing the sign of β,

$$\cos (\alpha - \beta) = \cos \alpha \cos \beta + \sin \alpha \sin \beta \qquad \ldots\ldots\text{(vii)},$$

since it can be shown easily from the relations in para. 10 that $\cos (- \beta) = \cos \beta$, and that $\sin (- \beta) = - \sin \beta$.

Again, by changing α to $\tfrac{1}{2}\pi + \alpha$ in (vi),

$$\cos (\tfrac{1}{2}\pi + \alpha + \beta) = \cos (\tfrac{1}{2}\pi + \alpha) \cos \beta - \sin (\tfrac{1}{2}\pi + \alpha) \sin \beta,$$

i.e. $\qquad \sin (\alpha + \beta) = \sin \alpha \cos \beta + \cos \alpha \sin \beta \qquad \ldots\ldots\text{(viii)},$

and, by writing $- \beta$ for β in (viii),

$$\sin (\alpha - \beta) = \sin \alpha \cos \beta - \cos \alpha \sin \beta \qquad \ldots\ldots\text{(ix)}.$$

The corresponding formulae for the tangents of the compound angles may be obtained thus:

$$\tan (\alpha + \beta) = \frac{\sin (\alpha + \beta)}{\cos (\alpha + \beta)} = \frac{\sin \alpha \cos \beta + \cos \alpha \sin \beta}{\cos \alpha \cos \beta - \sin \alpha \sin \beta}$$

$$= \frac{\dfrac{\sin \alpha \cos \beta}{\cos \alpha \cos \beta} + \dfrac{\cos \alpha \sin \beta}{\cos \alpha \cos \beta}}{\dfrac{\cos \alpha \cos \beta}{\cos \alpha \cos \beta} - \dfrac{\sin \alpha \sin \beta}{\cos \alpha \cos \beta}} = \frac{\tan \alpha + \tan \beta}{1 - \tan \alpha \tan \beta} \qquad \ldots\ldots\text{(x)},$$

and similarly $\tan (\alpha - \beta) \qquad = \dfrac{\tan \alpha - \tan \beta}{1 + \tan \alpha \tan \beta} \qquad \ldots\ldots\text{(xi)}.$

Note. We have proved the addition theorems for the following ranges of angles: (1) $\alpha + \beta < \tfrac{1}{2}\pi$; (2) $\alpha < \tfrac{1}{2}\pi$ and $\tfrac{1}{2}\pi < \beta < \pi$. The method of projection can be applied in a similar manner to prove the theorems for angles of any magnitude.

15. Sum and Difference formulae.

We have

$$\sin(\alpha + \beta) = \sin\alpha\cos\beta + \cos\alpha\sin\beta,$$
$$\sin(\alpha - \beta) = \sin\alpha\cos\beta - \cos\alpha\sin\beta;$$

therefore, by addition,

$$\sin(\alpha + \beta) + \sin(\alpha - \beta) = 2\sin\alpha\cos\beta.$$

Let $\alpha + \beta = \gamma$ and $\alpha - \beta = \delta$.

Then $\sin\gamma + \sin\delta = 2\sin\frac{1}{2}(\gamma + \delta)\cos\frac{1}{2}(\gamma - \delta)$ ......(xii).

By subtraction, we have, similarly,

$$\sin\gamma - \sin\delta = 2\cos\tfrac{1}{2}(\gamma + \delta)\sin\tfrac{1}{2}(\gamma - \delta) \quad ......\text{(xiii)}.$$

From formulae (vi) and (vii) it can be shown in the same manner that

$$\cos\gamma + \cos\delta = 2\cos\tfrac{1}{2}(\gamma + \delta)\cos\tfrac{1}{2}(\gamma - \delta) \quad ......\text{(xiv)},$$
$$\cos\gamma - \cos\delta = 2\sin\tfrac{1}{2}(\gamma + \delta)\sin\tfrac{1}{2}(\delta - \gamma)$$
$$= -2\sin\tfrac{1}{2}(\gamma + \delta)\sin\tfrac{1}{2}(\gamma - \delta)......\text{(xv)}.$$

These formulae can be proved by projection on the same lines as those adopted for the proofs of the addition formulae.

16. Double angles and half angles.

From formula (vi) we have, by putting $\beta = \alpha$,

$$\cos 2\alpha = \cos^2\alpha - \sin^2\alpha,$$

or, since $\cos^2\alpha + \sin^2\alpha = 1$,

$$\cos 2\alpha = 2\cos^2\alpha - 1 = 1 - 2\sin^2\alpha \quad ......\text{(xvi)}.$$

Again, from the formula for $\sin(\alpha + \beta)$, putting $\alpha = \beta$,

$$\sin 2\alpha = 2\sin\alpha\cos\alpha \quad ......\text{(xvii)}.$$

The tangent formula (x) gives

$$\tan 2\alpha = 2\tan\alpha/(1 - \tan^2\alpha) \quad ......\text{(xviii)}.$$

By replacing 2α by α convenient formulae in terms of half angles can at once be obtained, thus:

$$\sin\alpha = 2\sin\tfrac{1}{2}\alpha\cos\tfrac{1}{2}\alpha,$$
$$1 = \cos^2\tfrac{1}{2}\alpha + \sin^2\tfrac{1}{2}\alpha;$$

$$\therefore \sin \alpha = \frac{2 \sin \tfrac{1}{2}\alpha \cos \tfrac{1}{2}\alpha}{\cos^2 \tfrac{1}{2}\alpha + \sin^2 \tfrac{1}{2}\alpha}$$

$$= \frac{\dfrac{2 \sin \tfrac{1}{2}\alpha \cos \tfrac{1}{2}\alpha}{\cos^2 \tfrac{1}{2}\alpha}}{\dfrac{\cos^2 \tfrac{1}{2}\alpha}{\cos^2 \tfrac{1}{2}\alpha} + \dfrac{\sin^2 \tfrac{1}{2}\alpha}{\cos^2 \tfrac{1}{2}\alpha}}$$

$$= \frac{2 \tan \tfrac{1}{2}\alpha}{1 + \tan^2 \tfrac{1}{2}\alpha} \qquad \qquad \dots \dots (\text{xix}).$$

Similarly
$$\cos \alpha = \frac{1 - \tan^2 \tfrac{1}{2}\alpha}{1 + \tan^2 \tfrac{1}{2}\alpha} \qquad \dots \dots (\text{xx}),$$

and, by division,
$$\tan \alpha = \frac{2 \tan \tfrac{1}{2}\alpha}{1 - \tan^2 \tfrac{1}{2}\alpha} \qquad \dots \dots (\text{xxi}).$$

17. Examples.

Some examples illustrative of the use of the above formulae for the proving of identities and for the solution of trigonometrical equations are given below.

Example 6.

Prove that
$$\frac{\sin 5\alpha + \sin \alpha}{\sin 3\alpha - \sin \alpha} = 1 + 2 \cos 2\alpha.$$

$$\frac{\sin 5\alpha + \sin \alpha}{\sin 3\alpha - \sin \alpha} = \frac{2 \sin \tfrac{1}{2}(5\alpha + \alpha) \cos \tfrac{1}{2}(5\alpha - \alpha)}{2 \cos \tfrac{1}{2}(3\alpha + \alpha) \sin \tfrac{1}{2}(3\alpha - \alpha)}$$

$$= \frac{2 \sin 3\alpha \cos 2\alpha}{2 \cos 2\alpha \sin \alpha} = \frac{\sin 3\alpha}{\sin \alpha}.$$

But $\sin 3\alpha = \sin(2\alpha + \alpha) = \sin 2\alpha \cos \alpha + \cos 2\alpha \sin \alpha$

$$= 2 \sin \alpha \cos^2 \alpha + (1 - 2 \sin^2\alpha) \sin \alpha$$

$$= 2 \sin \alpha (1 - \sin^2\alpha) + (1 - 2 \sin^2\alpha) \sin \alpha$$

$$= 3 \sin \alpha - 4 \sin^3 \alpha.$$

$$\therefore \sin 3\alpha / \sin \alpha = 3 - 4 \sin^2\alpha = 3 + 2(1 - 2 \sin^2\alpha) - 2$$

$$= 1 + 2 \cos 2\alpha.$$

Example 7.

If $\cos \alpha + \cos \beta + \cos \gamma + \cos \alpha \cos \beta \cos \gamma = 0,$

prove that $\tan \tfrac{1}{2}\alpha \tan \tfrac{1}{2}\beta \tan \tfrac{1}{2}\gamma = \pm 1.$

Now
$$\cos \alpha = \frac{1 - \tan^2 \tfrac{1}{2}\alpha}{1 + \tan^2 \tfrac{1}{2}\alpha}.$$

Let $\tan \tfrac{1}{2}\alpha = a, \ \tan \tfrac{1}{2}\beta = b, \ \tan \tfrac{1}{2}\gamma = c.$

Then the condition that

$$\cos \alpha + \cos \beta + \cos \gamma + \cos \alpha \cos \beta \cos \gamma = 0$$

is the same condition as

$$\frac{1 - a^2}{1 + a^2} + \frac{1 - b^2}{1 + b^2} + \frac{1 - c^2}{1 + c^2} + \frac{(1 - a^2)(1 - b^2)(1 - c^2)}{(1 + a^2)(1 + b^2)(1 + c^2)} = 0.$$

By a simple algebraic transformation this becomes

$$\frac{4(1 - a^2 b^2 c^2)}{(1 + a^2)(1 + b^2)(1 + c^2)} = 0,$$

i.e. $$1 - a^2 b^2 c^2 = 0,$$

$$a^2 b^2 c^2 = 1,$$

or $$abc = \pm 1;$$

i.e. $$\tan \tfrac{1}{2}\alpha \tan \tfrac{1}{2}\beta \tan \tfrac{1}{2}\gamma = \pm 1,$$

which proves the proposition.

Example 8.

Prove that, if $\alpha + \beta + \gamma = \pi$, then

$$\frac{1 - \cos \alpha + \cos \beta + \cos \gamma}{1 - \cos \beta + \cos \gamma + \cos \alpha} = \frac{\tan \tfrac{1}{2}\alpha}{\tan \tfrac{1}{2}\beta}.$$

If $\alpha + \beta + \gamma = \pi$, then $\tfrac{1}{2}\alpha = \tfrac{1}{2}\pi - \tfrac{1}{2}(\beta + \gamma)$, so that

$$\sin \tfrac{1}{2}\alpha = \cos \tfrac{1}{2}(\beta + \gamma) \quad \text{and} \quad \cos \tfrac{1}{2}\alpha = \sin \tfrac{1}{2}(\beta + \gamma).$$

$$\frac{(1 - \cos \alpha) + (\cos \beta + \cos \gamma)}{(1 + \cos \alpha) + (\cos \gamma - \cos \beta)} = \frac{2\sin^2 \tfrac{1}{2}\alpha + 2\cos \tfrac{1}{2}(\beta + \gamma)\cos \tfrac{1}{2}(\beta - \gamma)}{2\cos^2 \tfrac{1}{2}\alpha - 2\sin \tfrac{1}{2}(\beta + \gamma)\sin \tfrac{1}{2}(\gamma - \beta)}$$

Substituting for $\sin \tfrac{1}{2}\alpha$ and $\cos \tfrac{1}{2}\alpha$ as above, and dividing through by

$\dfrac{\cos \tfrac{1}{2}(\beta + \gamma)}{\sin \tfrac{1}{2}(\beta + \gamma)}$, i.e. by $\cot \tfrac{1}{2}(\beta + \gamma)$ or $\tan \tfrac{1}{2}\alpha$, we obtain

$$\cot \tfrac{1}{2}(\beta + \gamma)\frac{\cos \tfrac{1}{2}(\beta + \gamma) + \cos \tfrac{1}{2}(\beta - \gamma)}{\sin \tfrac{1}{2}(\beta + \gamma) + \sin \tfrac{1}{2}(\beta - \gamma)}$$

$$= \tan \tfrac{1}{2}\alpha \frac{2\cos \tfrac{1}{2}\gamma \cos \tfrac{1}{2}\beta}{2\cos \tfrac{1}{2}\gamma \sin \tfrac{1}{2}\beta} = \frac{\tan \tfrac{1}{2}\alpha}{\tan \tfrac{1}{2}\beta}.$$

Example 9.

Solve the equation $\sin 9x + \sin 5x + 2\sin^2 x = 1$.

$$\sin 9x + \sin 5x = 1 - 2\sin^2 x$$

$$= \cos 2x,$$

i.e. $$2\sin 7x \cos 2x = \cos 2x;$$

therefore, either $$\cos 2x = 0 \qquad \qquad \dots\dots(a),$$

or $$\sin 7x = \tfrac{1}{2} \qquad \qquad \dots\dots(b).$$

From (a) $\qquad 2x = \tfrac{1}{2}\pi,$

or $\qquad\qquad x = \pi/4$ and generally $x = \tfrac{1}{2}\left(2n \pm \tfrac{1}{2}\right)\pi,$

and from (b) $\qquad 7x = \pi/6,$

or $\qquad\qquad x = \pi/42 \qquad ,, \qquad x = \tfrac{1}{7}\left[n + (-\ \mathrm{I})^n\,\tfrac{1}{6}\right]\pi.$

Example 10.

Express the function $A\cos\gamma + B\sin\gamma$ in terms of a single function of a single angle.

Let $A = r\cos\delta$, and $B = r\sin\delta$.

Then, since $\cos^2\delta + \sin^2\delta = 1$, we have $A^2 + B^2 = r^2$,

and, by division, $\qquad\qquad \tan\delta = B/A,$

i.e. $\qquad\qquad\qquad \delta = \tan^{-1}(B/A).$

We may write, therefore,

$$A\cos\gamma + B\sin\gamma = r\cos\gamma\cos\delta + r\sin\gamma\sin\delta = r\cos(\gamma - \delta),$$

where $\qquad\qquad\qquad r = \pm\ \sqrt{A^2 + B^2}.$

Similarly $\qquad A\cos\gamma - B\sin\gamma = r\cos(\gamma + \delta).$

Example 11.

To expand $\cos nx$ in an ascending series of powers of $\cos x$ and $\sin x$, where n is a positive integer.

Now, $\cos 2x = \cos^2 x - \sin^2 x,$

$$\begin{aligned}
\cos 3x &= 4\cos^3 x - 3\cos x \\
&= \cos^3 x + 3\cos^3 x - 3\cos x \\
&= \cos^3 x - 3\cos x\,(1 - \cos^2 x) \\
&= \cos^3 x - 3\cos x\sin^2 x = \cos^3 x - \frac{3\cdot 2}{2!}\cos x\sin^2 x,
\end{aligned}$$

$$\begin{aligned}
\cos 4x &= \cos^2 2x - \sin^2 2x \\
&= \cos^4 x - 2\cos^2 x\sin^2 x + \sin^4 x - 4\sin^2 x\cos^2 x \\
&= \cos^4 x - 6\cos^2 x\sin^2 x + \sin^4 x \\
&= \cos^4 x - \frac{4\cdot 3}{2!}\cos^2 x\sin^2 x + \frac{4\cdot 3\cdot 2}{4!}\sin^4 x.
\end{aligned}$$

This suggests the general form

$$\cos nx = \cos^n x - n_{(2)}\cos^{n-2} x\sin^2 x + n_{(4)}\cos^{n-4} x\sin^4 x - \dots$$
$$+ (-\ \mathrm{I})^m n_{(2m)}\cos^{n-2m} x\sin^{2m} x + \dots,$$

where $n_{(r)}$ stands for $\dfrac{1}{r!}\,n\,(n-1)\,\dots\,(n-r+1).$

Similarly, by expressing $\sin 2x$, $\sin 3x$ and $\sin 4x$ in terms of powers of $\cos x$ and $\sin x$, the general form for $\sin nx$ would appear to be

$$\sin nx = n_{(1)}\cos^{n-1} x\sin x - n_{(3)}\cos^{n-3} x\sin^3 x + \dots$$
$$+ (-\ \mathrm{I})^{m-1} n_{(2m-1)}\cos^{n-(2m-1)} x\sin^{2m-1} x + \dots.$$

Assume these two formulae true for the positive integral value n. Then

$$\cos(n+1)\,x = \cos nx \cos x - \sin nx \sin x$$
$$= \cos x\,(\cos^n x - n_{(2)} \cos^{n-2} x \sin^2 x + \ldots)$$
$$- \sin x\,(n_{(1)} \cos^{n-1} x \sin x - n_{(3)} \cos^{n-3} x \sin^3 x + \ldots),$$

where the coefficient of $\cos^{n-2m+1} x \sin^{2m} x$ is $(-1)^m\,(n_{(2m)} + n_{(2m-1)})$, which is $(-1)^m\,(n+1)_{(2m)}$.

Similarly for $\sin(n+1)\,x$.

If, therefore, the series are true for n they are true for $n+1$. But they are true for 2, 3, 4, ...; therefore they are true for 5, 6, ... and for any positive integer.

EXAMPLES 1

1. Write down the sine, cosine and tangent of the following angles:
$$150°, \qquad 135°, \qquad 750°, \qquad 210°.$$

2. Express the angles in the above question in radian measure.

3. Explain carefully why the following relations are impossible:
 (a) $\sin A = 1\cdot2$; (b) $\sin^2 A = 2 - \cos^2 A$;
 (c) $\sin A = \cdot8$ and $\cos A = \cdot7$; (d) $\tan A = \cdot8$ and $\sec A = \cdot9$;
 (e) $\sin A = \cdot5$, $\cos A = \cdot4$ and $\tan A = \cdot6$.

4. Give in radians the smallest positive angle satisfying the equations:
 (a) $\sin x = \frac{1}{2}$; (b) $\sin \frac{1}{2}x = \sqrt{3}/2$;
 (c) $\tan 4x = 1$; (d) $\operatorname{cosec} x = \sqrt{2}$;
 (e) $\cos 8x = 1$.

5. Determine $\operatorname{cosec} \beta$:
 (a) $\sec \beta = 8$; (b) $\cos \beta = \cdot108$; (c) $\tan \beta = \cdot501$.

6. Prove the identities:
 (i) $\sin^4 a - \sin^2 a = \cos^4 a - \cos^2 a$;
 (ii) $\cos^2 a - \sin^2 a = 2 \cos^2 a - 1 = 1 - 2 \sin^2 a$;
 (iii) $\sin^3 a - \cos^3 a = (1 + \sin a \cos a)(\sin a - \cos a)$;
 (iv) $\sin \gamma \cos \gamma = \tan \gamma / (1 + \tan^2 \gamma)$;
 (v) $\sin^2 \beta \tan^2 \beta + \sin^2 \beta = \tan^2 \beta$;
 (vi) $(\tan A - \tan B) \cos A \cos B = \sin A \cos B - \cos A \sin B$;
 (vii) $\cos^2 \beta\,(3 - \tan^2 \beta) = 3 - 4 \sin^2 \beta$;
 (viii) $\dfrac{\cos^2 \beta - \sin^2 \gamma}{\sin^2 \beta \sin^2 \gamma} = \dfrac{1 - \tan^2 \beta \tan^2 \gamma}{\tan^2 \beta \tan^2 \gamma}$;
 (ix) $2 \cos A - \sec A = (\cos A - \sin A)(1 + \tan A)$;
 (x) $(\sec \beta + \tan \beta)(\operatorname{cosec} \beta - \cot \beta) = (\sec \beta - 1)(\operatorname{cosec} \beta + 1)$.

7. Write down the complete solutions of the following equations:

    (i) $\sin x = 1/\sqrt{2}$;   (ii) $\sec x = 2$;

    (iii) $\tan x = -1/\sqrt{3}$;   (iv) $\cos\left(\frac{1}{4}\pi + \theta\right) = 0$;

    (v) $\sin\theta = \cos\theta$.

8. Complete the identities:

    (i) $\sin^{-1}\frac{1}{2} + \sin^{-1}\sqrt{3}/2 =$ (ii) $\cos^{-1} 0 + \cos^{-1} 1 =$

    (iii) $\tan^{-1}\sqrt{3} + \tan^{-1} 1/\sqrt{3} =$

    (iv) $\sin^{-1}(-1) + \cos^{-1} 0 =$ (v) $\cos^{-1}\frac{1}{2} + 2\sin^{-1}\frac{1}{2} =$

    (vi) $\cot^{-1}\infty + \tan^{-1} 1 =$

    (vii) $\cos^{-1}\left(-\frac{1}{2}\right) + 4\sec^{-1}\left(-2/\sqrt{3}\right) =$

  (viii) $\sin^{-1}(-1) + \sin^{-1}\left(-\frac{1}{2}\right) =$

    (ix) $\sec^{-1} 2 + \sec^{-1}(-2) + \sec^{-1}(-1) =$

    (x) $3\operatorname{cosec}^{-1} 2 + \operatorname{cosec}^{-1}(-2) + \operatorname{cosec}^{-1}(-1) =$

9. Solve the equations:

    (i) $\cos 4x = \sin 5x$;   (ii) $\sin x = \cos 10x$;

    (iii) $\tan x = \cot\left(\frac{1}{4}\pi + x\right)$;   (iv) $\operatorname{cosec} x = \sec(3\pi - 2x)$;

    (v) $\sin(n\pi - 3x) = \cos(2n\pi - 4x)$.

10. Write down, in terms of ratios of the angle θ alone,

$\sin(3\pi/2 + \theta)$; $\cos(3\pi/2 - \theta)$; $\tan(5\pi - \theta)$; $\cot(5\pi/2 - \theta)$;

 $\operatorname{cosec}(2\pi + \theta)$; $\sec(7\pi/2 + \theta)$; $\cot(-\theta)$; $\sin(-3\pi - \theta)$;

$$\cos\left(-\tfrac{1}{2}\pi + \theta\right).$$

11. Show that

        (i) given $A = \sin^{-1} 3/5$, $\cos A = 4/5$;

        (ii) ,, $B = \cos^{-1} 12/13$, $\sin B = 5/13$;

      (iii) ,, $C = \sin^{-1} 8/17$, $\cos C = 15/17$;

      (iv) ,, $D = \tan^{-1}\frac{1}{2}$, $\sin D = 1/\sqrt{5}$.

12. Find the values of

 $\sin(A + B)$ where $A = \sin^{-1} 3/5$ and $B = \cos^{-1} 12/13$;

 $\cos(A + B)$,, $A = \cos^{-1} 3/5$ $B = \sin^{-1} 8/17$;

 $\sin(A - B)$,, $A = \sin^{-1} 12/13$ $B = \sin^{-1} 1/\sqrt{5}$;

 $\cos(A - B)$,, $A = \sin^{-1} 5/13$ $B = \tan^{-1}\frac{1}{2}$;

 $\sin 2A$,, $A = \sin^{-1} 15/17$;

 $\cos 2A$,, $A = \cot^{-1} 2$;

 $\tan(A + B)$,, $A = \sec^{-1} 5/4$ $B = \cot^{-1} 12/5$;

 $\tan(A - B)$,, $A = \sin^{-1} 3/5$ $B = \operatorname{cosec}^{-1}\sqrt{5}$;

 $\tan 2A$,, $A = \sin^{-1} \cdot 83$;

 $\cot(A - B)$,, $A = \cos^{-1} \cdot 7$ $B = \sec^{-1} 3$.

Prove the following identities:

13. $\sin (A - B) \cos B + \cos (A - B) \sin B = \sin A$;

14. $\dfrac{\tan (A + B) - \tan A}{1 + \tan (A + B) \tan A} = \tan B$;

15. $\sin 3a = 3 \sin a - 4 \sin^3 a$;

16. $\tan 3a (1 - 3 \tan^2 a) = 3 \tan a - \tan^3 a$;

17. $\sin \pi/6 + \sin \pi/3 = 2 \sin \frac{1}{4}\pi \cos \pi/12$;

18. $\sin 3\beta + \sin 5\beta = 2 \sin 4\beta \cos \beta$;

19. $\tan \frac{1}{2}\theta = (1 - \cos \theta)/\sin \theta$;

20. $\sin (\theta + \frac{1}{4}\pi) - \cos (\theta - \frac{1}{4}\pi) = 0$;

21. $\cos (\frac{1}{4}\pi + \theta) + \cos (\frac{1}{4}\pi - \theta) = \sqrt{2} \cos \theta$;

22. $\cos (a + \beta) + \sin (a - \beta) = 2 \sin (\frac{1}{4}\pi + a) \cos (\frac{1}{4}\pi + \beta)$;

23. $\cos A + \cos 3A + \cos 5A + \cos 7A = 4 \cos A \cos 2A \cos 4A$;

24. $(\cos A + \cos 3A) \cos 4A = (\cos 3A + \cos 5A) \cos 2A$;

25. $\tan A + \tan B = \sin (A + B)/\cos A \cos B$;

26. $\cos 2\beta \cos \beta - \sin 4\beta \sin \beta = \cos 2\beta \cos 3\beta$;

27. $\cos 4\delta = \cos^4 \delta - 6 \cos^2 \delta \sin^2 \delta + \sin^4 \delta$;

28. $(a + b) + (a - b) \tan^2 \theta = (a + b \cos 2\theta) \sec^2 \theta$;

29. $\cos 4A = 3 + 4 \sin 2A - 2 (\cos A + \sin A)^4$;

30. $\tan \frac{1}{2} (A + B) - \tan \frac{1}{2} (A - B) = 2 \sin B/(\cos A + \cos B)$;

31. $(\tan A + \tan B) \sin (A - B) = (\tan A - \tan B) \sin (A + B)$;

32. $(\cot^2 A - \tan^2 B) \sin^2 A \cos^2 B = \cos (A + B) \cos (A - B)$.

Solve the equations:

33. $2 \sin x + 5 \cos x = 2$;

34. $\cos (a + x) - \sin (a + x) = \sqrt{2}$;

35. $\cos^{-1} x = \frac{1}{4}\pi - \cot^{-1} 2$;

36. $4 \cos x = 2 \tan x + 3 \sec x$;

37. $\sin x \sin 3x = \sin 5x \sin 7x$;

38. $\tan^{-1} \dfrac{x + 1}{x - 1} + \tan^{-1} \dfrac{x - 1}{x} = \tan^{-1} (- 7)$;

39. $\cos x + \cos 2x + \cos 3x + \cos 4x = 0$.

40. $x = \tan^{-1} \frac{1}{2} + \tan^{-1} \frac{1}{4} + \tan^{-1} \frac{1}{13}$. Express x in the form $\tan^{-1} k$.

41. Prove by projection that
$$\cos A + \cos (2\pi/3 + A) + \cos (2\pi/3 - A) = 0.$$

42. Plot the curve $\sin x/\cos 2x$ from 0 to π and hence solve approximately the equation
$$2x \cos 2x = \sin x.$$

43. Show that
$$2 \cos \tfrac{1}{2}A = (\pm \sqrt{1 + \sin A} \pm \sqrt{1 - \sin A}).$$

How would you find the cosine of the half-angle, given the sine of the whole angle, from this formula? Explain your answer by obtaining $\cos \pi/12$.

44. If $A + B + C = \pi$, prove that $\Sigma' \tan A = \tan A \tan B \tan C$. Prove also that $\Sigma \sin 2A = 4 \sin A \sin B \sin C$.

45. Prove that $2 \tan^{-1} \left\{ \dfrac{(a-b)^{\frac{1}{2}}}{(a+b)^{\frac{1}{2}}} \tan \frac{1}{2}x \right\} = \cos^{-1} \left\{ \dfrac{b + a \cos x}{a + b \cos x} \right\}$.

46. Solve the equation $8 \sin x + \sqrt{3} \sec x = \operatorname{cosec} x$.

47. If $\sin (B + C - A)$, $\sin (C + A - B)$, $\sin (A + B - C)$ are in arithmetic progression, prove that $\tan A$, $\tan B$, $\tan C$ are also in arithmetic progression; and conversely.

48. Solve the equation $\sin^{-1} (1 - x^2)^{\frac{1}{2}} + \tan^{-1} 2x = \frac{1}{2}\pi$.

49. Obtain α and β from the equations
$$\sin (\alpha + \beta) \cos (\alpha - \beta) = \tfrac{3}{4},$$
$$\cos (\alpha + \beta) \sin (\alpha - \beta) = \tfrac{1}{4}.$$

50. By multiplying all the way through by $2 \sin \frac{1}{2}\beta$, sum the series
$$\sin \alpha + \sin (\alpha + \beta) + \sin (\alpha + 2\beta) + \ldots \text{ to } n \text{ terms.}$$

Show that
$$\cos \alpha + \cos (\alpha + 2\pi/n) + \cos (\alpha + 4\pi/n) + \ldots + \cos (\alpha + \overline{2n - 1}\pi/n) = 0.$$

51. Use the tables to verify the results of Qu. 44 and Qu. 47 when $\tan A = 1$, $\tan B = 2$, $\tan C = 3$.

52. If $A + B + C = \pi$, prove that
$$\tan \frac{B}{2} \tan \frac{C}{2} + \tan \frac{C}{2} \tan \frac{A}{2} + \tan \frac{A}{2} \tan \frac{B}{2} = 1,$$
and verify this numerically when
$$A = 10°, \quad B = 40°, \quad C = 130°.$$

CHAPTER II

FUNCTIONS AND LIMITS

1. In most mathematical operations there are two classes of quantities. One class consists of those quantities which have the same value throughout the operation, and the other of quantities which may take different values. The first class are *constants* and the second are *variables*. If for example throughout a particular investigation $y = 5$, then wherever y occurs we may substitute the value 5 and y is said to be constant. If however $y = x + 2$, then to any particular value of x there corresponds a different value of y. In this example, if x may take up any value that we care to give it, then x is called an *independent variable*. On the other hand, y will vary according to the value that we assign to x and is said to be a *function* of x, or simply a *dependent variable*. A function of x is generally expressed in either of the following notations: $f(x)$, $F(x)$, $\phi(x)$, ... or u_x, v_x, U_x, ... There may be more than one independent variable on which the value of the function depends. Suppose that $y = x \sin \alpha + z \cos \beta$, where x, z, α, β all vary: then x, z, α, β are the independent variables and y may be written as $f(x, z, \alpha, \beta)$ or $u_{xz\alpha\beta}$.

A rational integral function is a simple form of function depending upon one variable.

$y = a + bx + cx^2 + dx^3 + ... + kx^n$ is a *rational integral function* of the nth degree in x, where a, b, c, d, ... k are constants and the indices are positive integers, n being the greatest.

It should be noted that for any one value of x in such a function there is one and only one value of y.

An alternative name for a rational integral function is a polynomial. A polynomial in x is generally written as $P_n(x)$.

When represented graphically, the curve $y = a + bx + cx^2 + ...$ is said to be of the parabolic form.

2. Algebraic functions.

A function $y = f(x)$ is an *algebraic function* of x if it is the root of an equation of the form

$$\alpha + \beta y + \gamma y^2 + ... + \kappa y^n + ... = 0,$$

where the coefficients $\alpha, \beta, \gamma, \ldots \kappa, \ldots$ are rational integral functions of x. In such cases y will usually have more than one value for any given value of x. y is then called a multiple-valued function of x. A simple example is $y^2 + 2\alpha y + \beta = 0$, where α, β are functions of x: for any value of x, y may have either of the values

$$- \alpha \pm (\alpha^2 - \beta)^{\frac{1}{2}}.$$

In the majority of examples that will occur subsequently the algebraic functions involved will be defined by simple forms of equations (e.g.

$$ax + by + c = 0; \quad y^2 - 4ax = 0; \quad x^2 + y^2 = r^2),$$

and it will generally be unnecessary to consider the multiple-valued function $Ay^n + By^{n-1} + \ldots = 0$.

The relation between a function of x and its argument may be expressed in one of two different forms. Consider for example the function y defined by $y = f(x) = a + bx + cx^2 + dx^3$. For any value of x the value of y becomes evident by simple substitution. Where this is so, y is said to be an *explicit* function of x. On the other hand, if the relation connecting x and y is of the form $\phi(x, y) = a + bxy + cx^2y + dy^3 = 0$, we cannot find y by an immediate substitution of a value of x. A further process is necessary—in this example the solution of a cubic equation in y—before the value or values of y can be obtained. $\phi(x, y) = 0$ defines an *implicit* function of x and y. It should be noted that plane curves can be represented either by an explicit function of one variable, $y = f(x)$; or by an implicit function of two variables defined by $\phi(x, y) = 0$. Similarly, an explicit function of two variables, $z = f(x, y)$ and an implicit function of three variables defined by $\phi(x, y, z) = 0$ represent surfaces in three-dimensional geometry.

A familiar type of rational integral function is a homogeneous function.

$f(x, y, z, \ldots)$ is a homogeneous function of the nth degree in $x, y, z, \ldots$ if, when the variables $x, y, z, \ldots$ are replaced by $\lambda x, \lambda y, \lambda z, \ldots$ respectively, the resulting function is $\lambda^n f(x, y, z, \ldots)$.

A simple example is

$$L(x^3 + y^3 + z^3) + M(x^2y + y^2z + z^2x + xy^2 + yz^2 + zx^2)$$
$$+ Nxyz;$$

this is a homogeneous function of the third degree in x, y and z.

3. Transcendental functions.

Any function that is not an algebraic function is called a *transcendental function*. Examples that occur at once are the trigonometrical ratios sin x, cos x, etc., and the exponential and logarithmic functions e^x, log x. Since c^x is also an exponential function, $y = f(x) = a + bc^x$ is a transcendental function. The forms $a + bc^x$ and $a + bx + kc^x$ are of frequent occurrence in actuarial processes.

4. Rates.

Suppose that successive values of a function y and its argument x are given by the table

$$
\begin{array}{ccccc}
x & a & b & c & d & \ldots \\
y & a' & b' & c' & d' & \ldots
\end{array}
$$

If we denote the differences between successive values of x by Δx and those between successive values of y by Δy, then for the first interval, $\Delta x = b - a$, and $\Delta y = b' - a'$: for the second interval $\Delta x = c - b$, $\Delta y = c' - b'$, ... and so on. If for every interval, whatever the values of $a, b, c, d, ..., \Delta y/\Delta x$ is constant, then y is said to vary at a *constant rate* with respect to x.

It is evident that this constant variation will occur only in a limited number of instances. A well-known example is that of uniform motion in a straight line. If x represents time-intervals and y distance-intervals, the ratio $\Delta y/\Delta x$ represents the speed of the moving body, and if this ratio is constant, the body is said to be moving uniformly or at a constant rate.

More commonly, rates will be variable and the successive values of $\Delta y/\Delta x$ will not be equal. We can, however, assign a meaning to $\Delta y/\Delta x$ by considering each interval separately. For example, giving numerical values to x and y, uniform variation is illustrated by

$$
\begin{array}{ccccc}
x & 1 & 2 & 3 & 4 & \ldots \\
y & 5 & 10 & 15 & 20 & \ldots
\end{array}
$$

for $\Delta y/\Delta x = 5 =$ constant.

On the other hand, if corresponding values of x and y are

$$
\begin{array}{ccccc}
x & 1 & 2 & 3 & 4 & \ldots \\
y & 5 & 12 & 30 & 60 & \ldots
\end{array}
$$

$\Delta y/\Delta x$ takes the values 7, 18, 30, ... for successive intervals, and is variable. If, however, we were to consider the range 1 to 4 for x, we could say that over this range of values of x, y increases from 5 to 60, and that the average rate of increase of y over this range $= (60 - 5)/(4 - 1) = 55/3$.

We are led therefore to the following definition:

Given corresponding increments h and k in the values of x and y for the function $y = f(x)$, the average rate of variation of y with x is the uniform rate which would give an increment k in the value of y for the increment h in x.

5. The average rate of variation over an interval has been illustrated above by a body moving with variable speed. This is the speed over an interval of time, and its meaning can easily be appreciated. Another conception of the term " speed " is that of speed at a particular moment of time. Suppose that the distance travelled by a moving body varies with the square of the time that has elapsed since the beginning of the motion, so that $s = t^2$. The average speed over an interval Δt will be

$$\frac{(t + \Delta t)^2 - t^2}{(t + \Delta t) - t} \quad \text{or} \quad 2t + \Delta t.$$

Giving Δt the values 1, ·1, ·01, ·001, ... we may construct the following table:

Interval	t to $t+1$	t to $t+$·1	t to $t+$·01	t to $t+$·001 ...
Average speed over interval	$2t + 1$	$2t + $·1	$2t + $·01	$2t + $·001 ...

Now the average speed over an interval tends to become more nearly equal to the speed at the beginning of the interval as the interval is reduced. The average speed over the interval tends to the value $2t$, and this must therefore be the value of the speed at the beginning of the interval.

More generally, the average rate of variation over an interval tends to the rate of change at a particular point (the beginning of the interval) as the interval is reduced.

It should be noted that although the value of

$$\frac{(t + \Delta t)^2 - t^2}{(t + \Delta t) - t}$$

tends to $2t$ as Δt is reduced, we cannot put $\Delta t = 0$ at once, for we then obtain $\frac{0}{0}$ which is meaningless in algebra. (This is what might be expected, for the average speed over a non-existent interval has no meaning.)

Suppose now that for the function $y = f(x)$ we take two successive values of the argument, namely, x and $x + h$. Then the average rate of variation of $f(x)$ in the interval x to $x + h$ will be

$$\frac{f(x+h) - f(x)}{(x+h) - x} = \frac{f(x+h) - f(x)}{h},$$

which tends to the rate of change of $f(x)$ at the point x as h is reduced. This rate of change is therefore the *limiting value* of the average rate of change as h tends to zero, and we must reach this limiting value by a process other than by direct substitution of $h = 0$ in the algebraic expression.

6. Certain limiting values may be illustrated by the application of the methods of elementary geometry.

Example 1.

Let A be a fixed point on a plane curve and let B_1AC_1 be any straight line drawn through A cutting the curve again at B_1. Let B_1 move down the curve towards A so that the secant takes up the successive positions

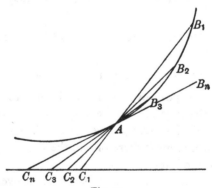

Fig. 13.

$B_2AC_2, B_3AC_3, \ldots$. Then the lengths of the secants cut off by the curve, namely $B_1A, B_2A, B_3A, \ldots$, become successively smaller. When, however, the two points BA virtually coincide, the secant approaches the position B_nAC_n, the tangent to the curve at the point A. In other words, the tangent $B_n AC_n$ is the limiting position of the secant $B_r AC_r$ as B moves along the curve to A.

Example 2.

Prove that $\sin \theta < \theta < \tan \theta$.

Let KOA be the angle $\theta \left(< \dfrac{\pi}{2} \right)$.

Draw a circle with OA as radius and let AB be a chord of the circle. Draw AT, BT, the tangents to the circle at A and B respectively, meeting at T. Then evidently the chord $AB <$ arc $AB < AT + TB$;

i.e. $HA <$ arc $AK < AT$.

$$\therefore \quad \frac{HA}{OA} < \frac{\text{arc } AK}{\text{radius } OA} < \frac{AT}{OA},$$

or $\quad \sin \theta < \theta < \tan \theta$.

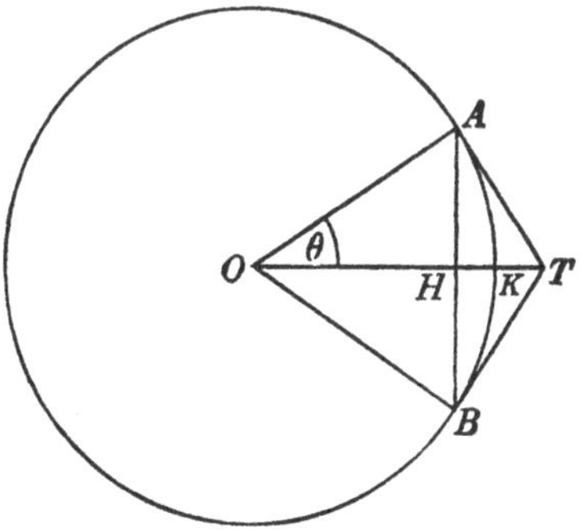

Fig. 14.

From these inequalities we have

$$1 < \frac{\theta}{\sin \theta} < \frac{1}{\cos \theta};$$

i.e. $$1 > \frac{\sin \theta}{\theta} > \cos \theta.$$

Therefore $\dfrac{\sin \theta}{\theta}$ lies between 1 and $\cos \theta$. In the limiting case when θ is zero, $\cos \theta$ is 1. (See Chapter I, para. 11.)

Therefore when θ approaches the limit zero, $\dfrac{\sin \theta}{\theta}$ has 1 as its limiting value.

7. Continuous functions.

Before proceeding further to the consideration of limits and limiting values it is necessary to distinguish between those functions which vary continuously between two values of the argument and those which do not.

If we wished to plot the curve of the function $y = x^2$ for all real values of x, we could give x certain values, and by substituting these values in the equation $y = x^2$ we could obtain the corresponding values of y. It would be necessary to plot only a limited number of points (x, y) and by drawing a smooth curve through these points the graph of the function $y = x^2$ would result. Suppose, however, that a limitation were imposed upon the values of x, namely, that x

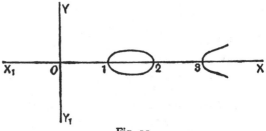

Fig. 15.

should always be a positive integer. The graphical representation of the values of x and y would be a series of isolated points, and a curve could not be drawn between any two successive values of (x, y).

Again, consider the function $y^2 = (x - 1)(x - 2)(x - 3)$. If y is to be real we have the following conditions (1) x must not be less than 1; (2) x must not lie between the values $x = 2$ and $x = 3$. This second condition shows that while x may have any value between 1 and 2 and any value greater than 3, for real values of y, there is no value of y corresponding to values of x between 2 and 3. y is said to be discontinuous between the values $x = 2$ and $x = 3$, and the curve will take the above shape (Fig. 15).

A type of function which, for a certain value of the variable, ceases to be continuous is $y = 1/x$. If x be zero, the function takes the form $1/0$ which is, strictly speaking, meaningless. As, however, $1/x$ becomes successively greater on decreasing x, it is possible to make $1/x$ greater than any finite value, by making x sufficiently small. The function is then said to "tend to infinity" or to "increase indefinitely" as x tends to zero.

8. Limits.

We are now in a position to give a clearer definition of what is meant by a limit. A simple definition is as follows:

If $y = f(x)$ and y tends continuously towards a certain value l, and can be made to differ as little as we please from that value by making x approach some fixed value a, then l is said to be the limiting value of $f(x)$ as x tends to the value a.

This may be expressed shortly as

$$\underset{x \to a}{\text{Lt}} \ f(x) = l.$$

For example, we have

$$\underset{h \to 0}{\text{Lt}} \ \frac{f(x+h) - f(x)}{h} = 2x \ \text{when} f(x) = x^2.$$

This definition is not sufficiently precise, and may prove inadequate in certain instances. Consider for example the following illustration.

The curve $y = \dfrac{\sin x}{x}$ is represented geometrically (see Fig. 16).

For large values of x the curve becomes indistinguishable from the axis of x and the value of y tends to zero, notwithstanding that, however large x may be, y may be sometimes increasing numerically. It is obvious that the phrase "tends continuously towards a certain value l" does not mean "constantly increases (or decreases) to the value l."

Fig. 16.

Now take the curve $y = \sin x$.

Here y does not tend to a limit as x becomes indefinitely great. It might be claimed, however, that y (i.e. $\sin x$) tends to unity for sufficiently large values of x. If this were countered by the argument that for a very large value of x, $\sin x$ was, say, $\frac{1}{2}$, the reply might be that the value of x was not sufficiently large, and that by

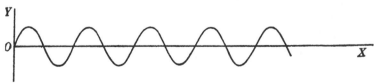

Fig. 17.

taking a larger value of x, sin x would differ from unity by as little as we pleased. The rejoinder to this would be that by taking a still larger value of x, sin x could be made to differ from $\frac{1}{2}$, or zero, or $-\frac{1}{2}$, etc. by as little as we pleased; and so on.

By the statement that $\underset{x \to \infty}{\text{Lt}} \dfrac{\sin x}{x}$ is zero and that $\dfrac{\sin x}{x}$ can be made to differ from zero by as little as we please, we imply that, given a number, say, ·01, we must be able to find a value of x such that, *for all greater values of x,* $\dfrac{\sin x}{x}$ will differ from zero by less than ·01. In other words, the whole of the graph of $y = \dfrac{\sin x}{x}$ after this point will be contained within the two ordinates $y = $ ·01 and $y = -$ ·01. Similarly, if the number ·001 were chosen, a value of x must be found such that for all greater values of x, the graph will be contained in the limits $y = $ ·001 and $y = -$ ·001.

It is clear that the graph of $y = \dfrac{\sin x}{x}$ would satisfy such a series of tests, but that the graph of $y = \sin x$ would not.

This leads directly to the more rigorous definition of a limit:

Let $f(x)$ be a function such that x lies between two fixed values a and b (i.e. $a < x < b$) and let x' be any value of x satisfying these conditions. Then if l be a number such that corresponding to an arbitrary positive number ϵ, a positive number η can be found such that $f(x)$ differs from l by less than ϵ whenever $x - x' < \eta$, then l is said to be the limit of $f(x)$ as $x \to x'$.

It should be emphasized that the limit of $f(x)$ as $x \to a$ is not defined as a value of $f(x)$, and in particular is not necessarily equal to $f(a)$. It is a quantity quite distinct from the values of $f(x)$ although it is defined by means of these values in the neighbourhood of $x = a$. As a rule, the limit of $f(x)$ as $x \to a$ is required in circumstances in which $f(a)$ has no meaning.

9. It is a simple matter to prove that the algebraic sum, product or quotient of the limits of any finite number of functions is the limit of the sum, product or quotient respectively of the functions, provided that, when considering quotients, the limit of the divisor is not zero. The definition of a limit and these corollaries form the basis of the infinitesimal calculus.

The following elementary examples are typical of the methods employed in the evaluation of limits.

Example 3.

Find $$\underset{x \to a}{\text{Lt}} \frac{x^3 - a^3}{x - a}.$$

We may not put $x = a$ immediately, for in that event the divisor will be zero and we shall arrive at the form $\frac{0}{0}$. If we divide throughout by $x - a$ the function becomes $x^2 + ax + a^2$ and if we let $x \to a$ in this expression we obtain $3a^2$. This is the limit when $x \to a$ of $\frac{x^3 - a^3}{x - a}$. Although it should be proved that a positive number η can be found such that $\frac{x^3 - a^3}{x - a} - 3a^2$ is less than any arbitrary number ϵ whenever $x - a < \eta$, it may be taken for granted that this criterion holds in all the examples that will be dealt with subsequently, and that we may proceed straight to the limit as above.

Example 4.

Find $\underset{n \to \infty}{\text{Lt}} \left[\frac{1}{n^4} \Sigma n^3 \right]$ where n is a positive integer.

$$\Sigma n^3 = 1^3 + 2^3 + 3^3 + \dots + n^3 = \frac{n^2 (n + 1)^2}{4} = \frac{n^2 + 2n^3 + n^4}{4}.$$

$$\therefore \frac{1}{n^4} \Sigma n^3 = \frac{1}{4} \left[\frac{1}{n^2} + \frac{2}{n} + 1 \right] = \frac{1}{4n^2} + \frac{1}{2n} + \frac{1}{4}.$$

$$\therefore \underset{n \to \infty}{\text{Lt}} \frac{1}{n^4} \Sigma n^3 = \underset{n \to \infty}{\text{Lt}} \frac{1}{4n^2} + \underset{n \to \infty}{\text{Lt}} \frac{1}{2n} + \underset{n \to \infty}{\text{Lt}} \frac{1}{4}$$

by the proposition above

$$= 0 + 0 + \tfrac{1}{4}$$
$$= \tfrac{1}{4}.$$

Example 5.

Show that $$\underset{x \to 1}{\text{Lt}} \frac{x^6 - 5x + 4}{x^3 - 2x + 1} = 1.$$

If we put $x = 1$ immediately we obtain the form $\frac{0}{0}$. As in Example 3, we could divide numerator and denominator by $x - 1$ and then find the limit. An alternative method is as follows:

Put $x = 1 + h$; then the function becomes a function of h instead of a function of x and we have to find the limit of the new function when $h \to 0$.

$$\frac{x^6 - 5x + 4}{x^3 - 2x + 1} = \frac{(1+h)^6 - 5(1+h) + 4}{(1+h)^3 - 2(1+h) + 1}$$

$$= \frac{1 + 6h + 15h^2 + \dots - 5 - 5h + 4}{1 + 3h + 3h^2 + h^3 - 2 - 2h + 1}$$

$$= \frac{h + 15h^2 + \dots}{h + 3h^2 + \dots}$$

$$= \frac{1 + 15h + \dots}{1 + 3h + \dots}$$

and the limit of this expression when $h \to 0$ is 1.

10. Limit of a sequence.

Let $u_1 + u_2 + u_3 + u_4 + \dots$ be an infinite series. If s_n be the sum of the first n terms, we can form an unending *sequence* of values, $s_1, s_2, s_3 \dots s_n \dots$. If $u_n \to 0$ as $n \to \infty$ s_n may tend to a finite number. For example, the series

$$1 + \tfrac{1}{2} + (\tfrac{1}{2})^2 + (\tfrac{1}{2})^3 + \dots + (\tfrac{1}{2})^{n-1} = [1 - (\tfrac{1}{2})^n]/(1 - \tfrac{1}{2}) = 2 - (\tfrac{1}{2})^{n-1},$$

so that s_n, the sum to n terms, differs from 2 by the small quantity $(\tfrac{1}{2})^{n-1}$.

The larger the value of n, the more nearly the sum to n terms is equal to 2; the sum $\to 2$ as $n \to \infty$.

A series of a different type is

$$1 + 2 + 3 + 4 + \dots + n.$$

The sum to n terms is $\tfrac{1}{2}n(n+1)$, and there is no fixed number to which the sum of the series tends: if n be very large $\tfrac{1}{2}n(n+1)$ is very large.

In the first example the limit of the sequence as n increases indefinitely is said to be 2, and the series is said to be *convergent*. In the second example there is no limit to the sum of the series, and the series is said to be *divergent*.

The definition of the limit of a sequence is as follows:

If $u_1, u_2, u_3, \dots u_n, \dots$ be an unending sequence of real or imaginary numbers, and if a number l exists such that corresponding to every positive number ϵ (however small) a number k can be found such that u_n differs from l by less than ϵ for all values of $n > k$, the sequence $u_1, u_2, u_3, \dots u_n, \dots$ is said to tend to the limit l as $n \to \infty$.

The limits of algebraic and other expansions are of the utmost importance in mathematical work, and while it is beyond the present scope to examine fully the convergence or otherwise of even the more important series, reference to them is essential for the proper understanding of the calculus.

11. $\dfrac{(x+h)^n - x^n}{h}$.

If n be a positive integer, this expression becomes

$$\frac{1}{h}\left[n_{(1)}hx^{n-1} + n_{(2)}h^2x^{n-2} + n_{(3)}h^3x^{n-3} + \ldots + h^n\right]$$

$$= n_{(1)}x^{n-1} + n_{(2)}hx^{n-2} + n_{(3)}h^2x^{n-3} + \ldots + h^{n-1},$$

which evidently tends to nx^{n-1} when $h \to 0$.

Suppose, however, that n be other than a positive integer. Then there will not be a limited number of terms, and we have

$$\operatorname*{Lt}_{h\to 0}\frac{(x+h)^n - x^n}{h} = \operatorname*{Lt}_{h\to 0}x^n\left[\frac{\left(1+\dfrac{h}{x}\right)^n - 1}{h}\right]$$

$$= \operatorname*{Lt}_{h\to 0}\frac{x^n}{h}\left[n_{(1)}\left(\frac{h}{x}\right) + n_{(2)}\left(\frac{h}{x}\right)^2 + n_{(3)}\left(\frac{h}{x}\right)^3 + \ldots\right].$$

This involves a *double limit*, for the number of terms inside the bracket is not finite, and we are not entitled to assume that the limit of the sum of the terms is equal to the sum of the limits of the terms.

The investigation of a double limit requires further mathematical analysis, and the consideration of the limit of the above expression when n is not a positive integer will be deferred to a later chapter.

12. $\left(1 + \dfrac{1}{n}\right)^n$.

For all values of r it may be shown that

$$\operatorname*{Lt}_{n\to\infty}\left(1 + \frac{1}{n}\right)^n$$

lies between

$$1 + 1 + \frac{1}{2!} + \frac{1}{3!} + \ldots + \frac{1}{r!}$$

and
$$1 + 1 + \frac{1}{2!} + \frac{1}{3!} + \dots + \frac{1}{r!} + \frac{1}{r.r!}.$$

The expression
$$\operatorname*{Lt}_{n \to \infty} \left(1 + \frac{1}{n}\right)^n$$
is denoted by e, so that
$$e = 1 + 1 + \frac{1}{2!} + \frac{1}{3!} + \dots + \frac{1}{r!} + R,$$

where
$$R < \frac{1}{r.r!}.$$

Since, however,
$$\operatorname*{Lt}_{r \to \infty} \frac{1}{r.r!}$$
is zero, e may be considered as the sum of the infinite series
$$1 + 1 + \frac{1}{2!} + \frac{1}{3!} + \dots + \frac{1}{r!} + \dots.$$

Again it may be shown that, if x is positive,
$$\operatorname*{Lt}_{n \to \infty} \left(1 + \frac{x}{n}\right)^n > 1 + x + \frac{x^2}{2!} + \frac{x^3}{3!} + \dots + \frac{x^r}{r!},$$

but
$$< 1 + x + \frac{x^2}{2!} + \frac{x^3}{3!} + \dots + \frac{x^r}{r!} + \frac{x^{r+1}}{(r+1-x)r!},$$

and that
$$e^x = \operatorname*{Lt}_{n \to \infty} \left(1 + \frac{x}{n}\right)^n = 1 + x + \frac{x^2}{2!} + \frac{x^3}{3!} + \dots + \frac{x^r}{r!} + \dots,$$
if x is not zero.

In the inequalities above put $r = 1$.

Then if x is a positive fraction
$$e^x > 1 + x \text{ and } < 1 + x + \frac{x^2}{(2-x)}.$$

$$\therefore\ e^x - 1 > x \text{ and } < x + \frac{x^2}{2-x},$$

i.e.
$$\frac{e^x - 1}{x} > 1 \text{ and } < 1 + \frac{x}{2-x},$$

so that if x be positive $\operatorname*{Lt}_{x \to 0} \frac{e^x - 1}{x} = 1$.

If x is negative we can replace x by $-y$ and obtain
$$\operatorname*{Lt}_{x \to 0} \frac{e^x - 1}{x} = \operatorname*{Lt}_{y \to 0} \frac{e^{-y} - 1}{-y} = \operatorname*{Lt}_{y \to 0} \frac{1}{e^y} \cdot \frac{e^y - 1}{y} = 1.$$

13. We may now proceed to a more formal definition of a continuous function.

(i) For continuity at a particular value of x, say at $x = a$, $f(a)$ must be a finite number (not infinity) and $\underset{x \to a}{\text{Lt}}\ f(x)$ must be equal to $f(a)$.

(ii) $f(x)$ is continuous for a given range from $x = a$ to $x = b$ if it is continuous for every value of x between a and b, i.e. for all values of x such that $a < x < b$.

(It should be noted that $\underset{x \to a}{\text{Lt}}\ f(x)$ must equal $f(a)$ whether x approaches a from the right or from the left.)

If the criterion (i) does not hold for the point whose abscissa is a, then the function is said to be discontinuous at the point.

For example, let $y = 1/x$, and let x pass through all values between $x = -1$ and $x = 1$. Then at one point intermediate between -1 and $+1$, namely where $x = 0$, y takes the value $1/0$, which is not a finite number. The function is therefore discontinuous at the point $x = 0$ (cf. para. 7 above).

14. Asymptotes.

Consider the curve $\qquad y = \dfrac{x^2}{(x-1)^2}.$

Here y tends to infinity as $x \to 1$, and since we may write the equation as $y = \dfrac{1}{[1 - 1/x]^2}$, y tends to the value 1 when x tends to infinity in either direction.

The curve is of the following shape.

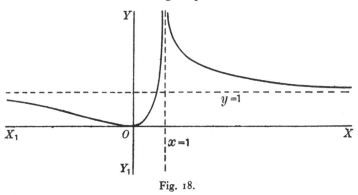

Fig. 18.

Discontinuities in the value of y when $x = 1$ and of x when $y = 1$ are apparent. It will be seen that the curve gradually approaches indefinitely near to the straight lines $x = 1$ and $y = 1$ but does not actually meet them at any finite distance from the origin.

Such lines are called *asymptotes* to the curve.

Example 6.

Find the asymptotes to the curve $y = \dfrac{(3x - 1)(x - 2)}{(x - 3)(x + 3)}$.

The equation of the curve may be written

$$y = 3 + \frac{29 - 7x}{(x - 3)(x + 3)} = 3 + \frac{4}{3(x - 3)} - \frac{25}{3(x + 3)}.$$

Then if x tend to infinity in either direction, the curve approaches the straight line $y = 3$. Hence $y = 3$ is an asymptote.

Further, if x is positive and greater than 29/7, the value of y is less than 3. Therefore, on the right the curve approaches $y = 3$ from underneath. If x is negative, on the left the curve approaches $y = 3$ from above.

Again, from the second form of the equation to the curve, it will be seen that $x = 3$ and $x = -3$ are asymptotes to the curve, since the curve gradually approaches these straight lines but does not meet them at a finite distance from the origin.

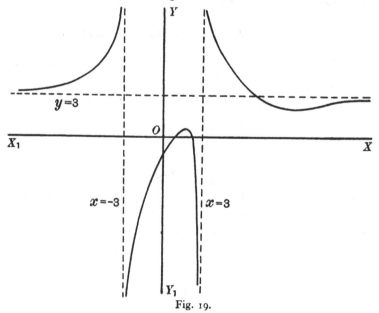

Fig. 19.

EXAMPLES 2

1. Find $\underset{x \to a}{Lt} \dfrac{x^p - a^p}{x^q - a^q}$ where p and q are positive integers.

2. Obtain $\overset{r=n}{\underset{r=1}{\Sigma}} \dfrac{r^2}{n^3}$ and hence show that the limit of the sum when $n \to \infty$ is finite.

3. Evaluate $\underset{x \to 0}{Lt} \dfrac{a^x - 1 - x \log a}{x^2}$.

4. Prove that $\underset{\theta \to 0}{Lt} \dfrac{\sin r\theta}{\theta} = r$.

5. Find the limiting value of
$$\sqrt{x^4 + ax^2 + bx + c} - \sqrt{x^4 + kx^2 + mx + n}$$
when x is indefinitely increased.

6. Prove that $1 > \cos \theta > 1 - \tfrac{1}{2}\theta^2$.

7. Show that $\underset{x \to 0}{Lt}\ x \log x = 0$ and hence find the limit of $\sin x \log x$ as $x \to 0$.

Find the following limiting values:

8. $\underset{x \to \infty}{Lt}\ \{x\sqrt{x^2 + a^2} - \sqrt{x^4 + a^4}\}$.

9. $\underset{x \to b}{Lt} \dfrac{(2x + b)^{\frac{1}{2}} - (3x)^{\frac{1}{2}}}{(x + 3b)^{\frac{1}{2}} - 2(x)^{\frac{1}{2}}}$.

10. $\underset{x \to \infty}{Lt}\ \sqrt{x}\,(\sqrt{x + 1} - \sqrt{x})$.

11. $\underset{x \to 1}{Lt} \dfrac{x^{\frac{3}{2}} - 1 + (x - 1)^{\frac{3}{2}}}{(x^2 - 1)^{\frac{1}{2}} - x + 1}$.

12. $\underset{x \to 0}{Lt} \dfrac{e^{ax} - e^{bx}}{a^{ex} - b^{ex}}$.

13. $\underset{\theta \to 0}{Lt}\ \tan m\theta \cot n\theta$.

14. $\underset{x \to 0}{Lt}\ x^x$.

15. $\underset{x \to a}{Lt} \dfrac{(3x - a)^{\frac{1}{2}} - (x + a)^{\frac{1}{2}}}{x - a}$.

16. $\underset{y \to 0}{Lt} \dfrac{\log(1 + y + y^2)}{y^2(1 - 2y)}$.

17. $\underset{n \to \infty}{Lt} \left[\left(1 + \dfrac{1}{n}\right)^n - \left(1 + \dfrac{1}{n}\right)^{-n} \right]$.

18. Show that $\dfrac{1.3.5 \ldots 2n - 1}{2.4.6 \ldots 2n} < \dfrac{2.4.6 \ldots 2n}{3.5.7 \ldots 2n + 1}$

and that $\dfrac{3.5.7 \ldots 2n + 1}{2.4.6 \ldots 2n} > \dfrac{4.6.8 \ldots 2n + 2}{3.5.7 \ldots 2n + 1}$.

19. From the inequalities in Qu. 18 prove that

$$\text{Lt}_{n \to \infty} \frac{1.3.5 \dots 2n - 1}{2.4.6 \dots 2n} = 0$$

and

$$\text{Lt}_{n \to \infty} \frac{3.5.7 \dots 2n + 1}{2.4.6 \dots 2n} = \infty.$$

Prove also that the limit when $n \to \infty$ of the product of these two functions lies between $\frac{1}{2}$ and 1.

20. Evaluate

$$\text{Lt}_{n \to \infty} n \left[1 - \log \left(1 + \frac{1}{n} \right)^{n-1} \right].$$

CHAPTER III

DIFFERENTIAL CALCULUS
DEFINITIONS; STANDARD FORMS;
SUCCESSIVE DIFFERENTIATION

1. We have seen in the previous chapter that if $y = f(x)$ be a continuous function of x, the average rate of change of y with x is

$$\frac{f(x+h) - f(x)}{h},$$

or $\Delta y / \Delta x$, where $\Delta x = h$.

The limit of this function when the interval tends to zero (which we may call the rate of change) is called the differential coefficient of y with respect to x. If we denote this result by Dy, we have

$$Dy = \mathop{\text{Lt}}_{\Delta x \to 0} \Delta y / \Delta x = \mathop{\text{Lt}}_{h \to 0} \frac{f(x+h) - f(x)}{h},$$

and we are said to have "differentiated y with respect to x."

The usual notation for the differential coefficient is $\dfrac{dy}{dx}$, but for convenience in working alternative methods of denoting $\dfrac{dy}{dx}$ are often used. For example,

$$y', \dot{y}, Dy; \quad f'(x), Df(x), \frac{d}{dx} f(x),$$

represent the same result.

It should be noted that, although $\Delta y / \Delta x$ is the result of the division of a definite quantity Δy by another definite quantity Δx, $\dfrac{dy}{dx}$ represents an operation performed on the function y, the operator being $\dfrac{d}{dx}$. At this stage neither dy nor dx should be considered to have a separate meaning.

The differential coefficient of y with respect to x is sometimes called the "first derivative" or the "first derived function" of y with respect to x.

2. Before proceeding to examine the values of the differential coefficients of various functions, it will be of advantage to consider the geometrical interpretation of the operation of differentiation.

Let B_1AB represent the continuous curve $y = f(x)$ and let the coordinates of a point A on the curve be (x, y) or $\{x, f(x)\}$. Let B be a near point on the curve whose coordinates are $\{x + h, f(x + h)\}$.

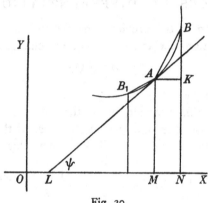

Fig. 20.

Then it is evident from the figure that, if θ be the angle BAK,

$$\tan \theta = BK/AK = \frac{BN - NK}{MN} = \frac{BN - MA}{ON - OM}$$

$$= \frac{f(x + h) - f(x)}{h}.$$

Now as the point B moves along the curve so as ultimately to coincide with the point A, the secant BA takes up the position of the tangent AL to the curve (see Ex. 1 of Chapter II). The angle θ then becomes the angle ψ which the tangent AL makes with the axis of x.

But the limit of $\dfrac{f(x + h) - f(x)}{h}$ when B coincides with A is the limit of this expression as $h \to 0$.

Also $$\underset{h \to 0}{\text{Lt}} \frac{f(x + h) - f(x)}{h} = \frac{d}{dx} f(x).$$

Therefore $\dfrac{d}{dx} f(x) = \tan \psi$

= the tangent of the angle that the tangent to the curve $y = f(x)$ at the point (x, y) makes with the x-axis.

The tangent to a curve at any point measures the slope or gradient of the curve at that point. The differential coefficient of y with respect to x is often referred to as the gradient of the curve $y = f(x)$ at the point (x, y).

It may happen that near the point A of the curve the curve is continuous as x increases, but that there is a discontinuity in the other direction—as in Fig. 21. If we were to consider the effect

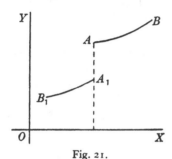

Fig. 21.

of allowing the point B_1 to approach A_1—the x coordinate of which is the same as that of the point A—the value of the differential coefficient might be different from that found by assuming B to coincide with A.

For this reason it is probably better to define the differential coefficient thus:

If $f(x)$ be a continuous function of x and if $\operatorname*{Lt}\limits_{h \to 0} \dfrac{f(x + h) - f(x)}{h}$ is equal to $\operatorname*{Lt}\limits_{h \to 0} \dfrac{f(x) - f(x - h)}{h}$, then either of these limits is called the differential coefficient of y with respect to x.

Another method of obtaining $\dfrac{dy}{dx}$ (when it exists) is to consider two points

$$B_1 \quad \{(x - h), f(x - h)\}$$

and $\quad B \quad \{(x + h), f(x + h)\}$

which approach A simultaneously. By reference to Fig. 20 it will be seen that

$$\tan \psi = \frac{dy}{dx} = \operatorname*{Lt}_{h \to 0} \frac{f(x+h) - f(x-h)}{2h}.$$

This form is of advantage when the evaluation of

$$f(x+h) - f(x-h)$$

is simpler than the evaluation of $f(x+h) - f(x)$.

3. The following propositions are of general application:

(i) If a is any constant, then $\dfrac{da}{dx} = 0$.

This is obvious, since there can be no rate of change of a constant quantity.

(ii) $\dfrac{d}{dx} af(x) = a \dfrac{d}{dx} f(x)$, where a is a constant.

$$\frac{d}{dx} af(x) = \operatorname*{Lt}_{h \to 0} \frac{af(x+h) - af(x)}{h}$$

$$= a \operatorname*{Lt}_{h \to 0} \frac{f(x+h) - f(x)}{h}$$

$$= a \frac{d}{dx} f(x).$$

(iii) If $y = f(x) + \phi(x) + \psi(x) + \dots,$

then $\dfrac{dy}{dx} = \dfrac{d}{dx} f(x) + \dfrac{d}{dx} \phi(x) + \dfrac{d}{dx} \psi(x) + \dots.$

Since $y = f(x) + \phi(x) + \psi(x) + \dots,$

$\quad\quad\quad\quad \Delta y = \Delta f(x) + \Delta \phi(x) + \Delta \psi(x) + \dots.$

$$\therefore \frac{\Delta y}{\Delta x} = \frac{\Delta f(x)}{\Delta x} + \frac{\Delta \phi(x)}{\Delta x} + \frac{\Delta \psi(x)}{\Delta x} + \dots.$$

The limit of this expression as $\Delta x \to 0$ is

$$\frac{dy}{dx} = \frac{d}{dx} f(x) + \frac{d}{dx} \phi(x) + \frac{d}{dx} \psi(x) + \dots.$$

(iv) If $y = uv$, where u, v are both functions of x, then

$$\frac{dy}{dx} = u \frac{dv}{dx} + v \frac{du}{dx}.$$

$$\Delta y = \Delta \ (uv)$$

$$= (u + \Delta u) \ (v + \Delta v) - uv$$

$$= u \Delta v + v \Delta u + \Delta u \Delta v.$$

$$\therefore \ \frac{\Delta y}{\Delta x} = u \frac{\Delta v}{\Delta x} + v \frac{\Delta u}{\Delta x} + \Delta u \frac{\Delta v}{\Delta x}$$

$$= (u + \Delta u) \frac{\Delta v}{\Delta x} + v \frac{\Delta u}{\Delta x}.$$

Therefore since in the limit $\Delta x \to 0$, $u + \Delta u$ will become u,

$$\frac{dy}{dx} = u \frac{dv}{dx} + v \frac{du}{dx}.$$

As a corollary we have, by successive applications of (iv),

$$\frac{d}{dx} uvw \ldots = uv \ldots \frac{dw}{dx} + vw \ldots \frac{du}{dx} + uw \ldots \frac{dv}{dx} + \ldots.$$

(v) If $y = \dfrac{u}{v}$, then $\dfrac{dy}{dx} = \left\{ \dfrac{v \dfrac{du}{dx} - u \dfrac{dv}{dx}}{v^2} \right\}.$

Now $\quad \Delta y = \Delta \left(\dfrac{u}{v} \right) = \dfrac{u + \Delta u}{v + \Delta v} - \dfrac{u}{v}$

$$= \frac{(u + \Delta u) \ v - (v + \Delta v) \ u}{v \ (v + \Delta v)}$$

$$= \frac{v \Delta u - u \Delta v}{v \ (v + \Delta v)}.$$

$$\therefore \ \frac{\Delta y}{\Delta x} = \frac{v \dfrac{\Delta u}{\Delta x} - u \dfrac{\Delta v}{\Delta x}}{v \ (v + \Delta v)}.$$

I.e. $\quad \dfrac{dy}{dx} = \dfrac{v \dfrac{du}{dx} - u \dfrac{dv}{dx}}{v^2}$

when $\Delta x \to 0$.

Putting $u = 1$, we have

$$\frac{d}{dx} \frac{1}{v} = - \frac{1}{v^2} \frac{dv}{dx}.$$

(vi) If y is a function of x and z is a function of y, then

$$\frac{dz}{dx} = \frac{dz}{dy} \cdot \frac{dy}{dx}.$$

Since

$$\frac{\Delta z}{\Delta x} = \frac{\Delta z}{\Delta y} \cdot \frac{\Delta y}{\Delta x},$$

$$\frac{dz}{dx} = \frac{dz}{dy} \cdot \frac{dy}{dx}$$

when $\Delta x \to$ o.

It follows that

$$\frac{dz}{dt} = \frac{dz}{dy} \cdot \frac{dy}{dx} \cdot \frac{dx}{du} \cdot \frac{du}{dv} \cdots \frac{dr}{ds} \cdot \frac{ds}{dt},$$

where s is a function of t, r a function of s, etc.

(vii)

$$\frac{dy}{dx} = \frac{1}{\dfrac{dx}{dy}}.$$

We have

$$\frac{\Delta y}{\Delta x} = \frac{1}{\dfrac{\Delta x}{\Delta y}}.$$

$\therefore$ If $\dfrac{\Delta x}{\Delta y}$ be not equal to zero,

$$\frac{dy}{dx} = \frac{1}{\dfrac{dx}{dy}}.$$

Note. If more than one value of y correspond to a given value of x (e.g. if $y = \sin^{-1} x$), and/or more than one value of z to a given value of y, then in taking the changes in value Δx, Δy, Δz we must keep them consistent in assuming that $\dfrac{\Delta z}{\Delta x} = \dfrac{\Delta z}{\Delta y} \cdot \dfrac{\Delta y}{\Delta x}$, or that

$$\frac{\Delta y}{\Delta x} = \frac{1}{\dfrac{\Delta x}{\Delta y}}.$$

4. Standard forms: Algebraic.

We will now proceed to obtain the differential coefficients of some standard functions.

(i) $y = x^n$.

(a) n a positive integer.

This follows directly from the proof on page 33 where it was shown that

$$\underset{h \to 0}{\text{Lt}} \frac{(x + h)^n - x^n}{h} = nx^{n-1}.$$

(b) n a positive fraction.

Let $n = \dfrac{p}{q}$ where p, q are positive integers.

Then
$$y = x^n = x^{p/q}.$$

$$\therefore y^q = x^p = z, \quad \text{say.}$$

We have
$$\left.\begin{array}{l} \dfrac{dz}{dx} = px^{p-1} \\[2mm] \dfrac{dz}{dy} = qy^{q-1} \end{array}\right\} \text{ from } (a) \text{ above.}$$

and

But
$$\frac{dy}{dx} = \frac{dy}{dz} \cdot \frac{dz}{dx} = \frac{1}{\dfrac{dz}{dy}} \cdot \frac{dz}{dx}$$

$$= \frac{px^{p-1}}{qy^{q-1}} = \frac{p}{q} \cdot \frac{x^p}{y^q} \cdot \frac{y}{x}$$

$$= \frac{p}{q} \cdot \frac{y}{x} = \frac{p}{q} \cdot x^{\frac{p}{q} - 1}$$

$$= nx^{n-1}.$$

(c) n negative.

Let $n = -m$ where m is positive (integral or fractional).

$$y = x^n = x^{-m} = \frac{1}{x^m}.$$

$$\therefore x^m y = 1,$$

and
$$\frac{d}{dx}(x^m y) = mx^{m-1}y + x^m \frac{dy}{dx},$$

since m is positive.

But $x^m y = 1 = \text{constant}.$

$$\therefore \frac{d}{dx}(x^m y) = 0.$$

$$\therefore\ mx^{m-1}y + x^m\frac{dy}{dx} = 0.$$

$$\therefore\ \frac{dy}{dx} = -\frac{mx^{m-1}y}{x^m} = -\frac{my}{x}$$

$$= nx^{n-1}.$$

I.e. $\frac{dx^n}{dx} = nx^{n-1}$ for all values of n positive or negative, integral or fractional.

For example,
$$\frac{d}{dx}x^5 = 5x^4,$$

$$\frac{d}{dx}x^{-5} = -5x^{-6},$$

$$\frac{d}{dx}x^{\frac{1}{5}} = \tfrac{1}{5}x^{-\frac{4}{5}},$$

$$\frac{d}{dx}x^{-\frac{1}{5}} = -\tfrac{1}{5}x^{-\frac{6}{5}}.$$

(ii) $y = e^x$.

$$\frac{d}{dx}e^x = \operatorname*{Lt}_{h\to 0}\frac{e^{x+h}-e^x}{h} = e^x\operatorname*{Lt}_{h\to 0}\frac{e^h-1}{h}$$

$$= e^x, \text{ since } \operatorname*{Lt}_{h\to 0}\frac{e^h-1}{h} = 1 \quad (\text{p. } 34).$$

Corollary:
$$\frac{da^x}{dx} = a^x\log_e a.$$

For $a^x = e^{x\log a}$ and $\frac{da^x}{dx} = \frac{de^{x\log a}}{dx} = \frac{de^{x\log a}}{d(x\log a)}\cdot\frac{d(x\log a)}{dx}$

$$= e^{x\log a}.\log a = a^x\log a.$$

(iii) $y = \log_e x$.

$$\frac{d}{dx}\log_e x = \operatorname*{Lt}_{h\to 0}\frac{\log(x+h)-\log x}{h}$$

$$= \operatorname*{Lt}_{h\to 0}\frac{\log x + \log\left(1+\frac{h}{x}\right) - \log x}{h}$$

$$= \operatorname*{Lt}_{h\to 0}\frac{\log\left(1+\frac{h}{x}\right)}{h}.$$

Now put $\frac{h}{x} = \frac{1}{k}$ so that if $x \neq 0$, $\operatorname*{Lt}_{h\to 0}$ is the same as $\operatorname*{Lt}_{k\to\infty}$.

Then

$$\operatorname*{Lt}_{h \to 0} \frac{\log\left(1 + \frac{h}{x}\right)}{h} = \operatorname*{Lt}_{k \to \infty} \left\{\frac{k}{x}\log\left(1 + \frac{1}{k}\right)\right\} = \frac{1}{x}\operatorname*{Lt}_{k \to \infty}\left\{k\log\left(1 + \frac{1}{k}\right)\right\}$$

$$= \frac{1}{x}\operatorname*{Lt}_{k \to \infty}\left\{\log\left(1 + \frac{1}{k}\right)^k\right\} = \frac{1}{x}\log\left\{\operatorname*{Lt}_{k \to \infty}\left(1 + \frac{1}{k}\right)^k\right\}$$

$$= \frac{1}{x}\log e = \frac{1}{x}.$$

Corollary: $\qquad \dfrac{d}{dx}\log_a x = \dfrac{1}{\log_e a}\cdot\dfrac{1}{x}.$

5. Standard forms: Trigonometrical.

(i) $y = \sin x.$

For the differentiation of $\sin x$ we adopt the alternative form

$$\frac{d}{dx}f(x) = \operatorname*{Lt}_{h \to 0} \frac{f(x + h) - f(x - h)}{2h}.$$

Then $\qquad \dfrac{d}{dx}\sin x = \operatorname*{Lt}_{h \to 0} \dfrac{\sin(x + h) - \sin(x - h)}{2h}$

$$= \operatorname*{Lt}_{h \to 0} \frac{2\cos x \sin h}{2h} \qquad \text{(p. 14)}$$

$$= \cos x \operatorname*{Lt}_{h \to 0} \frac{\sin h}{h}$$

$$= \cos x, \text{ since } \operatorname*{Lt}_{h \to 0} \frac{\sin h}{h} = 1 \qquad \text{(p. 27)}.$$

Similarly $\qquad \dfrac{d}{dx}\cos x = -\sin x.$

(ii) $y = \tan x.$

$$\frac{dy}{dx} = \operatorname*{Lt}_{h \to 0} \frac{\tan(x + h) - \tan(x - h)}{2h}$$

$$= \operatorname*{Lt}_{h \to 0} \frac{\sin(x + h)\cos(x - h) - \cos(x + h)\sin(x - h)}{2h\cos(x + h)\cos(x - h)}$$

$$= \operatorname*{Lt}_{h \to 0} \frac{\sin 2h}{2h}\cdot\frac{1}{\cos(x + h)\cos(x - h)}$$

$$= \frac{1}{\cos^2 x}$$

$$= \sec^2 x.$$

Similarly $\qquad\qquad \dfrac{d}{dx}\cot x = -\operatorname{cosec}^2 x.$

(iii) $y = \sin^{-1} x.$

If $\qquad\qquad\qquad y = \sin^{-1}x,$ then $\sin y = x.$

Therefore, differentiating both sides with respect to x,

$$\cos y \frac{dy}{dx} = \frac{dx}{dx} = 1,$$

and $\qquad\qquad \dfrac{dy}{dx} = \dfrac{1}{\cos y} = \dfrac{1}{\sqrt{1 - x^2}}.$

In the same manner it may be proved that

$$\frac{d}{dx}\cos^{-1} x = -\frac{1}{\sqrt{1 - x^2}} \quad\text{and}\quad \frac{d}{dx}\tan^{-1} x = \frac{1}{1 + x^2}.$$

6. Miscellaneous examples of differentiation.

Example 1.

Differentiate with respect to x:

$$(a)\ \sqrt{a^2 - x^2}, \qquad (b)\ \frac{1}{\sqrt{a^2 - x^2}}, \qquad (c)\ \frac{x}{\sqrt{a^2 - x^2}}.$$

$(a)\ \dfrac{d}{dx}\sqrt{a^2 - x^2} = \dfrac{d\,(a^2 - x^2)^{\frac{1}{2}}}{d\,(a^2 - x^2)} \cdot \dfrac{d\,(a^2 - x^2)}{dx}$

$$= \tfrac{1}{2}(a^2 - x^2)^{-\frac{1}{2}}.(-2x)$$

$$= -\frac{x}{\sqrt{a^2 - x^2}}.$$

$(b)\ \dfrac{d}{dx}\dfrac{1}{\sqrt{a^2 - x^2}} = \dfrac{d\,(a^2 - x^2)^{-\frac{1}{2}}}{d\,(a^2 - x^2)} \cdot \dfrac{d\,(a^2 - x^2)}{dx}$

$$= -\tfrac{1}{2}(a^2 - x^2)^{-\frac{3}{2}}.(-2x) = x\,(a^2 - x^2)^{-\frac{3}{2}}.$$

$(c)\ \dfrac{d}{dx}\dfrac{x}{\sqrt{a^2 - x^2}} = x.\dfrac{d}{dx}\dfrac{1}{\sqrt{a^2 - x^2}} + \dfrac{1}{\sqrt{a^2 - x^2}}.\dfrac{dx}{dx}$

$$= x.\frac{x}{(a^2 - x^2)^{\frac{3}{2}}} + \frac{1}{\sqrt{a^2 - x^2}}.1$$

$$= \frac{x^2 + a^2 - x^2}{(a^2 - x^2)^{\frac{3}{2}}} = \frac{a^2}{(a^2 - x^2)^{\frac{3}{2}}}.$$

Example 2.

Find $\dfrac{dy}{dx}$ where $y = \dfrac{2x + 5}{x^2 - 3x + 2}.$

The differentiation can be performed at once by treating y as the quotient of two functions of x, thus:

$$\frac{dy}{dx} = \frac{(x^2 - 3x + 2)\frac{d}{dx}(2x + 5) - (2x + 5)\frac{d}{dx}(x^2 - 3x + 2)}{(x^2 - 3x + 2)^2}$$

$$= \frac{2(x^2 - 3x + 2) - (2x + 5)(2x - 3)}{(x^2 - 3x + 2)^2}$$

$$= \frac{-2x^2 - 10x + 19}{(x^2 - 3x + 2)^2},$$

or, alternatively, we can split $\frac{2x + 5}{x^2 - 3x + 2}$ into partial fractions and differentiate each fraction separately;

$$\frac{dy}{dx} = \frac{d}{dx} \cdot \frac{2x + 5}{x^2 - 3x + 2} = \frac{d}{dx} \cdot \frac{2x + 5}{(x - 1)(x - 2)}$$

$$= \frac{d}{dx}\left(\frac{9}{x - 2} - \frac{7}{x - 1}\right) = -\frac{9}{(x - 2)^2} + \frac{7}{(x - 1)^2}$$

$$= \frac{-9x^2 + 18x - 9 + 7x^2 - 28x + 28}{(x - 2)^2 (x - 1)^2}$$

$$= \frac{-2x^2 - 10x + 19}{(x^2 - 3x + 2)^2}, \text{ as before.}$$

Example 3.

$$y = b^{c^x}. \quad \text{Find } \frac{dy}{dx}.$$

For this type of function it is useful to employ the process known as *logarithmic differentiation*. Here we take logarithms of both sides of the equation before differentiating and write

$$\log y = c^x \log b.$$

Let
$$z = \log y.$$

Then
$$\frac{dz}{dx} = \frac{dz}{dy} \cdot \frac{dy}{dx} = \frac{d(\log y)}{dy} \cdot \frac{dy}{dx} = \frac{1}{y} \cdot \frac{dy}{dx}.$$

Also
$$\frac{d}{dx}(c^x \log b) = c^x \log c \log b.$$

$$\therefore \frac{1}{y}\frac{dy}{dx} = c^x \log c \log b.$$

$$\therefore \frac{dy}{dx} = yc^x \log c \log b = b^{c^x}c^x \log c \log b.$$

Example 4.

Differentiate $\tan^{-1} \dfrac{1}{\sqrt{x^2 - 1}}$ with respect to x.

$$\frac{dy}{dx} = \frac{d \tan^{-1} (x^2 - 1)^{-\frac{1}{2}}}{d (x^2 - 1)^{-\frac{1}{2}}} \cdot \frac{d (x^2 - 1)^{-\frac{1}{2}}}{d (x^2 - 1)} \cdot \frac{d (x^2 - 1)}{dx}$$

$$= \frac{1}{1 + \dfrac{1}{x^2 - 1}} \cdot - \tfrac{1}{2} (x^2 - 1)^{-\frac{3}{2}} \cdot 2x$$

$$= - \frac{1}{x \sqrt{x^2 - 1}}.$$

Example 5.

Find $\dfrac{dy}{dx}$ where $y = x^x + x^{\frac{1}{x}}$.

It is important to note that $\dfrac{d}{dx} x^n = n x^{n-1}$ only where n is *a constant*, and it is therefore incorrect to state that $\dfrac{d}{dx} x^x = x . x^{x-1}$. To obtain $\dfrac{d}{dx} x^x$ we must employ the method of logarithmic differentiation. Moreover, y is the sum of two functions of x, and if we are to employ this method we must differentiate each of the functions separately. It would be incorrect to take logarithms of each side of the equality as it stands, for if $y = u + v$ then $\log y \neq \log u + \log v$.

Let $\qquad\qquad y = x^x + x^{\frac{1}{x}} = u + v.$

Then $\qquad\qquad \log u = x \log x$ and $\log v = \dfrac{1}{x} \log x.$

$$\frac{1}{u} \frac{du}{dx} = x . \frac{1}{x} + \log x = 1 + \log x.$$

$$\therefore \ \frac{du}{dx} = x^x (1 + \log x);$$

similarly $\qquad \dfrac{1}{v} \dfrac{dv}{dx} = \dfrac{1}{x} . \dfrac{1}{x} + \log x . - \dfrac{1}{x^2} = \dfrac{1}{x^2} (1 - \log x).$

$$\therefore \ \frac{dv}{dx} = x^{\frac{1}{x}} . \frac{1}{x^2} (1 - \log x).$$

$$\therefore \ \frac{dy}{dx} = x^x (1 + \log x) + x^{\frac{1}{x}} \frac{(1 - \log x)}{x^2}.$$

Example 6.

Differentiate $x \sin x$ with respect to $\tan x$.

$$\frac{d\,(x\sin x)}{d\tan x} = \frac{d\,(x\sin x)}{dx}\cdot\frac{dx}{d\tan x}$$

$$= \frac{\dfrac{d\,(x\sin x)}{dx}}{\dfrac{d\tan x}{dx}} = \frac{x\cos x + \sin x}{\sec^2 x} = x\cos^3 x + \sin x\cos^2 x.$$

7. Successive differentiation.

If we differentiate dy/dx with respect to x we obtain a new function which is called the second differential coefficient of y with respect to x. By analogy with the symbolic notation adopted in finite differences, we write

$$\frac{d}{dx}\frac{dy}{dx} \quad\text{as}\quad \frac{d^2y}{dx^2},$$

where, it should be remembered, the independent variable is still x and not x^2. Similarly, the third differential coefficient of y with respect to x is $\frac{d^3y}{dx^3}$, and if y is differentiated n times with respect to x, the nth differential coefficient is $\frac{d^ny}{dx^n}$. In the alternative notation we have

$$D^2y,\ D^3y,\ \dots D^ny,$$
$$f''(x),\ f'''(x),\ \dots f^{(n)}(x).$$

A notation frequently employed for the nth derivative is y_n.

8. Successive differential coefficients of many simple functions can be found by an inductive process.

Example 7.

Find $\dfrac{d^n}{dx^n}\log x$.

$$y = \log x;\quad y_1 = 1/x;\quad y_2 = (-1).1/x^2;$$
$$y_3 = (-1)(-2).1/x^3;\quad y_4 = (-1)(-2)(-3).1/x^4;$$

and so on.

Therefore by induction $y_n = (-1)^{n-1}\dfrac{(n-1)!}{x^n}$.

Example 8.

$$y = (2x+5)/(x^2-3x+2).\ \text{Find } y_n.$$

It is imperative where higher differential coefficients than the first are required to use the second method given in Example 2 of para. 6, and to express y in partial fractions before differentiating.

$$y = \frac{9}{x-2} - \frac{7}{x-1},$$

$$y_1 = -\frac{9\cdot 1}{(x-2)^2} + \frac{7\cdot 1}{(x-1)^2},$$

$$y_2 = \frac{9\cdot 1\cdot 2}{(x-2)^3} - \frac{7\cdot 1\cdot 2}{(x-1)^3},$$

$$y_3 = -\frac{9\cdot 1\cdot 2\cdot 3}{(x-2)^4} + \frac{7\cdot 1\cdot 2\cdot 3}{(x-1)^4},$$

$$\ldots\ldots\ldots\ldots\ldots\ldots$$

$$\therefore\ y_n = (-1)^n\, n!\left[\frac{9}{(x-2)^{n+1}} - \frac{7}{(x-1)^{n+1}}\right].$$

Example 9.

Show that if y be a rational integral function of the nth degree in x, then the nth differential coefficient of y with respect to x is constant.

If
$$y = a + bx + cx^2 + \ldots + kx^n,$$
$$y_1 = b + 2cx + \ldots + knx^{n-1},$$
$$y_2 = 2c + \ldots + kn\,(n-1)\,x^{n-2},$$
$$\ldots\ldots\ldots\ldots\ldots\ldots\ldots,$$

and each time that we differentiate we lower the degree of the function by unity. Hence after n differentiations we shall lower the degree of the function by n.

$$\therefore\ y_n = kn\,(n-1)\,(n-2)\ldots(n-\overline{n-1})\,x^{n-n}$$
$$= kn!\ \text{which is constant.}$$

If we denote $\dfrac{d^n y}{dx^n}$ by $D^n y$ we may write $D^m x^m = m!$.

9. Leibnitz's Theorem.

Let D_1 and D_2 represent the operations of differentiating u and v respectively, where D_1 operates only on u and its successive differential coefficients and D_2 operates only on v and its successive differential coefficients.

Then
$$Duv = uDv + vDu$$

$$= D_1\,(uv) + D_2\,(uv).$$

$$\therefore\ D \equiv D_1 + D_2,$$

so that

$$D^n \equiv (D_1 + D_2)^n$$

$$\equiv D_1{}^n + n_1 D_1{}^{n-1} D_2 + n_2 D_1{}^{n-2} D_2{}^2 + \dots + n_r D_1{}^{n-r} D_2{}^r + \dots + D_2{}^n.$$

But $D_1{}^{n-r} D_2{}^r (uv) = \dfrac{d^{n-r}}{dx^{n-r}} u \cdot \dfrac{d^r}{dx^r} v.$

$$\therefore \frac{d^n y}{dx^n} = D^n (uv) = \frac{d^n u}{dx^n} v + n_1 \frac{d^{n-1}u}{dx^{n-1}} \cdot \frac{dv}{dx} + n_2 \frac{d^{n-2}u}{dx^{n-2}} \cdot \frac{d^2 v}{dx^2} + \dots$$

$$+ n_r \frac{d^{n-r}u}{dx^{n-r}} \cdot \frac{d^r v}{dx^r} + \dots + u \frac{d^n v}{dx^n}.$$

This is Leibnitz's Theorem for the successive differentiation of the product of two functions of x.

10. Application of Leibnitz's Theorem.

Example 10.

If $y = x^2 e^x$ find $\dfrac{d^n y}{dx^n}$.

In the general expansion above let $x^2 = v$ and $e^x = u$.

Then
$$v = x^2, \qquad\qquad u = e^x,$$

$$\frac{dv}{dx} = 2x, \qquad\qquad \frac{du}{dx} = e^x,$$

$$\frac{d^2 v}{dx^2} = 2, \qquad\qquad \frac{d^2 u}{dx^2} = e^x.$$

$\dfrac{d^3 v}{dx^3}$ and higher derivatives are zero.

$$\therefore \frac{d^n}{dx^n} (x^2 e^x) = x^2 e^x + n.2x.e^x + \frac{n(n-1)}{2}.2e^x$$

$$= e^x (x^2 + 2nx + n^2 - n).$$

Example 11.

If
$$y = \log \{(x - 1)^{\frac{1}{2}} + (x + 1)^{\frac{1}{2}}\}$$

prove that
$$(x^2 - 1)\frac{d^2 y}{dx^2} + x\frac{dy}{dx} = 0$$

and that
$$(x^2 - 1)\frac{d^{n+2}y}{dx^{n+2}} + (2n + 1) x\frac{d^{n+1}y}{dx^{n+1}} + n^2 \frac{d^n y}{dx^n} = 0.$$

$$y = \log \{(x - 1)^{\frac{1}{2}} + (x + 1)^{\frac{1}{2}}\}.$$

$$\therefore \frac{dy}{dx} = \frac{1}{(x - 1)^{\frac{1}{2}} + (x + 1)^{\frac{1}{2}}} \cdot \{\tfrac{1}{2}(x - 1)^{-\frac{1}{2}} + \tfrac{1}{2}(x + 1)^{-\frac{1}{2}}\} = \tfrac{1}{2}(x^2 - 1)^{-\frac{1}{2}}.$$

$$\therefore \frac{d^2y}{dx^2} = \frac{d}{dx}\{\tfrac{1}{2}(x^2-1)^{-\frac{1}{2}}\} = -\tfrac{1}{2}x(x^2-1)^{-\frac{3}{2}}.$$

$$\therefore (x^2-1)\frac{d^2y}{dx^2} + x\frac{dy}{dx} = 0;$$

Differentiate each of the products $(x^2-1)\dfrac{d^2y}{dx^2}$ and $x\dfrac{dy}{dx}$ n times by Leibnitz's Theorem.

Then $(x^2-1)y_{n+2} + n.2x.y_{n+1} + \dfrac{n(n-1)}{2}.2.y_n$

$$+ x.y_{n+1} + ny_n = 0;$$

i.e. $(x^2-1)y_{n+2} + (2n+1)xy_{n+1} + n^2y_n = 0.$

11. We will conclude this chapter with some miscellaneous examples of differentiation.

Example 12.

If y, z are both functions of x and if $y^2 + z^2 = k^2$ prove that

$$y.\frac{d}{dx}\left(\frac{y}{k}\right) + \frac{d}{dx}\left(\frac{z^2}{k}\right) = \frac{z}{k}.\frac{dz}{dx}.$$

$$y.\frac{d}{dx}\left(\frac{y}{k}\right) + \frac{d}{dx}\left(\frac{z^2}{k}\right) = y.\frac{d}{dx}\frac{y}{\sqrt{y^2+z^2}} + \frac{d}{dx}\frac{z^2}{\sqrt{y^2+z^2}}$$

$$=y.\left[\frac{\dfrac{dy}{dx}\sqrt{y^2+z^2} - \dfrac{y\left\{y\dfrac{dy}{dx}+z\dfrac{dz}{dx}\right\}}{\sqrt{y^2+z^2}}}{(y^2+z^2)}\right] + \frac{2z\dfrac{dz}{dx}\sqrt{y^2+z^2} - \dfrac{z^2\left\{y\dfrac{dy}{dx}+z\dfrac{dz}{dx}\right\}}{\sqrt{y^2+z^2}}}{(y^2+z^2)}$$

$$=\frac{1}{(y^2+z^2)^{\frac{3}{2}}}\Bigg[y\frac{dy}{dx}(y^2+z^2) - y^2\left(y\frac{dy}{dx}+z\frac{dz}{dx}\right) + 2z\frac{dz}{dx}(y^2+z^2)$$

$$- z^2\left(y\frac{dy}{dx}+z\frac{dz}{dx}\right)\Bigg]$$

which simplifies to

$$\frac{1}{(y^2+z^2)^{\frac{3}{2}}}\left\{z\frac{dz}{dx}(y^2+z^2)\right\} = \frac{z}{k}.\frac{dz}{dx}.$$

Example 13.

Prove that if n be a positive integer, and a and b have any values, then

$$(a+b)(a+b-1)\dots(a+b-n+1)$$

$$= \sum_{p=0}^{p=n}\left[\frac{n!}{p!q!}a(a-1)\dots(a-p+1).b(b-1)\dots(b-q+1)\right]$$

where $p+q=n$.   (Vandermonde's Theorem.)

Now $D^n(uv) = \Sigma\left[\dfrac{n!}{p!\,q!}\,D^p(u)\,D^q(v)\right]$ by Leibnitz's Theorem.

Let $u = x^a$ and $v = x^b$ so that $uv = x^{a+b}$. Then

$(a+b)(a+b-1)\ldots(a+b-n+1)\,x^{a+b-n}$

$= \Sigma\left[\dfrac{n!}{p!\,q!}\,a(a-1)\ldots(a-p+1)\,x^{a-p}.b(b-1)\ldots(b-q+1)\,x^{b-q}\right]$

$= \Sigma\left[\dfrac{n!}{p!\,q!}\,a(a-1)\ldots(a-p+1).b(b-1)\ldots(b-q+1)\,x^{a+b-p-q}\right].$

Since $p+q=n$ we may divide through by x^{a+b-n} and the proposition is proved.

Example 14.

If $y = f(x)$ obtain $\dfrac{d^2x}{dy^2}$ and $\dfrac{d^3x}{dy^3}$ in terms of $\dfrac{dy}{dx}, \dfrac{d^2y}{dx^2}$ and $\dfrac{d^3y}{dx^3}$.

Let y_1, y_2, y_3 stand for $\dfrac{dy}{dx}, \dfrac{d^2y}{dx^2}, \dfrac{d^3y}{dx^3}$ respectively.

(i) $\qquad\qquad \dfrac{dx}{dy} = \dfrac{1}{y_1}.$

(ii) $\qquad \dfrac{d^2x}{dy^2} = \dfrac{d}{dy}\left(\dfrac{dx}{dy}\right) = \dfrac{d}{dy}\left(\dfrac{1}{y_1}\right) = \dfrac{d}{dx}\left(\dfrac{1}{y_1}\right)\dfrac{dx}{dy}$

$\qquad\qquad\qquad = -\dfrac{1}{y_1^2}.y_2.\dfrac{1}{y_1} = -\dfrac{y_2}{y_1^3}.$

(iii) $\qquad \dfrac{d^3x}{dy^3} = \dfrac{d}{dy}\left(\dfrac{d^2x}{dy^2}\right) = \dfrac{d}{dx}\left(-\dfrac{y_2}{y_1^3}\right)\dfrac{dx}{dy}$

$\qquad\qquad\qquad = -\dfrac{y_3 y_1^3 - 3y_1^2 y_2^2}{y_1^6}.\dfrac{1}{y_1}$

$\qquad\qquad\qquad = \dfrac{3y_2^2 - y_1 y_3}{y_1^5}.$

EXAMPLES 3

1. If y represent the number of gallons of water in a leaking tank and x the number of hours since the tank was full, what does $\dfrac{dy}{dx}$ represent, and is it positive or negative?

2. Let x denote the annual expenditure, and y the annual receipts of a trading company. If $\dfrac{dy}{dx}$ be positive, and $\dfrac{d^2y}{dx^2}$ be negative for a given

value of x, what inference would you draw? What additional statement could you make if you also knew whether $\frac{dy}{dx}$ were greater or less than unity?

3. Prove that, when b tends to a, the limit of $\frac{(b^{\frac{1}{2}} - a^{\frac{1}{2}})}{b - a}$ is $\frac{1}{2}a^{-\frac{1}{2}}$ and deduce the differential coefficient of $\sqrt{x}$.

4. If a body in motion moves a distance of s feet in t seconds what are the meanings of $\frac{ds}{dt}$ and $\frac{d^2s}{dt^2}$?

5. Find from first principles the first differential coefficients with respect to x of $x\sqrt{a^2 - x^2}$ and $e^{x \log x}$.

6. (i) Give a geometrical interpretation of the differential coefficient of a function of x with respect to x.

(ii) Find, from first principles,

$$\frac{d}{dx}(x^5); \qquad \frac{d}{dx}(ax + b)^n; \qquad \frac{d}{dx}(x^x).$$

Differentiate with respect to x:—

7. $(a + bx)^n$; $\quad a^{nx}$; $\quad \sqrt[n]{a^2 + x^2}$; $\quad \log \frac{x}{a^x}$.

8. $(x + 1/x)^2$; $\quad x^m(1 - x)^n$; $\quad x^m e^x$; $\quad x^n \log x$.

9. $\log_x a$; $\quad \log x^{x^2}$; $\quad 10^{10^x}$; $\quad \frac{\log x}{x}$.

10. $\sin^2 x$; $\quad \sin 2x$; $\quad \cos^3 x$; $\quad x^2 \sec x$.

11. $\sin^{-1} x^2$; $\quad \sqrt{x \sin x}$; $\quad \tan x \tan 2x$.

12. $x \cos^{-1} x$; $\quad x^2 \tan^{-1} x$; $\quad \sin x (\tan^{-1} x)^2$.

13. $(5 + 4x)^{\log x}$; $\quad \dfrac{x^m}{(1 - \sqrt{1 - x^2})^m}$; $\quad \log(\log x)$.

14. $a^x + x^a$; $\quad x^x + (1 - x^2)^m$; $\quad x^{x^n}$.

15. $\tan^{-1} \dfrac{3x}{1 + 4x^2}$; $\quad x\sqrt{x}\sqrt{\cos^{-1} x}$.

16. If $\qquad y = x\sqrt{x^2 + a^2} + a^2 \log(x + \sqrt{x^2 + a^2})$,

prove that $\qquad \dfrac{dy}{dx} = 2\sqrt{x^2 + a^2}$.

17. Show that the result of differentiating the expression

$$\frac{x+1}{(x-1)(x-2)}$$

as it stands and differentiating the same expression when split up into partial fractions is the same.

18. Find $\dfrac{dy}{dx}$ given $y = x^y$.

19. Differentiate $\log \dfrac{xe^x}{e^x - 1}$ with respect to x.

20. A ladder, AB, 13 feet long, rests against a vertical wall, having its lower extremity B distant 5 feet from the wall. If B be made to slide outwards from the wall at the rate of $1\frac{1}{2}$ feet per second, find at what rate the upper end A will begin to slide down the wall.

21. Find $\dfrac{dy}{dx}$:

(i) $y = \dfrac{x \sqrt{x^2 - 4a^2}}{\sqrt{x^2 - a^2}}$;
    (ii) $e^y = \dfrac{(a + bx^n)^{\frac{1}{2}} - a^{\frac{1}{2}}}{(bx^n)^{\frac{1}{2}}}$.

22. If S_n equals the sum of a G.P. to n terms, of which r is the common ratio, prove that $(r - 1) \dfrac{dS_n}{dr} = (n - 1) S_n - nS_{n-1}$.

23. $y = \log \tan^{-1} \left\{ \dfrac{2x^2 + a}{2ax^2 - 1} \right\}$. Find $\dfrac{dy}{dx}$.

24. (i) Find $\dfrac{dy}{dx}$ where $y = x^{e^x}$.

(ii) Find $\dfrac{dy}{dx}$ where $y = x \log \dfrac{y}{1 + x}$.

25. Prove that if $x + \sqrt{a^2 - y^2} = a \log \dfrac{a + \sqrt{a^2 - y^2}}{y}$ then

$$\frac{dy}{dx} = - \frac{y}{\sqrt{a^2 - y^2}}.$$

26. Differentiate $x^{(\log x)^2}$ with respect to $\log x$.

27. Differentiate $\tan^{-1} \left\{ \dfrac{\sqrt{1 + x^2} - 1}{x} \right\}$ with regard to $\tan^{-1} x$.

28. If $t = \tan \dfrac{x}{2}$ differentiate the following with regard to t: $\sin x$; $\cos x$; $\sec^2 x$; x. Express the results in terms of t.

29. Differentiate $\log \sqrt[3]{\dfrac{a^3 + a^2 x + ax^2 + x^3}{a^2 + ax + x^2}}$ with respect to x.

30. Differentiate $\log_{10} x$ with respect to x^2 and

$$\frac{(1 + x^2)^{\frac{1}{2}} + (1 - x^2)^{\frac{1}{2}}}{(1 + x^2)^{\frac{1}{2}} - (1 - x^2)^{\frac{1}{2}}}$$

with respect to $(1 - x^4)^{\frac{1}{2}}$.

31. If $\sqrt{1 - x^2} + \sqrt{1 - y^2} = a(x - y)$, prove that $\dfrac{dy}{dx} = \sqrt{\dfrac{1 - y^2}{1 - x^2}}$.

32. Differentiate $\log \dfrac{e^x + \sqrt{e^{2x} - a^2}}{e^x - \sqrt{e^{2x} - a^2}}$ with respect to x.

33. Find $\dfrac{dy}{dx}$ where $y(y^2 + x^2) = x + y$.

34. Differentiate (i) $\log \sin x$; (ii) $\tan^{-1} \left\{ \dfrac{4x(1 - x^2)}{1 - 6x^2 + x^4} \right\}$.

35. Determine the coefficients $a_0, a_1, a_2, \ldots a_n$, so that

$$\frac{d}{dx} \left[\frac{a_0 x^n + a_1 x^{n-1} + a_2 x^{n-2} + \ldots + a_n}{e^x} \right] \text{ shall equal } \frac{x^n}{e^x}.$$

36. Differentiate $\tan^{-1}(\sin a/x + \cos a/x)$ with respect to x.

37. If $y^2 = a^2 x^2 + c$, differentiate with respect to x the functions (i) $\log(ax + y)$; (ii) xy, and express the results in terms of y.

38. $x = e^{\tan^{-1} z}$, where $z = (y - x^2)/x^2$. Find $\dfrac{dy}{dx}$.

39. Differentiate e^{a^x} with respect to (i) x; (ii) e^x; (iii) x^x.

40. If u_1, v_1, u_2, v_2 represent functions of x show that

$$\frac{d}{dx} \left[\frac{u_1 u_2}{v_1 v_2} \right] = \frac{u_1 u_2}{v_1 v_2} \left\{ \left[\frac{1}{u_1} \frac{du_1}{dx} - \frac{1}{v_1} \frac{dv_1}{dx} \right] + \left[\frac{1}{u_2} \frac{du_2}{dx} - \frac{1}{v_2} \frac{dv_2}{dx} \right] \right\}.$$

41. Find $\dfrac{d^3 y}{dx^3}$ when

$$\text{(i) } y = \frac{ax + b}{cx + d}; \qquad \text{(ii) } y = \frac{\log x}{x}.$$

42. If $y = \sin(\log x)$, prove that $x^2 \dfrac{d^2 y}{dx^2} + x \dfrac{dy}{dx} + y = 0$.

43. If $y = ax \cos \left[\dfrac{n}{x} + b \right]$, show that $x^4 \dfrac{d^2 y}{dx^2} + n^2 y = 0$.

44. Find the second differential coefficient of $x(x-4)$ with regard to $\log x$.

45. Show that the equation $\dfrac{d^2y}{dx^2} - 2m\dfrac{dy}{dx} + m^2y = e^x$ is satisfied by

$$y = (A + Bx)\,e^{mx} + \frac{e^x}{(m-1)^2}.$$

46. If $y = a + x\log y$, prove that, when $x = 0$, $y_1 = \log a$ and find y_2.

47. If $y = (x + \sqrt{x^2 + 1})^n$, prove that $(x^2 + 1)\dfrac{d^2y}{dx^2} + x\dfrac{dy}{dx} - n^2y = 0$

48. If
$$A = a\cos(x + k) + b\sin(x + k),$$
$$B = a\sin(x + k) - b\cos(x + k),$$

show that
$$-\frac{d^2A}{dB^2} = \frac{B^2 + A^2}{A^3}.$$

49. If $y = \dfrac{3x + 4}{5x + 6}$, prove that $\dfrac{d^2y}{dx^2} \cdot \dfrac{d^3y}{dx^3} = \dfrac{1}{2}\dfrac{dy}{dx} \cdot \dfrac{d^4y}{dx^4}$.

50. $y = x\log\dfrac{x}{a + bx}$. Find the value of $x^3\dfrac{d^2y}{dx^2} - \left(y - x\dfrac{dy}{dx}\right)^2$.

51. Find the nth differential coefficient of $\dfrac{px + q}{(x - a)(x - b)(x - c)}$.

52. Find the nth differential coefficient of $x(x + 1)(x^2 - 3x + 2)^{-1}$.

53. Find $\dfrac{d^ny}{dx^n}$, where $y = \dfrac{(x - a)(x - b)}{(x - c)(x - d)}$.

54. Find $\dfrac{d^4y}{dx^4}$ if $y = \dfrac{1}{(2x + 1)(1 - x)}$.

55. If $y = (x^2 - 1)^n$, prove

(a) $(x^2 - 1)\dfrac{dy}{dx} = 2nxy$;

(b) $(x^2 - 1)\dfrac{d^{n+2}y}{dx^{n+2}} + 2x\dfrac{d^{n+1}y}{dx^{n+1}} - n(n + 1)\dfrac{d^ny}{dx^n} = 0$.

56. If $y = A(x + \sqrt{x^2 - 1})^m + B(x - \sqrt{x^2 - 1})^m$, prove that
$$(x^2 - 1)\frac{d^2y}{dx^2} + x\frac{dy}{dx} - m^2y = 0,$$

and that
$$(x^2 - 1)\frac{d^{n+2}y}{dx^{n+2}} + (2n + 1)x\frac{d^{n+1}y}{dx^{n+1}} + (n^2 - m^2)\frac{d^ny}{dx^n} = 0.$$

57. Find $\dfrac{d^ny}{dx^n}$, where y equals

(i) $x^2\log x \quad (n > 3)$; (ii) $\dfrac{6x^3 + 5x^2 - 7}{3x^2 - 2x - 1}$.

58. Prove that $\dfrac{d^n}{dx^n}(e^{ax}u_x) = e^{ax}\left\{\dfrac{d}{dx}+a\right\}^n u_x.$

59. If $y = e^{ax}[a^2 x^2 - 2nax + n(n+1)]$, find $\dfrac{d^n y}{dx^n}$.

60. Find the nth differential coefficient of $\dfrac{1}{(x-a)^2(x-b)}$.

61. If $y = x^n (\log x)^2$, prove that $x^2 \dfrac{d^{n+2} y}{dx^{n+2}} + x \dfrac{d^{n+1} y}{dx^{n+1}} = 2(n!).$

62. If $y = \sin(a \sin^{-1} x)$, show that

   (i) $(1-x^2)\dfrac{d^2 y}{dx^2} - x\dfrac{dy}{dx} + a^2 y = 0;$

   (ii) $(1-x^2)\dfrac{d^{n+2} y}{dx^{n+2}} - (2n+1)x\dfrac{d^{n+1} y}{dx^{n+1}} + (a^2 - n^2)\dfrac{d^n y}{dx^n} = 0.$

63. If $y = \dfrac{\sin^{-1} x}{(1-x^2)^{\frac{1}{2}}}$, prove that $(1-x^2)\dfrac{dy}{dx} = xy+1$; and if y_n denotes the nth differential coefficient of y, prove that, when $x = 0$, $y_n = (n-1)^2 y_{n-2}.$

64. Prove that, if $x + y = 1$,
$$\dfrac{d^n}{dx^n}(x^n y^n) = n![y^n - (n_1)^2 y^{n-1} x + (n_2)^2 y^{n-2} x^2 - \ldots].$$

65. Prove that, if $y = e^{\tan^{-1} x}$,
$$(1+x^2)\dfrac{d^{n+1} y}{dx^{n+1}} = (1-2nx)\dfrac{d^n y}{dx^n} - n(n-1)\dfrac{d^{n-1} y}{dx^{n-1}}.$$

66. If $u = \sin(m \tan^{-1} x)$, prove that
$$\dfrac{d^2 u}{dx^2}(1+x^2)^2 + \dfrac{du}{dx}(2x + 2x^3) + m^2 u = 0,$$
and thence, by use of Leibnitz's Theorem, show that, if A_n denote the value of $\dfrac{d^n u}{dx^n}$ when x is put equal to zero,
$$A_{n+2} + (2n^2 + m^2) A_n + n(n-1)^2(n-2) A_{n-2} = 0.$$

67. Prove that, if $\sin^{-1} y = a + b \sin^{-1} x$, then, when x is zero, $y_{n+2} = (n^2 - b^2) y_n.$

68. $y = xe^x \log x$. Prove that
$$x(y_4 - 4y_3 + 6y_2 - 4y_1 + y) = -2(y_3 - 3y_2 + 3y_1 - y).$$

69. If $y^3 + 3x^2 y + 1 = 0$, prove that $(x^2 + y^2)^3 \dfrac{d^2 y}{dx^2} + 2(x^2 - y^2) = 0.$

70. If $u = ks^x g^{c^x}$, show that the ratio between $\dfrac{d^2u}{dx^2}$ and u can be expressed in the form $p + qc^x + rc^{2x}$, and find p, q and r.

71. Differentiate:

(i) $\sin^{-1} (\operatorname{cosec} \theta \sqrt{\cos 2\theta})$; (ii) $\tan^{-1} \dfrac{x}{1 + (1 + x^2)^{\frac{1}{2}}}$.

72. Prove that $\left(\dfrac{d}{dx}\right)^n (e^{ax} x^r) = \left(\dfrac{a}{x}\right)^{n-r} \left(\dfrac{d}{dx}\right)^r (e^{ax} x^n)$.

73. Differentiate with respect to x:

$$\tan^{-1} \left[\frac{3 \tan x - \tan^3 x}{1 - 3 \tan^2 x} \right].$$

74. In the curve $b^2 y = \frac{1}{3}x^3 - ax^2$, find the coordinates of the points at which the tangent to the curve is parallel to the axis of x.

75. The equation to a curve is $4x^2 + 9y^2 + 16x - 18y - 11 = 0$. Find the points on the graph of the curve where the tangent is (i) parallel, (ii) perpendicular to the axis of x.

76. If $ax^2 + 2hxy + by^2 + 2gx + 2fy + c = 0$, show that

$$(hx + by + f)^3 \frac{d^2y}{dx^2}$$

is constant.

77. $y = \tan^{-1} [(e^x + 1)/(e^x - 1)]^{\frac{1}{2}}$. Prove that

$$y_3 = y_1 (1 + 12 y_1^2) (1 + 4 y_1^2).$$

78. If $y = (\sqrt{x} - 1) e^{\sqrt{x}}$, show that $2x \dfrac{d^2y}{dx^2} = \frac{1}{2} y + \dfrac{dy}{dx}$.

79. If $y = \dfrac{ax + b}{Ax + B}$ and $z = \dfrac{ay + b}{Ay + B}$, show that

$$\frac{z'''}{z'} - \frac{3}{2} \left(\frac{z''}{z'}\right)^2 = \frac{y'''}{y'} - \frac{3}{2} \left(\frac{y''}{y'}\right)^2 = 0,$$

where accents denote differentiations with respect to x.

80. Prove by induction that $\dfrac{d^n}{dx^n} (x^{n-1} \log x) = \dfrac{(n-1)!}{x}$.

CHAPTER IV

EXPANSIONS

1. It is often necessary to express the function $f(x+h)$ in a series of ascending powers of h and of the successive differential coefficients of $f(x)$.

It was shown in the last chapter that the function $y=f(x)$ could have a unique differential coefficient at the point $x=a$ only if y were finite and continuous at that point and as a result we must be careful in dealing with expansions involving differential coefficients that the conditions of continuity hold.

2. Rolle's Theorem.

Before proceeding to obtain the general expansion of $f(x+h)$ in terms of $f(x)$ and its derivatives it will be necessary to consider some simple theorems connected with the first and second differential coefficients of the function. The first of these theorems is Rolle's Theorem, which states that

If $f(x)$ and $f'(x)$ $\left(\text{i.e. } \dfrac{d}{dx} f(x)\right)$ are continuous over the range $x = a$ to $x = b$, and if $f(x) = 0$ when $x = a$ and when $x = b$, then for at least one value of x between a and b, $f'(x)$ will be zero.

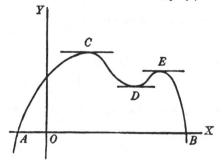

Fig. 22.

The proof is as follows:

Since $f(a) = f(b) = 0$, $f(x)$ cannot always be increasing or decreasing. Hence for at least one value between $x = a$ and $x = b$

there will be a change from an increase to a decrease or vice versa. For the particular value of x for which this is so, $f'(x)$ must be zero, which proves the proposition.

That the theorem is self-evident may be seen from the diagram above (Fig. 22).

If the curve represents the continuous function $y=f(x)$ and if $y=f(x)=0$ for the values $x=a$ and $x=b$ (i.e. at the points A and B), then at the points C, D, E the tangents to the curve are parallel to the x-axis. That is, at these points $f'(x)$ is zero.

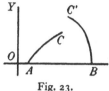

Fig. 23.

It should be noted that $f(x)$ must be continuous within the given range. If there be a discontinuity such as at the points C and C' in Fig. 23 there is no unique differential coefficient; consequently the theorem does not apply and $f'(x)$ is not necessarily zero in the range.

Since difficulties may arise in dealing with multiple-valued functions, it is advisable to restrict the above proof to single-valued functions of x.

3. Mean Value Theorem.

As before, let $f(x)$ and $f'(x)$ be continuous in the range $x = a$ to $x = b$ and let $m = \dfrac{f(b) - f(a)}{b - a}$, so that

$$f(b) - f(a) - m(b - a) = 0.$$

Replace b by x in the left-hand side of this expression and let

$$\phi(x) = f(x) - f(a) - m(x - a).$$

Then obviously $\phi(a) = 0$ and we have shown that $\phi(b) = 0$.

Therefore Rolle's Theorem holds, since $f(x)$ and $f'(x)$ are continuous in the given range.

Hence $\phi'(x)$ will be zero for at least one value of x (x_1 say) between a and b.

But $\qquad \phi(x) = f(x) - f(a) - m(x - a).$

Therefore $\phi'(x) = f'(x) - m$ on differentiating.

Hence since $\phi'(x_1) = 0$, then $f'(x_1) = m$.

Therefore $\qquad \dfrac{f(b) - f(a)}{b - a} = f'(x_1).$

This is the Mean Value Theorem, and may be stated thus:

If $f(x)$ and $f'(x)$ are continuous in the range $x = a$ to $x = b$, then there is at least one value of x (x_1 say) between $x = a$ and $x = b$ such that $\dfrac{f(b) - f(a)}{b - a} = f'(x_1)$.

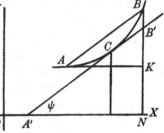

Fig. 24.

This is equivalent to saying that if $y = f(x)$ is a continuous curve between the values A ($x = a$) and B ($x = b$), then there is at least one value of x, (x_1), where $a < x < b$, for which the tangent to the curve is parallel to the chord AB. That is, if the tangent at this point C make an angle ψ with the x-axis,

$$\tan \psi = \frac{B'N}{A'N} = \frac{BK}{AK} = \frac{f(b) - f(a)}{b - a}.$$

A more convenient form may be obtained for the result of this theorem. Since x_1 lies between a and b we may write

$$x_1 = a + \theta_1 (b - a),$$

where θ_1 is a positive proper fraction.

The mean value theorem becomes therefore

$$\frac{f(b) - f(a)}{b - a} = f'[a + \theta_1 (b - a)],$$

or if $b - a = h$, so that $b = a + h$, then

$$f(a + h) - f(a) = hf'(a + \theta_1 h);$$

i.e. $\qquad f(a + h) = f(a) + hf'(a + \theta_1 h).$

4. We may extend the mean value theorem to include higher derivatives of $f(x)$, thus:

If $f(x)$, $f'(x)$ and $f''(x)$ are continuous in the range $x = a$ to $x = b$, then there is at least one value x_2 between $x = a$ and $x = b$ such that

$$f(b) = f(a) + (b - a)f'(a) + \tfrac{1}{2}(b - a)^2 f''(x_2).$$

Let $\qquad p = \dfrac{f(b) - f(a) - (b - a)f'(a)}{\tfrac{1}{2}(b - a)^2},$

and let $\quad \phi(x) = f(x) - f(a) - (x - a)f'(a) - \tfrac{1}{2}(x - a)^2 p.$

Then $\phi(a) = 0$ and $\phi(b) = 0$; and $\phi(x)$ satisfies the conditions of Rolle's Theorem.

Therefore for a value x_1 say between $x = a$ and $x = b$, $\phi'(x_1) = 0$.

But $$\phi'(x) = f'(x) - f'(a) - (x - a)p,$$

and this vanishes for the values a and x_1.

Therefore $\phi''(x) = 0$ for some value of x (x_2 say) between a and x_1, i.e. between a and b.

But $$\phi''(x) = f''(x) - p.$$

Hence since $\phi''(x_2) = 0$, then $p = f''(x_2)$.

$$\therefore \ f(b) - f(a) - (b - a)f'(a) = \tfrac{1}{2}(b - a)^2 f''(x_2).$$

If as before we put $x_2 = a + \theta_2(b - a)$ and $b - a = h$, we have

$$f(b) = f(a) + hf'(a) + \tfrac{1}{2}h^2 f''(a + \theta_2 h).$$

5. Taylor's Theorem.

It is evident that we can extend the above process as long as the successive differential coefficients are continuous throughout the given range, and can thus obtain expressions for $f(b)$ in terms of $f(a)$ and its higher derivatives.

Consider the general case, where all the derivatives are continuous:

Let

$$q = \frac{f(b) - \left[f(a) + (b - a)f'(a) + \dfrac{(b - a)^2}{2!}f''(a) + \ldots + \dfrac{(b - a)^{n-1}}{(n - 1)!}f^{(n-1)}(a)\right]}{(b - a)^n}.$$

and let

$$\phi(x) = f(b) - f(x) - (b - x)f'(x) - \frac{(b - x)^2}{2!}f''(x) - \ldots$$
$$- \frac{(b - x)^{n-1}}{(n - 1)!}f^{(n-1)}(x) - (b - x)^n q.$$

As before $\phi(a)$, $\phi(b)$ are both zero. Since $\phi(x)$, $\phi'(x)$ are continuous, $\phi'(x)$ is zero for a value x_1 in the given range.

But by differentiation

$$\phi'(x) = -\frac{(b - x)^{n-1}}{(n - 1)!}f^{(n)}(x) + n(b - x)^{n-1}q,$$

all the remaining terms in the expression for $\phi(x)$ vanishing on differentiation.

FI

5

$$\therefore \quad -\frac{(b-x_1)^{n-1}}{(n-1)!}f^{(n)}(x_1) + n(b-x_1)^{n-1}q = 0.$$

$$\therefore \quad q = \frac{f^{(n)}(x_1)}{n!} \quad \text{since } b \neq x_1.$$

If $x_1 = a + \theta(b-a)$ and $b - a = h$ we see that

$$f(b) = f(a) + hf'(a) + \frac{h^2}{2!}f''(a) + \dots$$
$$+ \frac{h^{n-1}}{(n-1)!}f^{(n-1)}(a) + \frac{h^n}{n!}f^{(n)}(a+\theta h).$$

An expansion for $f(x+h)$ in terms of $f(x)$ and ascending powers of h is at once evident. Replace b by $x+h$ and write x for a so that $b - a = (x+h) - x = h$ as before.

Then

$$f(x+h) = f(x) + hf'(x) + \frac{h^2}{2!}f''(x) + \frac{h^3}{3!}f'''(x) + \dots$$
$$+ \frac{h^{n-1}}{(n-1)!}f^{(n-1)}(x) + \frac{h^n}{n!}f^{(n)}(x+\theta h).$$

This is Taylor's Theorem.

If in the above expansion we put $x = 0$ we have

$$f(h) = f(0) + hf'(0) + \frac{h^2}{2!}f''(0) + \frac{h^3}{3!}f'''(0) + \dots$$
$$+ \frac{h^{n-1}}{(n-1)!}f^{(n-1)}(0) + \frac{h^n}{n!}f^{(n)}(\theta h),$$

or putting x for h

$$f(x) = f(0) + xf'(0) + \frac{x^2}{2!}f''(0) + \frac{x^3}{3!}f'''(0) + \dots$$
$$+ \frac{x^{n-1}}{(n-1)!}f^{(n-1)}(0) + \frac{x^n}{n!}f^{(n)}(\theta x).$$

In this form the expansion is known as Stirling's or Maclaurin's Theorem.

6. It will be noticed that the first n terms in Taylor's Theorem are of the form $\dfrac{h^r}{r!}f^{(r)}(x)$. The $(n+1)$th term is of the same form but involves a different value of the variable. This term is called the "remainder" term after n terms and is denoted by $R_n(x)$. If $\underset{n \to \infty}{\text{Lt }} R_n(x)$ is zero, then $f(x + h)$ can be expanded as an infinite series, and will be convergent. We may state therefore that if $f(x)$ and its successive differential coefficients are continuous within the given range, then

$$f(x) + hf'(x) + \frac{h^2}{2!}f''(x) + \ldots + \frac{h^{n-1}}{(n-1)!}f^{(n-1)}(x) + \ldots$$

converges to the limit $f(x + h)$, provided that $\underset{n \to \infty}{\text{Lt }} R_n(x)$ is zero.

7. Other forms for $R_n(x)$.

The form $\dfrac{h^n}{n!}f^{(n)}(x + \theta h)$ is called Lagrange's form of the remainder after n terms.

If the denominator in the expression for q in paragraph 5 be $(b - a)^p$ instead of $(b - a)^n$ it can be shown that

$$R_n(x) = \frac{h^n (1 - \theta)^{n-p}}{(n-1)! \, p} f^{(n)}(x + \theta h).$$

This is Schlömilch's form. The Lagrange form follows immediately by putting $p = n$. If we put $p = 1$ we obtain another form,

$$R_n(x) = \frac{h^n (1 - \theta)^{n-1}}{(n-1)!} f^{(n)}(x + \theta h),$$

due to Cauchy.

8. Examples on the above theorems.

In obtaining expansions for various functions of x it is more convenient to use Maclaurin's form than to use Taylor's. Moreover, since the condition for a convergent series applies equally to both forms, it is strictly necessary to prove that $\underset{n \to \infty}{\text{Lt }} R_n(x)$, i.e.

$\underset{n \to \infty}{\text{Lt }} \dfrac{x^n}{n!} f^{(n)}(\theta x)$, is zero before assuming that an infinite series can represent the function. For example, on expanding $(1 + x)^n$ by Maclaurin's Theorem different conditions arise according to the values of x and n, and a complete investigation of the convergency of the various series involves further mathematical analysis. In the examples that follow it will be assumed that $\underset{n \to \infty}{\text{Lt }} R_n(x)$ is zero and that the function in question is the sum of an infinite convergent series.

Example 1.

Expand $\log (1 + x + x^2)$ as far as the term involving x^3.

$$f(x) = \log (1 + x + x^2), \text{ and } f(0) = 0,$$

$$f'(x) = \frac{1 + 2x}{1 + x + x^2}, \qquad f'(0) = 1,$$

$$f''(x) = \frac{1 - 2x - 2x^2}{(1 + x + x^2)^2} = \frac{-2}{(1 + x + x^2)} + \frac{3}{(1 + x + x^2)^2}, \qquad f''(0) = 1,$$

$$f'''(x) = \frac{2(1 + 2x)}{(1 + x + x^2)^2} + \frac{-6(1 + 2x)}{(1 + x + x^2)^3}, \qquad f'''(0) = -4.$$

By Maclaurin's Theorem:

$$f(x) = f(0) + xf'(0) + \frac{x^2}{2!}f''(0) + \frac{x^3}{3!}f'''(0) + \dots.$$

$$\therefore \quad \log (1 + x + x^2) = x + \frac{x^2}{2} - \frac{2x^3}{3} + \dots.$$

Notes on this example:

(i) The expansion is true only if x is numerically less than unity.

(ii) Since $1 + x + x^2 = (1 - x^3)/(1 - x)$, an alternative method would be to expand $\log (1 - x^3) - \log (1 - x)$ by algebra.

(iii) It is simpler to differentiate products than to differentiate quotients. We might write

$$f'(x) = \frac{1 + 2x}{1 + x + x^2}$$

as $\qquad (1 + x + x^2)f'(x) = 1 + 2x$, so that $f'(0) = 1$.

Differentiate:

$$(1 + x + x^2)f''(x) + (1 + 2x)f'(x) = 2, \qquad f''(0) = 1,$$

$$(1 + x + x^2)f'''(x) + 2(1 + 2x)f''(x) + 2f'(x) = 0, \qquad f'''(0) = -4,$$

and so on.

(iv) For an expansion involving higher powers of x we may continue the differentiation in (iii) by applying Leibnitz's Theorem, or we may adopt other methods, as in Example 3 below.

Example 2.

Prove that if x is any positive quantity

$$(x + 2)\log (1 + x) > 2x.$$

Now if θ is a positive proper fraction,
$$f(x) = f(0) + xf'(0) + \tfrac{1}{2}x^2 f''(\theta x).$$

Let $\quad f(x) = (x + 2) \log (1 + x) - 2x$, so that $f(0) = 0$.

Then $\quad f'(x) = \log (1 + x) + \dfrac{x+2}{1+x} - 2, \quad f'(0) = 0,$

and $\quad f''(x) = \dfrac{1}{1+x} - \dfrac{1}{(1+x)^2} = \dfrac{x}{(1+x)^2}.$

$$\therefore \quad f(x) = \tfrac{1}{2}x^2 \dfrac{\theta x}{(1 + \theta x)^2}.$$

But for all positive values of x this is positive, since θ is a positive proper fraction.

$\therefore \quad (x + 2) \log (1 + x) - 2x$ is positive when x is positive,

i.e. $\quad\quad\quad\quad (x + 2) \log (1 + x) > 2x.$

9. Formation of a differential equation.

This method can be employed with advantage for the expansion of certain functions without the use of the above series. It must be assumed that the given function $f(x)$ can be expanded in the form $a_0 + a_1 x + a_2 x^2 + \dots + a_r x^r + \dots$, and if on differentiating $f(x)$ a simple relation between the coefficients is evident, we can obtain the required expansion. It should be noted that the first one or two terms of the expansion may have to be found by a different method, such as by substitution of numerical values on both sides of the identity.

Example 3.

Expand $\log (1 + x + x^2)$ in ascending powers of x. (Cf. Ex. 1, p. 68.)

Let
$$\log (1 + x + x^2) = a_0 + a_1 x + a_2 x^2 + a_3 x^3 + \dots + a_r x^r + \dots.$$
Then by differentiating,
$$\frac{1 + 2x}{1 + x + x^2} = a_1 + 2a_2 x + 3a_3 x^2 + \dots + ra_r x^{r-1} + \dots,$$
or $\quad 1 + 2x = (1 + x + x^2)(a_1 + 2a_2 x + 3a_3 x^2 + \dots + ra_r x^{r-1} + \dots).$

Equating coefficients of powers of x,
$$a_1 = 1, \quad\quad a_1 = 1,$$
$$2a_2 + a_1 = 2, \quad\quad a_2 = \tfrac{1}{2},$$
$$3a_3 + 2a_2 + a_1 = 0, \quad\quad a_3 = -\tfrac{2}{3},$$
$$4a_4 + 3a_3 + 2a_2 = 0, \quad\quad a_4 = \tfrac{1}{4},$$
$$5a_5 + 4a_4 + 3a_3 = 0, \quad\quad a_5 = \tfrac{1}{5},$$

and so on, the law of formation of the coefficients being

$$r a_r + (r - 1) a_{r-1} + (r - 2) a_{r-2} = 0,$$

except for the first two terms.

$$\therefore \ \log (1 + x + x^2) = x + \frac{x^2}{2} - \frac{2x^3}{3} + \frac{x^4}{4} + \frac{x^5}{5}\dots,$$

since a_0 is obviously zero.

Example 4.

If $y = \log (1 + \sin x)$ obtain a relation between the first three differential coefficients of y with respect to x, and hence expand y in an ascending series of powers of x.

$$f(x) = y = \log (1 + \sin x), \qquad f'(x) = \frac{\cos x}{1 + \sin x},$$

$$f''(x) = -\frac{1}{1 + \sin x}, \qquad f'''(x) = \frac{\cos x}{(1 + \sin x)^2}.$$

$$\therefore \ f'''(x) + f'(x) f''(x) = 0.$$

Let $\quad f(x) = a_0 + a_1 x + a_2 x^2 + a_3 x^3 + a_4 x^4 + a_5 x^5 + \dots.$

Then $\quad f'(x) = a_1 + 2a_2 x + 3a_3 x^2 + 4a_4 x^3 + 5a_5 x^4 + \dots,$

$$f''(x) = 2a_2 + 6a_3 x + 12a_4 x^2 + 20a_5 x^3 + \dots,$$

$$f'''(x) = 6a_3 + 24a_4 x + 60a_5 x^2 + \dots.$$

Now
$$f(0) = 0, \qquad \text{or} \qquad a_0 = 0,$$
$$f'(0) = 1, \qquad \text{giving} \quad a_1 = 1,$$
$$f''(0) = -1, \qquad ,, \qquad a_2 = -\tfrac{1}{2},$$
$$f'''(0) = 1, \qquad ,, \qquad a_3 = \tfrac{1}{6}.$$

Since $f'''(x) + f'(x) f''(x) = 0$, we have, by multiplying together the expansions for $f'(x)$ and $f''(x)$ and equating coefficients of x,

$$4a_2{}^2 + 6a_1 a_3 = -24a_4, \quad \text{so that} \quad a_4 = -\tfrac{1}{12}.$$

Similarly, equating coefficients of x^2,

$$6a_2 a_3 + 12a_2 a_3 + 12a_1 a_4 = -60a_5 \quad \text{and} \quad a_5 = \tfrac{1}{24},$$

and so on.

$$\therefore \ \log (1 + \sin x) = x - \frac{x^2}{2} + \frac{x^3}{6} - \frac{x^4}{12} + \frac{x^5}{24}\dots.$$

10. The series $\dfrac{x}{e^x - 1}$.

The coefficients in the expansion of $\dfrac{x}{e^x - 1}$ are of great importance in the higher branches of mathematics, and the method of obtaining the series in ascending powers of x is an excellent example of the application of the above principles.

Consider
$$\frac{x}{e^x-1}+\frac{x}{2}=\frac{x}{2}\cdot\frac{e^x+1}{e^x-1}.$$

Let
$$\frac{x}{2}\cdot\frac{e^x+1}{e^x-1}=a_0+a_1x+a_2x^2+a_3x^3+a_4x^4+\ldots.$$

Change the sign of x: the left-hand side becomes

$$-\frac{x}{2}\cdot\frac{e^{-x}+1}{e^{-x}-1}\quad\text{or}\quad\frac{x}{2}\cdot\frac{e^x+1}{e^x-1}.$$

$$\therefore\ \frac{x}{2}\cdot\frac{e^x+1}{e^x-1}=a_0-a_1x+a_2x^2-a_3x^3+a_4x^4-\ldots.$$

Add: then on dividing both sides by 2, we have

$$\frac{x}{2}\cdot\frac{e^x+1}{e^x-1}=a_0+a_2x^2+a_4x^4+\ldots,$$

which shows that no odd powers of x occur in the expansion of

$$\frac{x}{2}\cdot\frac{e^x+1}{e^x-1}.$$

Let
$$f(x)=\frac{x}{e^x-1}+\frac{x}{2}=\frac{x}{2}\cdot\frac{e^x+1}{e^x-1}.$$

Then
$$e^x f(x)=f(x)+\tfrac{1}{2}x+\tfrac{1}{2}xe^x.$$

Differentiate with respect to x:

$$e^x\left[f(x)+f'(x)\right]=f'(x)+\tfrac{1}{2}+\tfrac{1}{2}e^x(1+x).$$

Similarly, on successive differentiation,

$$e^x\left[f''(x)+2f'(x)+f(x)\right]=f''(x)+\tfrac{1}{2}e^x(2+x),$$

$$e^x\left[f'''(x)+3f''(x)+3f'(x)+f(x)\right]=f'''(x)+\tfrac{1}{2}e^x(3+x),$$

and the law of formation is evident.

Moreover, if we expand $f(x)$ by Maclaurin's Theorem, we have

$$f(x)=f(0)+xf'(0)+\frac{x^2}{2!}f''(0)+\frac{x^3}{3!}f'''(0)+\ldots,$$

and since there are no odd powers of x in the expansion of $f(x)$, it follows that

$$f'(0)=f'''(0)=f^{\text{v}}(0)=\ldots=0.$$

Now $\qquad e^x\left[f(x)+f'(x)\right]=f'(x)+\tfrac{1}{2}+\tfrac{1}{2}e^x(1+x)$,

so that, when $x=0$,

$$f(0)=\tfrac{1}{2}+\tfrac{1}{2}=1 \text{ since } f'(0)=0.$$

Similarly, by substitution of $x=0$ in the next equation but one, we obtain

$$e^0\left[f'''(0)+3f''(0)+3f'(0)+f(0)\right]=f'''(0)+\tfrac{1}{2}e^0(3+0),$$

and, remembering that $f'(0)$ and $f'''(0)$ are zero, we find that $f''(0)=\tfrac{1}{6}$.

Similarly, $f^{iv}(0)=-\tfrac{1}{30}, f^{vi}(0)=\tfrac{1}{42}, f^{viii}(0)=-\tfrac{1}{30}, \ldots$

$$\therefore \frac{x}{e^x-1}+\frac{x}{2}=\frac{x}{2}\cdot\frac{e^x+1}{e^x-1}=1+\frac{1}{6}\cdot\frac{x^2}{2!}-\frac{1}{30}\cdot\frac{x^4}{4!}+\frac{1}{42}\cdot\frac{x^6}{6!}-\frac{1}{30}\cdot\frac{x^8}{8!}+\ldots$$

or $\qquad \dfrac{x}{e^x-1}=1-\dfrac{x}{2}+\dfrac{1}{6}\cdot\dfrac{x^2}{2!}-\dfrac{1}{30}\cdot\dfrac{x^4}{4!}+\dfrac{1}{42}\cdot\dfrac{x^6}{6!}-\dfrac{1}{30}\cdot\dfrac{x^8}{8!}+\ldots.$

The coefficients obtained above are denoted by $B_1, B_2, B_3, B_4 \ldots$; these are called Bernouilli's Numbers.

We have, therefore, that

$$\frac{x}{e^x-1}=1-\tfrac{1}{2}x+B_1\frac{x^2}{2!}-B_2\frac{x^4}{4!}+B_3\frac{x^6}{6!}-B_4\frac{x^8}{8!}+\ldots.$$

The expansion of $\dfrac{x}{e^x-1}$ may be obtained otherwise by assuming that

$$\frac{x}{e^x-1}=a_0+a_1x+a_2x^2+\ldots+a_rx^r+\ldots,$$

i.e. that

$$x=\left(x+\frac{x^2}{2!}+\frac{x^3}{3!}+\ldots\right)(a_0+a_1x+a_2x^2+\ldots+a_rx^r+\ldots),$$

and equating coefficients of powers of x on both sides of the identity.

11. Differentiation of a known series.

It can be shown that if an infinite series converges to a value $f(x)$ within a given range, then the series formed by differentiating each term of the original series is $f'(x)$, provided that the second series is convergent for all values of the variable within the given range.

It sometimes happens that the function whose expansion is required is the differential coefficient of a function whose expansion is known. By the application of the simple process of differentiating each term of the known expansion the required result is easily obtained.

Example 5.

If $\quad \log(1 - x - x^2) = -u_1 x - \tfrac{1}{2}u_2 x^2 - \tfrac{1}{3}u_3 x^3 - \dots,$

prove that $\quad\quad\quad\quad u_n = u_{n-1} + u_{n-2}.$

$$\frac{d}{dx} \log(1 - x - x^2) = -\frac{1 + 2x}{1 - x - x^2}.$$

But $\quad \dfrac{d}{dx} \log(1 - x - x^2) = -u_1 - u_2 x - u_3 x^2 - u_4 x^3 - \dots.$

$$\therefore \quad -\frac{1 + 2x}{1 - x - x^2} = -u_1 - u_2 x - u_3 x^2 - u_4 x^3 - \dots,$$

i.e. $\dfrac{1 + 2x}{1 - x - x^2}$ is the generating function of the series

$$u_1 + u_2 x + u_3 x^2 + \dots + u_{n-2} x^{n-3} + u_{n-1} x^{n-2} + u_n x^{n-1} + \dots.$$

$$\therefore \quad u_n - u_{n-1} - u_{n-2} = 0, \quad \text{or} \quad u_n = u_{n-1} + u_{n-2},$$

which proves the proposition.

12. Trigonometrical series.

Let $\quad\quad\quad\quad f(x) = \sin x.$

Then $\quad\quad\quad\quad f'(x) = \cos x = \sin\left(x + \dfrac{\pi}{2}\right),$

$$f''(x) = \cos\left(x + \frac{\pi}{2}\right) = \sin\left(x + 2\frac{\pi}{2}\right),$$

....

and the nth differential coefficient is $\sin\left(x + n\dfrac{\pi}{2}\right).$

$$\therefore \ f(0) = 0; \ f'(0) = \sin\frac{\pi}{2} = 1; \ f''(0) = \sin\frac{2\pi}{2} = 0;$$

$$f'''(0) = \sin\frac{3\pi}{2} = -1; \ f^{\text{iv}}(0) = \sin\frac{4\pi}{2} = 0,$$

and so on.

Even derivatives will obviously be zero, and odd derivatives $+1$ and -1 alternately.

Therefore by Maclaurin's Theorem,

$$\sin x = x - \frac{x^3}{3!} + \frac{x^5}{5!} - \frac{x^7}{7!} + \dots,$$

and it is easy to show that the series is convergent for all values of x.

Similarly $\qquad \cos x = 1 - \dfrac{x^2}{2!} + \dfrac{x^4}{4!} - \dfrac{x^6}{6!} + \ldots$

This result can be obtained by replacing $n\theta$ by a in the expansion for $\cos n\theta$ in Example 11, p. 17, and by then considering the limit of the expansion as $n \to \infty$. It will be seen, however, that by finding the limit $n \to \infty$ in the series

$$\cos a = (\cos a/n)^n - n_{(2)}(\cos a/n)^{n-2}(\sin a/n)^2 + n_{(4)}(\cos a/n)^{n-4}(\sin a/n)^4 - \ldots$$

a double limit is involved. It is therefore simpler to obtain the cosine and sine series by Maclaurin's Theorem as above. The series for $\tan x$ does not take a simple form: the first few terms can be obtained by division of the sine series by the cosine series, or by Maclaurin's Theorem.

EXAMPLES 4

1. Prove that $e^{x+h} = e^x + he^x + \dfrac{h^2}{2!}e^x + \ldots$.

2. Find the expansion of $\log(1 + e^x)$ in ascending powers of x as far as the term containing x^4.

3. Expand $(1 + x)^x$ by Maclaurin's Theorem as far as the term containing x^4.

4. Prove that
$$\frac{f(x+h) + f(x-h)}{2} = f(x) + \frac{h^2}{2!}f''(x) + \frac{h^4}{4!}f^{\mathrm{iv}}(x) + \ldots.$$

5. If $u = f(x)$, show that
$$f\left(\frac{x}{2}\right) = u - \frac{x}{2}\frac{du}{dx} + \frac{1}{2!}\left(\frac{x}{2}\right)^2\frac{d^2u}{dx^2} - \frac{1}{3!}\left(\frac{x}{2}\right)^3\frac{d^3u}{dx^3} + \ldots.$$

6. Assuming that $\dfrac{x}{\log(1+x)}$ can be expanded in ascending powers of x, find the first four terms of the expansion.

7. Expand $f(x)$ in powers of x as far as the term containing x^6, given that $f(0) = 1$; $f'(0) = 2$; $f''(0) = 3$ and $f'''(x) = f(x)$.

8. Prove that the first three terms in the expansion of $\log \dfrac{xe^x}{e^x - 1}$ are $\frac{1}{2}x - \frac{1}{24}x^2 + \frac{1}{2880}x^4$.

9. By means of a differential equation find a series for $\tan^{-1} x$.

10. If $\tan y = 1 + x + x^2$, expand y in terms of x as far as the term involving x^3.

11. Prove that
$$f(mx) = f(x) + (m-1)\, xf'(x) + (m-1)^2 \frac{x^2}{2!} f''(x) + \dots .$$

12. Show that if $y = \log (1 + \sin x)$, then $\dfrac{d^3y}{dx^3} + \dfrac{dy}{dx} \cdot \dfrac{d^2y}{dx^2} = 0$.
Use this formula to obtain the expansion
$$\log (1 + \sin x) = x - \frac{x^2}{2} + \frac{x^3}{6} - \frac{x^4}{12} + \frac{x^5}{24} \dots ,$$
and find the coefficient of x^6.

13. $ay^3 = xy + a$. Apply Maclaurin's Theorem to expand y in ascending powers of x as far as the term involving x^3.

14. If $\log y = \log \sin x - x^2$, prove that
$$\frac{d^2y}{dx^2} + 4x \frac{dy}{dx} + (4x^2 + 3)\, y = 0.$$
Hence expand y in terms of x as far as the term in x^5.

15. Prove that
$$\log (1 - x + x^2) = -x + \frac{x^2}{2} + \frac{2x^3}{3} + \frac{x^4}{4} - \frac{x^5}{5} - \frac{x^6}{3} - \frac{x^7}{7} + \frac{x^8}{8} \dots .$$

16. If $\sin y = a_1 x + a_2 x^2 + \dots + a_n x^n + \dots$ where $\tan y = x$, prove that
$$(n^2 + 3n + 2)\, a_{n+2} + (2n^2 + 1)\, a_n + (n^2 - 3n + 2)\, a_{n-2} = 0.$$

17. Show that $e^{x \cos x} = 1 + x + \dfrac{x^2}{2} - \dfrac{x^3}{3} \dots$, and find the coefficient of x^4.

18. Expand $\dfrac{\sqrt{1+x}}{(1-x)}$ in ascending powers of x by first forming a differential equation.

19. If $e^{\sin^{-1} x} = a_0 + a_1 x + a_2 x^2 + \dots + a_r x^r + \dots$, prove that
$$\frac{(n+2)\, a_{n+2}}{n^2 + 1} = \frac{a_n}{n+1}.$$

20. Expand $\dfrac{x}{e^x - 1}$ as far as the term involving x^6. Use the result to expand $\dfrac{1}{e^x + 1}$ to four terms.

21. Prove that if x is positive $x > \log (1 + x) > x - \frac{1}{2}x^2$.

22. Find the expansion of $e^{-x^2} \sin px$ in ascending powers of x as far as the term involving x^5.

CHAPTER V

MAXIMA AND MINIMA

1. In Chapter II, para. 13, a definition was given of a function $f(x)$ which is continuous at the point $x = a$. A property of such a function which is of frequent application in the calculus is as follows:

If $f(x)$ is a continuous function throughout the range of values considered, then for values of x near the point $x = a$, $f(x)$ has the same sign as $f(a)$, provided that $f(a)$ is not zero.

This proposition is almost self-evident. Since, *for a continuous function*, $\underset{x \to a}{\mathrm{Lt}}\, f(x)$ is equal to $f(a)$, it follows from the definition of a limit that there is a range of values over which $f(x)$ differs from $f(a)$ by less than ϵ where ϵ may be as small as we please. For any value of ϵ numerically less than $f(a)$ the sign of $f(x)$ for values of x within the corresponding range will be the same as that of $f(a)$.

Now let $y = f(x)$ be a continuous function of x.

Then
$$\frac{dy}{dx} = \underset{\Delta x \to 0}{\mathrm{Lt}} \frac{\Delta y}{\Delta x},$$

so that $\dfrac{\Delta y}{\Delta x} = \dfrac{dy}{dx} + \epsilon$ where ϵ is a small quantity whose limit as $\Delta x \to 0$ is zero.

If $\dfrac{dy}{dx}$ is not zero, the sign of $\dfrac{dy}{dx}$ will be the same as that of $\dfrac{\Delta y}{\Delta x}$ provided that we take Δx small enough; if $\Delta x \to 0$, the sign of Δy will be the same as that of $\Delta x \dfrac{dy}{dx}$.

Consequently if Δx is positive but $\to 0$, Δy will have the same sign as $\dfrac{dy}{dx}$.

But
$$\Delta y = f(x + \Delta x) - f(x).$$

Therefore $f(x + \Delta x) - f(x)$ will have the same sign as $\dfrac{dy}{dx}$ if Δx is positive, but $\to 0$.

If Δx is positive, $x + \Delta x$ is greater than x; i.e. x is increasing: and if $\frac{dy}{dx}$ is positive $f(x + \Delta x)$ is greater than $f(x)$; i.e. y is increasing.

Therefore $f(x)$ increases as x increases if $\frac{dy}{dx}$ is positive, and decreases as x increases if $\frac{dy}{dx}$ is negative.

Similarly, if Δx is negative, so that x is decreasing, $f(x)$ decreases as x decreases if $\frac{dy}{dx}$ is positive, and increases as x decreases if $\frac{dy}{dx}$ is negative.

Values of $f(x)$ at which the function ceases to increase (decrease) and begins to decrease (increase) are called *turning values* or *critical values*.

2. Maxima and Minima.

At the points where the function $y = f(x)$ ceases to increase and begins to decrease y is generally said to have a *maximum value*: conversely where the function ceases to decrease and begins to increase y is said to have a *minimum value*.

It should be noted that a maximum value need not necessarily be the greatest numerical value of the function, nor need a minimum value be the least. For example, in Fig. 25, there are maxima at the points A and C, and minima at B and D. The numerical value, however, of the 'ordinate at D is greater than that of the ordinate at A, although the function assumes a minimum value at D and a maximum value at A.

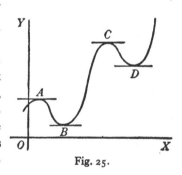

Fig. 25.

The following is a more correct definition of maximum and minimum values:

The function $y = f(x)$ has a maximum value at the point $x = a$, if $f(a)$ exceeds both $f(a + h)$ and $f(a - h)$ for all positive values of h less than a small finite quantity ϵ. Similarly, $f(x)$ has a minimum value when $x = a$, if $f(a)$ is less than both $f(a + h)$ and $f(a - h)$ for all positive values of h less than ϵ.

If therefore $f(a)$ is a maximum value of $y = f(x)$, (i) as x increases from $(a - h)$ to a, y increases and $\frac{dy}{dx}$ is positive; and (ii) as x increases from a to $(a + h)$, y decreases and $\frac{dy}{dx}$ is negative (para. 1). That is, as x increases $\frac{dy}{dx}$ changes from a positive to a negative value. The criterion for a maximum value at $x = a$ is therefore that $\frac{dy}{dx}$ changes sign from positive to negative as x passes through a. Conversely, for a minimum value $\frac{dy}{dx}$ changes from negative to positive.

Since a continuous function cannot change sign without passing through a zero value, we have that, for a critical value, $\frac{dy}{dx}$ must be zero provided that it be continuous.

If therefore $f(a)$ is a maximum or a minimum value of the function $y = f(x)$, and $f'(x)$ is continuous,

(i) $\left[\frac{dy}{dx}\right]_{x=a}$ must be zero;

(ii) $\frac{dy}{dx}$ must change from positive to negative for a maximum value;

(iii) $\frac{dy}{dx}$ must change from negative to positive for a minimum value.

Example 1.

Find the maximum and minimum values of
$$y = 4x^3 - 18x^2 + 24x + 11.$$

$$\frac{dy}{dx} = 12x^2 - 36x + 24.$$

We must equate $\frac{dy}{dx}$ to zero: this gives
$$12x^2 - 36x + 24 = 0,$$

i.e. $\qquad x^2 - 3x + 2 = 0,$

i.e. $\qquad x = 2 \text{ or } 1.$

These values of x give critical values to y.

To find which of these values gives a maximum and which a minimum we must proceed further.

Let $x = 2 - \Delta x$ and $2 + \Delta x$ in turn, where Δx is a small positive quantity.

(i) $\dfrac{dy}{dx} = (2 - \Delta x)^2 - 3(2 - \Delta x) + 2,$ when $x = 2 - \Delta x,$

$\qquad = 4 - 4\Delta x + (\Delta x)^2 - 6 + 3\Delta x + 2 = -\Delta x + (\Delta x)^2;$

(ii) $\dfrac{dy}{dx} = 4 + 4\Delta x + (\Delta x)^2 - 6 - 3\Delta x + 2 = \Delta x + (\Delta x)^2,$

when $x = 2 + \Delta x.$

Now since Δx is a small positive quantity,

$\qquad [-\Delta x + (\Delta x)^2]$ is negative

and $\qquad [\Delta x + (\Delta x)^2]$ is positive.

$\therefore \dfrac{dy}{dx}$ passes from negative to positive as x passes through the value 2.

$\therefore x = 2$ gives y a minimum value.

Similarly it may be shown that $x = 1$ gives y a maximum value.

The values required are therefore

$\qquad$ Maximum: $y = 4 \cdot 1^3 - 18 \cdot 1^2 + 24 \cdot 1 + 11 = 21.$

$\qquad$ Minimum: $y = 4 \cdot 2^3 - 18 \cdot 2^2 + 24 \cdot 2 + 11 = 19.$

3. An alternative method for determining the maximum or minimum values of a continuous function depends upon the rate of change of $\dfrac{dy}{dx}$. We have seen that if $f(a)$ is a maximum value, $\dfrac{dy}{dx}$ changes from positive as x passes through a. In other words $\dfrac{dy}{dx}$ is decreasing near the point, and consequently its differential coefficient, i.e. $\dfrac{d^2y}{dx^2}$, or $f''(x)$, must be negative. Therefore, by the proposition in para. 1, the sign of $f''(x)$ is the same as that of $f''(a)$ provided that $f''(a)$ is not zero.

We have therefore for a maximum value at the point $x = a$, $\dfrac{d^2y}{dx^2}$ must be negative: and conversely for a minimum value $\dfrac{d^2y}{dx^2}$ must be positive.

The test is easy to apply. For example, using the same function as in Ex. 1, we find that

$$\frac{d^2y}{dx^2} = \frac{d}{dx} \, 12 \, (x^2 - 3x + 2) = 12 \, (2x - 3).$$

This is positive when $x = 2$ and negative when $x = 1$. Consequently $x = 2$ gives a minimum value and $x = 1$ a maximum (as above).

4. The tests for maximum and minimum values are quite straightforward and their application to simple problems presents little difficulty. The following examples are illustrative of the methods employed.

Example 2.

A window is in shape a rectangle with a semicircle covering the top. If the perimeter of the window be a fixed length p, find its maximum area.

We have first to choose an independent variable. Let BO, the radius of the semicircle, be x. Then since the perimeter of the figure is a fixed length p,

$$p = 2BC + CD + AKB$$
$$= 2BC + 2x + \pi x,$$

so that $\qquad BC = \dfrac{p - (2 + \pi) \, x}{2}.$

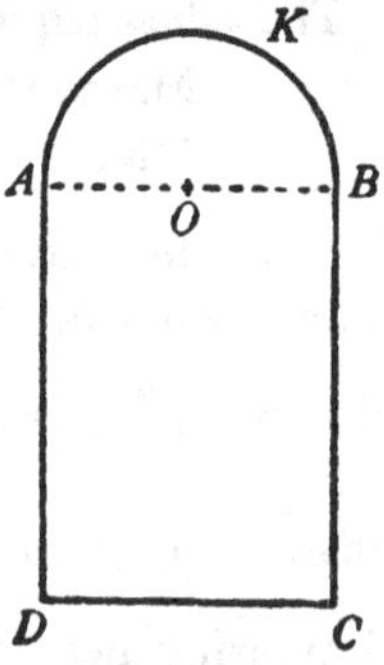

The area a will be [rectangle $ABCD$ + semicircle AKB],

i.e. $\qquad a = BC . CD + \tfrac{1}{2}\pi x^2$

$$= \frac{p - (2 + \pi) \, x}{2} . 2x + \tfrac{1}{2}\pi x^2$$

$$= xp - (2 + \pi) \, x^2 + \tfrac{1}{2}\pi x^2.$$

$$\therefore \quad \frac{da}{dx} = p - 2x \, (2 + \pi) + \pi x.$$

Fig. 26.

For a maximum or minimum value $\dfrac{da}{dx} = 0$,

i.e. $\qquad\qquad\qquad x = \dfrac{p}{4 + \pi}.$

It is evident that this will give a maximum value to a, for when $x = 0$ the area is zero. We need not therefore apply the second test.

Giving x the value above,

$$a = xp - (2 + \pi) x^2 + \tfrac{1}{2}\pi x^2$$
$$= \frac{p^2}{4 + \pi} - \frac{4 + \pi}{2} \cdot \frac{p^2}{(4 + \pi)^2} = \frac{p^2}{2(4 + \pi)}.$$

Example 3.

Given $u_{-1} = -5$; $u_1 = -1$; $u_2 = 4$; $u_5 = 175$; find the maximum and minimum values of u_x.

Since four values of u_x are given we must assume that the function is a rational integral function of the third degree in x.

Let
$$y = u_x = a + bx + cx^2 + dx^3.$$
Then
$$-5 = u_{-1} = a - b + c - d,$$
$$-1 = u_1 = a + b + c + d,$$
$$4 = u_2 = a + 2b + 4c + 8d,$$
$$175 = u_5 = a + 5b + 25c + 125d.$$

Solving these equations we obtain easily that

$$a = 0; \quad b = 0; \quad c = -3; \quad d = 2.$$
$$\therefore \ y = -3x^2 + 2x^3.$$

For critical values $\dfrac{dy}{dx} = 0$,

i.e. $\qquad\qquad -6x + 6x^2 = 0,$

giving $\qquad\qquad x = 0 \text{ or } 1.$

Also $\qquad\qquad \dfrac{d^2y}{dx^2} = -6 + 12x.$

When $x = 0$, $\dfrac{d^2y}{dx^2}$ is negative, giving a maximum value;

$x = 1$, $\dfrac{d^2y}{dx^2}$ is positive, giving a minimum value.

Therefore maximum value of y is 0;

minimum value of y is -1.

Example 4.

A ladder is to be carried in a horizontal position round a corner formed by two streets a feet and b feet wide meeting at right angles. Prove that the length of the longest ladder that will pass round the corner without jamming is $(a^{\frac{2}{3}} + b^{\frac{2}{3}})^{\frac{3}{2}}$ feet.

In this example it is advisable to take as the variable the angle that the ladder makes with the wall of the street. Call this angle α. Let x be the distance across the corner. The longest ladder will of course be the shortest distance across the corner, and the problem reduces to one of finding the minimum value of x. Then

$$x = AB = AC + CB$$
$$= a \sec \alpha + b \operatorname{cosec} \alpha,$$

$$\frac{dx}{d\alpha} = a \sec \alpha \tan \alpha - b \operatorname{cosec} \alpha \cot \alpha;$$

i.e. for a maximum or minimum value,

$$a \sec \alpha \tan \alpha - b \operatorname{cosec} \alpha \cot \alpha = 0,$$

or $\qquad a \dfrac{\sin \alpha}{\cos^2 \alpha} - b \dfrac{\cos \alpha}{\sin^2 \alpha} = 0,$

from which $\qquad \tan \alpha = \dfrac{b^{\frac{1}{3}}}{a^{\frac{1}{3}}}.$

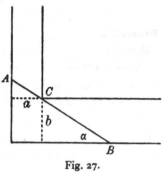

Fig. 27.

This evidently gives a minimum value to $a \sec \alpha + b \operatorname{cosec} \alpha$, the maximum value being ∞.

$$\therefore \quad \sin \alpha = \frac{b^{\frac{1}{3}}}{(a^{\frac{2}{3}} + b^{\frac{2}{3}})^{\frac{1}{2}}}; \quad \cos \alpha = \frac{a^{\frac{1}{3}}}{(a^{\frac{2}{3}} + b^{\frac{2}{3}})^{\frac{1}{2}}},$$

and $\qquad\qquad x = \dfrac{a}{\cos \alpha} + \dfrac{b}{\sin \alpha}$

$$= (a^{\frac{2}{3}} + b^{\frac{2}{3}})^{\frac{3}{2}}$$

on simplifying.

5. Points of inflexion.

It has been seen above that, for a critical value at $x = a$, $f'(a) = 0$ and that in order to ascertain whether this value is a maximum or a minimum, recourse must be had to the change of sign of $f'(x)$ as x passes through a, provided that $f''(a)$ is not zero. The question of what happens if $f''(a)$ is in fact zero now arises. Now $f''(a)$ will be zero if there is no rate of change of $f'(a)$. In that event $f(x)$ will not increase (decrease) and then decrease (increase) as x passes through a, although $f'(x) = 0$ for the value $x = a$. $f'(x)$ will have the same sign for

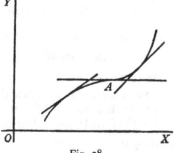

Fig. 28.

the value $x = a + h$ as for $x = a - h$ where h is small. There is therefore, as a rule, no maximum or minimum value at the point A, and A is said to be a *point of inflexion* on the curve.

In general there is a point of inflexion at $x = a$ if $f''(a)$ is zero: the exceptions depend upon the values of the higher derivatives.

Example 5.

Find the points of inflexion on the curve $y(1 + x^3) = 1$.

$$y = \frac{1}{1 + x^3},$$

$$\therefore \frac{dy}{dx} = \frac{-3x^2}{(1 + x^3)^2}.$$

Therefore for a critical value, $x = 0$.

But

$$\frac{d^2y}{dx^2} = -3\left[\frac{2x}{(1 + x^3)^2} - \frac{6x^4}{(1 + x^3)^3}\right]$$

which is zero when $x = 0$ or $x = \sqrt[3]{\frac{1}{2}}$. There are therefore points of inflexion where $x = 0$ and $\sqrt[3]{\frac{1}{2}}$.

6. We have illustrated the critical values of the function $y = f(x)$ by reference to the geometry of the curve. The problem may also be considered analytically.

By the extension of the Mean Value Theorem (p. 64)

$$f(a + h) = f(a) + hf'(a) + \tfrac{1}{2}h^2f''(a + \theta_1 h),$$

and

$$f(a - h) = f(a) - hf'(a) + \tfrac{1}{2}h^2f''(a - \theta_2 h),$$

where θ_1, θ_2 are positive proper fractions not necessarily equal.

Now for critical values $f'(a) = 0$.

Therefore

$$f(a + h) - f(a) = \tfrac{1}{2}h^2f''(a + \theta_1 h),$$

and

$$f(a - h) - f(a) = \tfrac{1}{2}h^2f''(a - \theta_2 h).$$

If h be made sufficiently small the right-hand side will have the same sign in both expressions. For a maximum value

$$f(a + h) - f(a) \text{ and } f(a - h) - f(a)$$

will both be negative. Therefore, since $\tfrac{1}{2}h^2$ is positive, the second differential coefficient must be negative. Similarly for a minimum value the second differential coefficient must be positive. If, however, $f''(a)$ is zero we must consider a further term: thus

$$f(a+h) = f(a) + hf'(a) + \frac{h^2}{2!}f''(a) + \frac{h^3}{3!}f'''(a + \theta_3 h),$$

$$f(a-h) = f(a) - hf'(a) + \frac{h^2}{2!}f''(a) - \frac{h^3}{3!}f'''(a - \theta_4 h),$$

which reduce to

$$f(a+h) - f(a) = \frac{h^3}{3!}f'''(a + \theta_3 h),$$

and
$$f(a-h) - f(a) = -\frac{h^3}{3!}f'''(a - \theta_4 h).$$

It will be seen that here there can be no maximum or minimum value if $f'''(a)$ is not zero, for since the sign of the right-hand side can be made to depend upon the sign of $\frac{h^3}{3!}f'''(a)$, the signs of $f(a+h) - f(a)$ and $f(a-h) - f(a)$ will be different and there will be a point of inflexion.

We may carry this proof further. If $f'''(a)$ is zero, the condition for maxima and minima will depend upon the sign of $f^{iv}(a)$—provided that $f^{iv}(a)$ is not zero—and so on. In general, therefore, we may say that

For a maximum or minimum value the first derivative that does not vanish must be of an even order: if in that event the derivative is negative the critical value is a maximum and if positive a minimum. Otherwise there will be a point of inflexion.

It is worthy of note that if $f(x)$ is a continuous function, maximum and minimum values (if any) occur alternately.

Example 6.

Examine the critical values of $y = x^2 - 3x^3 + 3x^4 - x^5$.

$$y = x^2 - 3x^3 + 3x^4 - x^5.$$

$$\therefore \frac{dy}{dx} = 2x - 9x^2 + 12x^3 - 5x^4.$$

Equating this to zero we obtain the four values $x = 0, 1, 1, \frac{2}{5}$.

$$\frac{d^2y}{dx^2} = 2 - 18x + 36x^2 - 20x^3;$$

when $x = 0$, $\dfrac{d^2y}{dx^2} = 2$, giving a minimum value;

$x = 1$, $\dfrac{d^2y}{dx^2} = 0$, which must be examined further;

$x = \frac{2}{5}$, $\dfrac{d^2y}{dx^2} = - \cdot 72$, giving a maximum value.

Again $\qquad \dfrac{d^3y}{dx^3} = - 18 + 72x - 60x^2;$

when $x = 1$, $\qquad \dfrac{d^3y}{dx^3} = - 6,$

and since this is not zero $x = 1$ gives a point of inflexion.

7. In the above demonstrations it has been assumed that the functions concerned have a differential coefficient for all values of the variable considered. There are, however, continuous functions which do not have a definite derivative for every value of the variable, although they may have a maximum or minimum value at some point for which there is no definite differential coefficient.

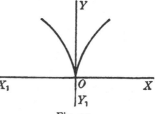

Fig. 29.

For example, there is a minimum value at the point $x = 0$ on the curve

$$y = x^{\frac{2}{3}},$$

although there is no definite derivative at that point. When $x = 0$, $\dfrac{dy}{dx}$ is infinite.

8. We will conclude this chapter with some miscellaneous applications of the above processes.

Example 7.

Find the maximum value of $(x - a)^2 (x - b)$.

$$y = (x - a)^2 (x - b),$$

$$\frac{dy}{dx} = 2 (x - a) (x - b) + (x - a)^2 = (x - a) (3x - 2b - a).$$

If $\dfrac{dy}{dx} = 0$, then $x = a$, or $\dfrac{a + 2b}{3}$;

$$\frac{d^2y}{dx^2} = 3x - 2b - a + 3(x - a) = 6x - 2b - 4a.$$

If $x = a$, $\qquad\qquad \frac{d^2y}{dx^2} = 2a - 2b,$

and if $x = \dfrac{a + 2b}{3}$, $\qquad \dfrac{d^2y}{dx^2} = 2b - 2a.$

We cannot therefore determine the sign of the second differential coefficient unless we know the relative magnitudes of a and b.

If $a > b$, $\quad x = \dfrac{a + 2b}{3}$ gives y a maximum value,

$\quad a < b$, $\quad x = a$ $\qquad\qquad$,, $\qquad$,,

$\quad a = b$, $\quad$ there is a point of inflexion for the value $x = a$.

The required values of $(x - a)^2(x - b)$ will be found by substitution of the values of x in the original expression.

Example 8.

Divide the number 21 into three parts a, b, c in continued proportion such that $3a + 6b + 4c$ may be a maximum.

Since a, b, c are in continued proportion, $a : b :: b : c$, so that we may write $a = bk$ and $b = ck$.

$$\therefore \quad a = ck^2.$$

But $\qquad\qquad\qquad\qquad a + b + c = 21.$

$$\therefore \quad (1 + k + k^2)c = 21 \quad\dots\dots\dots\dots\dots\dots(i).$$

We have to find the maximum value of $3a + 6b + 4c$ or, in terms of c and k, of $(4 + 6k + 3k^2)c$.

Let $\qquad\qquad\qquad (4 + 6k + 3k^2)c = z \dots\dots\dots\dots\dots\dots(ii).$

Then if there were one variable k, the necessary procedure would be to find the values of k which give $\dfrac{dz}{dk}$ a zero value. But c may vary as well as k, and if we differentiate z with respect to k a further differential coefficient, namely $\dfrac{dc}{dk}$, is involved. We can, however, make use of equation (i) and thus eliminate $\dfrac{dc}{dk}$ from our differential equations.

Differentiating equations (i) and (ii) respectively with respect to k,

$$(2k + 1)c + (1 + k + k^2)\frac{dc}{dk} = 0,$$

$$(6k + 6)c + (4 + 6k + 3k^2)\frac{dc}{dk} = \frac{dz}{dk} = 0$$

for a critical value.

Eliminating $\dfrac{dc}{dk}$, we obtain easily that

$$3k^2 + 2k - 2 = 0,$$

so that $k = \dfrac{-1 \pm \sqrt{7}}{3}$, the positive root giving a maximum value.

Substituting in (i) and simplifying,

$$c = 14 - \sqrt{7},$$

whence

$$a = 14 - 4\sqrt{7},$$

$$b = 5\sqrt{7} - 7,$$

and the required value of $3a + 6b + 4c$ becomes $56 + 14\sqrt{7}$.

(The minimum value, found from the value $k = \dfrac{-1 - \sqrt{7}}{3}$, is $56 - 14\sqrt{7}$).

Example 9.

Find the maximum value of $2(a - x)(x + \sqrt{x^2 + b^2})$ where x is real.

In certain circumstances it may happen that a simple and straightforward method of obtaining maximum or minimum values can be evolved by reference to algebra or geometry.

For example, although by differentiating the above expression and equating the result to zero the required value can be obtained, a neater proof results from the use of a well-known algebraic property.

$$(a - x)^2 \text{ and } x^2 + b^2 \text{ are positive since } x \text{ is real.}$$

$$\therefore \quad (a - x)^2 + (x^2 + b^2) \not< 2\sqrt{(a - x)^2(x^2 + b^2)},$$

i.e. $$\not< 2(a - x)\sqrt{x^2 + b^2},$$

i.e. $$a^2 - 2ax + x^2 + x^2 + b^2 \not< 2(a - x)\sqrt{x^2 + b^2},$$

or $$-2(a - x)x + a^2 + b^2 \not< 2(a - x)\sqrt{x^2 + b^2},$$

i.e. $$a^2 + b^2 \not< 2(a - x)(x + \sqrt{x^2 + b^2}).$$

In other words, $2(a - x)(x + \sqrt{x^2 + b^2})$ is not greater than $a^2 + b^2$, i.e. the maximum value of the expression is $a^2 + b^2$.

EXAMPLES 5

Find the maximum and minimum values, where such exist, of

1. $\dfrac{x}{(x^2 - 5x + 9)}$.

2. $\dfrac{x^3}{3} + ax^2 - 3a^2x$.

3. $\dfrac{x^2 + x + 1}{x^2 - x + 1}$.

4. $x^2(1 + x^2)^{-3}$.

5. $x^4 - 4x^2 + 73$.

6. $\dfrac{x^2 - 1}{(3 + x^2)^3}$.

7. $12x^5 - 45x^4 + 40x^3 + 6$.

8. $\dfrac{(x + a)(x + b)}{(x - a)(x - b)}$.

9. $x^3 - 5x^2 + 8x - 4$.

10. $ax + by$, where $xy = c^2$.

11. If $ux = a^2 + n^2x^2$, find the value of x which gives u its smallest value.

12. Find the maxima and minima of $1 + 2\sin\theta + 3\cos^2\theta$.

13. If $xy = 720$ find to one place of decimals the minimum value of $5x + 3y$.

14. Find the maximum value of $\dfrac{1}{x^x}$.

15. Show that $x^3 - 3x^2 + 6x + 3$ has neither a maximum nor a minimum value.

16. Find the minimum value of $9^x - 6x\log_e 3$.

17. Find the values of a and β in order that $x^6 + ax^5 + \beta x^4$ may have a maximum value when $x = 2$ and a minimum value when $x = 3$.

18. $ABCD$ is a rectangular field; AB is 200 yards, BC is 100 yards. A man has to walk from A to C. He can walk at 5 miles an hour down the side AB, but directly he leaves the path AB and strikes across the grass he can only go at 3 miles an hour. Find which is his quickest route.

19. An open box is to be made on a square base with vertical sides out of a given quantity of cardboard of area c^2. What is the maximum volume of the box?

20. Into how many parts must the number ne be divided so that their continued product may be a maximum; n being a positive integer and e the base of the Napierian logarithms?

21. A rectangular piece of cardboard, sides a, b, has an equal square cut out of each corner. Find the side of the square so that the remainder may form a box of maximum volume.

22. Find the length of the shortest straight line which can be drawn through the point (a, b) terminated by the rectilinear axes.

23. A man is 2 miles from the nearest point A of a straight road, and he wishes to reach a point B on the road 4 miles from A. He can walk at 4 miles per hour until he reaches the road and at 5 miles per hour on the road. Find the least time in which he can reach B.

24. Find the maximum and minimum values of y regarded as a function of the variable x, where $ax^2 + 2hxy + by^2 + 2cx = 0$.

25. A fixed point is taken on a circle of radius r, and a chord is drawn from this point to any other point on the circle. The tangent to the circle at the second point is constructed and a perpendicular is dropped from the fixed point on to the tangent. Prove that the maximum area of the triangle formed by the chord, the tangent and the perpendicular is $3\sqrt{3}r^2/8$.

26. In a submarine telegraph cable the speed of signalling varies as $x^2 \log \dfrac{1}{x}$, where x is the ratio of the radius of the core to that of the covering. Show that the greatest speed is attained when this ratio is $1 : e^{\frac{1}{2}}$.

27. A person being in a boat a miles from the nearest point A of the beach wishes to reach as quickly as possible a point B which is b miles from A along the shore. The ratio of his rate of walking to his rate of rowing is λ. Find the distance from A at which he should land.

28. A wire of given length is cut into two portions which are bent into the shapes of a circle and a square respectively. Show that if the sum of the areas be the least possible the side of the square is twice the radius of the circle.

29. An open tank is to be constructed with a square base and vertical sides so as to contain a given quantity of water. Show that the expense of lining it with lead will be least if the depth is made half the width.

30. Find the least value of $ae^{\kappa x} + be^{-\kappa x}$.

31. Find the maximum area of the rectangle which can be drawn with its sides passing through the four corners of a given rectangle whose sides are a and b in length respectively.

32. A train passes a station X at a rate of 30 miles per hour. Its speed increases and at any point exceeds the speed at X by a quantity proportional to the time elapsed since leaving X. At the end of a minute it passes Y, 3840 feet from X. A second train passes X 8 seconds after

the first and travels at a uniform speed of 45 miles per hour. Find the minimum distance between the two trains at any time.

33. A function y is the sum of two functions of which the first varies as the cube of x and the second inversely as the square of x. The least value of y is 5 which occurs when $x = 1$. Find the complete expression of y as a function of x.

34. Trace the curve $y = \dfrac{x^2 + 1}{x^2 + x + 1}$, finding the maximum and minimum values of y.

35. Find the maximum and minimum values of $y = x + \dfrac{4}{x + 2}$. Illustrate your results by drawing a graph of the function.

36. If x be the independent variable find the maximum and minimum values of y given

$$y - 12 - x^4 \left(5x^2 + 6x - 15\right) = 0.$$

37. Explain how to discriminate between the maxima and minima values of $f(x)$, if

$$\frac{df(x)}{dx} = (x - a)^4 (x - b)^3 (x - c),$$

and a, b, c be in ascending order of magnitude.

38. Explain what is meant by a "point of inflexion" on a curve and show how to find the points of inflexion, if any, on the curve $y = f(x)$.
Find the points of inflexion on the curve

$$y^2 = \frac{x^2}{a^2}(a^2 - x^2).$$

39. Draw a graph of the curve $y = e^{-x^2}$, and find the points of inflexion.

40. Find the points of inflexion on the curve $y = \dfrac{x^2}{1 + x^2}$ and illustrate by a diagram.

41. Prove that the triangle of maximum area inscribed in a circle is such that the tangents to the circle at the angular points are parallel to the opposite sides.

42. If $\dfrac{x^2}{a} + \dfrac{y^2}{b} = 1$, show that the maximum and minimum values of $x^2 + xy + y^2$ are the roots of the equation

$$4z^2 - 4z(a + b) + 3ab = 0.$$

43. $9y^2 + 6xy + 4x^2 - 24y - 8x + 4 = 0.$
Find the maximum and minimum values of y.

44. Given

$$\log_{10} e = \cdot 4343; \ \log_{10} 2 = \cdot 3010; \ \log_{10} 3 = \cdot 4771,$$

find the maximum and minimum values of

$$12 \left(\log_e x + 1\right) + x^2 - 10x.$$

45. Draw a rough sketch of a curve

$$y \left(2x^2 + 13x - 7\right) = 10x^2 + 30x,$$

and find the maximum and minimum values of y.

46. If $x^2 + y^2 = 1$, find the minimum value of $3x + 4y$.

47. Find the minimum value of

$$\frac{a^2 \cos^2 x + b^2 \sin^2 x}{\sin^2 x \cos^2 x}.$$

CHAPTER VI

MISCELLANEOUS THEOREMS

1. Indeterminate forms.

It has been demonstrated in Chapter II (para. 8) that the limit of $f(x)$ as $x \to a$ is frequently required although $f(a)$ itself has no meaning. Forms such as $\dfrac{0}{0}$ which result from the direct substitution of a for x in $f(x)$ are called *indeterminate forms*. To obtain $\underset{x \to a}{\text{Lt}} f(x)$, where $f(a)$ is an indeterminate form, we may resort to algebraic methods as previously shown, or we may adapt the processes of the differential calculus to the solution of the problem.

Let $\phi(x)$ and $\psi(x)$ be two functions of x continuous as far as the value $x = a$ and let $\phi(a) = 0 = \psi(a)$, so that $\dfrac{\phi(a)}{\psi(a)}$ is of the indeterminate form $\dfrac{0}{0}$.

Let $f(x) = \dfrac{\phi(x)}{\psi(x)}$. Write $a + h$ for x, so that $\underset{x \to a}{\text{Lt}}$ is the same as $\underset{h \to 0}{\text{Lt.}}$

Then $f(x) = \dfrac{\phi(x)}{\psi(x)} = \dfrac{\phi(a+h)}{\psi(a+h)} = \dfrac{\phi(a) + h\phi'(a + \theta_1 h)}{\psi(a) + h\psi'(a + \theta_2 h)}$.

But $\phi(a)$ and $\psi(a)$ are each zero.

Therefore $f(x) = \dfrac{\phi'(a + \theta_1 h)}{\psi'(a + \theta_2 h)}$ (dividing numerator and denominator by h).

Therefore $\underset{x \to a}{\text{Lt}} f(x) = \underset{h \to 0}{\text{Lt}} \dfrac{\phi(x)}{\psi(x)} = \dfrac{\phi'(a)}{\psi'(a)}$, since when $h \to 0$, $a + \theta_1 h$ and $a + \theta_2 h$ each $\to a$.

To obtain $\underset{x \to a}{\text{Lt}} f(x)$ when $f(a)$ is the indeterminate form $\dfrac{0}{0}$ we therefore differentiate numerator and denominator separately and put $x = a$ in the result.

If $\phi'(a)$ and $\psi'(a)$ are both zero (so that the form $\dfrac{0}{0}$ is again obtained) a further differentiation must be effected and a substituted for x in $\dfrac{\phi''(x)}{\psi''(x)}$; and so on if this be indeterminate.

2. The following examples are illustrative of the method.

Example 1.

Show that $\underset{x \to 1}{\text{Lt}} \dfrac{x^6 - 5x + 4}{x^3 - 2x + 1}$ is 1 (cf. Ex. 5, p. 31).

$\dfrac{x^6 - 5x + 4}{x^3 - 2x + 1}$ takes the form $\dfrac{0}{0}$ when 1 is substituted for x.

$$\therefore \quad \underset{x \to 1}{\text{Lt}} \frac{x^6 - 5x + 4}{x^3 - 2x + 1} = \underset{x \to 1}{\text{Lt}} \frac{6x^5 - 5}{3x^2 - 2} = \frac{1}{1} = 1.$$

Example 2.

Find $\underset{\theta \to 0}{\text{Lt}} \dfrac{\sin^{-1}\theta - \theta}{\theta^3}$.

$$\underset{\theta \to 0}{\text{Lt}} \frac{\sin^{-1}\theta - \theta}{\theta^3} \qquad \text{form } \frac{0}{0}.$$

Differentiating numerator and denominator separately:

$$= \underset{\theta \to 0}{\text{Lt}} \frac{\dfrac{1}{\sqrt{1 - \theta^2}} - 1}{3\theta^2} \qquad \text{form } \frac{0}{0}.$$

Differentiating again:
$$= \underset{\theta \to 0}{\text{Lt}} \frac{\theta(1 - \theta^2)^{-\frac{3}{2}}}{6\theta}$$

$$= \underset{\theta \to 0}{\text{Lt}} \frac{(1 - \theta^2)^{-\frac{3}{2}}}{6}, \text{ on dividing through by } \theta,$$

$$= \tfrac{1}{6}.$$

3. Other indeterminate forms: ∞/∞; $0 \times \infty$; $\infty - \infty$; 0^0; ∞^0; 1^∞.

In order to obtain the limits of functions which take these forms it is strictly necessary to consider each variation separately and to prove that we may in effect obtain the required limit by application of the calculus. It will be sufficient, however, simply to indicate the methods to be adopted for the solution of the problems.

(*a*) The form ∞/∞.

If $\underset{x \to a}{\text{Lt}} \dfrac{\phi(x)}{\psi(x)}$ take the form $\dfrac{\infty}{\infty}$, it can be shown that, as for the form $\dfrac{0}{0}$, $\qquad \underset{x \to a}{\text{Lt}} \dfrac{\phi(x)}{\psi(x)} = \underset{x \to a}{\text{Lt}} \dfrac{\phi'(x)}{\psi'(x)}.$

(For a proof of this theorem, see Gibson's *Elementary Treatise on the Calculus*, p. 420.)

(*b*) Form $0 \times \infty$.

Let $\underset{x \to a}{\mathrm{Lt}} \; \phi(x) \psi(x)$ take the form $0 \times \infty$, $(\phi(a) = 0; \psi(a) = \infty)$.

Then $\phi(x) \psi(x) = \dfrac{\phi(x)}{\dfrac{1}{\psi(x)}}$ which is of the form $\dfrac{0}{0}$, and the ordinary

processes may be adopted.

(*c*) $\infty - \infty$; 0°; ∞°; 1^∞.

These forms are best treated by algebraic methods, e.g. by expanding certain series, by taking logarithms, etc. It is advisable not to adopt any standard methods for evaluation of limits in these examples, but to consider each one separately as it arises.

Example 3.

Evaluate $\underset{x \to \infty}{\mathrm{Lt}} \; x^n e^{-x}$, where n is a positive integer.

$$\underset{x \to \infty}{\mathrm{Lt}} \; x^n e^{-x} = \underset{x \to \infty}{\mathrm{Lt}} \; \frac{x^n}{e^x} \qquad\qquad \text{form } \frac{\infty}{\infty}$$

$$= \underset{x \to \infty}{\mathrm{Lt}} \; \frac{n x^{n-1}}{e^x} \qquad\qquad \text{''}$$

$$= \underset{x \to \infty}{\mathrm{Lt}} \; \frac{n(n-1) x^{n-2}}{e^x} \qquad \text{''}$$

$$\cdots\cdots\cdots\cdots\cdots\cdots\cdots$$

$$= \underset{x \to \infty}{\mathrm{Lt}} \; \frac{n!}{e^x}$$

$$= 0.$$

Example 4.

Find $\underset{x \to 0}{\mathrm{Lt}} \; \left\{ \dfrac{1}{x} - \dfrac{1}{x^2} \log(1 + x) \right\}$.

$$\underset{x \to 0}{\mathrm{Lt}} \; \left\{ \frac{1}{x} - \frac{1}{x^2} \log(1 + x) \right\} \text{ is of the form } \infty - \infty.$$

Write it as $\underset{x \to 0}{\mathrm{Lt}} \; \dfrac{x - \log(1 + x)}{x^2} \qquad \text{form } \dfrac{0}{0}$

$$= \underset{x \to 0}{\mathrm{Lt}} \; \frac{1 - (1 + x)^{-1}}{2x} \qquad \text{''}$$

$$= \underset{x \to 0}{\mathrm{Lt}} \; \frac{(1 + x)^{-2}}{2} = \frac{1}{2}.$$

Example 5.

$$\underset{x \to 1}{\text{Lt}} \ (1 - x^2)^{\frac{1}{\log(1-x)}}.$$

This takes the form 0^0 when 1 is substituted for x.

Let
$$y = (1 - x^2)^{\frac{1}{\log(1-x)}}.$$

Then
$$\log y = \frac{1}{\log(1 - x)} \log(1 - x^2).$$

$$\therefore \ \underset{x \to 1}{\text{Lt}} \log y = \underset{x \to 1}{\text{Lt}} \ \frac{\log(1 - x^2)}{\log(1 - x)} \qquad \text{form } \frac{-\infty}{-\infty}$$

$$= \underset{x \to 1}{\text{Lt}} \ \frac{\dfrac{-2x}{1 - x^2}}{-\dfrac{1}{1 - x}},$$

which, on removing the common factor $\dfrac{1}{1 - x}$, is

$$\underset{x \to 1}{\text{Lt}} \ \frac{2x}{1 + x} = 1.$$

$$\therefore \ \underset{x \to 1}{\text{Lt}} \ y = e.$$

Note. Care must be taken in applying the principles of the differential calculus to indeterminate forms to remember that

(i) the method holds only when the function takes an indeterminate form when a is substituted for x. Otherwise $\underset{x \to a}{\text{Lt}} \ \dfrac{\phi(x)}{\psi(x)}$ will not be $\underset{x \to a}{\text{Lt}} \ \dfrac{\phi'(x)}{\psi'(x)}$;

(ii) the differentiation is performed on the numerator and denominator separately. $\dfrac{\phi(x)}{\psi(x)}$ must not be differentiated as the quotient of two functions of x.

4. Partial differentiation.

If $f(x, y) = 0$ defines an implicit function of x and y, we may obtain $\dfrac{dy}{dx}$ by differentiating in the usual manner and then solving the resulting equation for $\dfrac{dy}{dx}$.

For example, if
$$x^2 + xy + y^2 = 0,$$
then
$$2x + y + xy' + 2yy' = 0,$$
and
$$y' = - (2x + y)/(x + 2y).$$

Where there are two or more independent variables an alternative method can be adopted which is often simpler in its application. This is the method known as partial differentiation.

Consider the function $f(x, y) = x^2 + xy + y^2$ where x and y are independent variables. Then if we differentiate $f(x, y)$ with respect to x keeping y constant, the result is said to be the partial differential coefficient of $f(x, y)$ with respect to x; similarly, on differentiating with respect to y keeping x constant, we obtain the partial differential coefficient of $f(x, y)$ with respect to y.

The usual notation is $\dfrac{\partial}{\partial x} f(x, y)$; $\dfrac{\partial}{\partial y} f(x, y)$ for partial derivatives with respect to x and y respectively.

In the above example $\dfrac{\partial f}{\partial x} = 2x + y$ and $\dfrac{\partial f}{\partial y} = x + 2y$.

Generally, if u be written for $f(x, y)$,

$$\frac{\partial u}{\partial x} = \operatorname*{Lt}_{\Delta x \to 0} \frac{f(x + \Delta x, y) - f(x, y)}{\Delta x},$$

and

$$\frac{\partial u}{\partial y} = \operatorname*{Lt}_{\Delta y \to 0} \frac{f(x, y + \Delta y) - f(x, y)}{\Delta y}.$$

5. To prove that, if x and y be functions of a third variable z, then

$$\frac{du}{dz} = \frac{\partial u}{\partial x} \frac{dx}{dz} + \frac{\partial u}{\partial y} \frac{dy}{dz}.$$

Let x, y, u become $x + \Delta x$, $y + \Delta y$, $u + \Delta u$ respectively when z becomes $z + \Delta z$.

Now if we let x vary while $y + \Delta y$ remains constant, we have, by the Mean Value Theorem,

$$f(x + \Delta x, y + \Delta y) = f(x, y + \Delta y) + \Delta x \frac{\partial}{\partial x} f(x + \theta_1 \Delta x, y + \Delta y).$$

Similarly,

$$f(x, y + \Delta y) = f(x, y) + \Delta y \frac{\partial}{\partial y} f(x, y + \theta_2 \Delta y).$$

Adding these two results and dividing by Δz, we obtain

$$\frac{\Delta u}{\Delta z} = \frac{f(x + \Delta x, y + \Delta y) - f(x, y)}{\Delta z}$$

$$= \frac{\Delta x}{\Delta z} \frac{\partial}{\partial x} f(x + \theta_1 \Delta x, y + \Delta y) + \frac{\Delta y}{\Delta z} \frac{\partial}{\partial y} f(x, y + \theta_2 \Delta y).$$

Taking the limit $\Delta z \to 0$, so that $\Delta u, \Delta x, \Delta y$ also $\to 0$,

$$\frac{\Delta u}{\Delta z}, \frac{\Delta x}{\Delta z}, \frac{\Delta y}{\Delta z} \quad \text{become} \quad \frac{du}{dz}, \frac{dx}{dz}, \frac{dy}{dz} \text{ respectively,}$$

$$\frac{\partial}{\partial x} f(x + \theta_1 \Delta x, y + \Delta y) \quad \text{becomes} \quad \frac{\partial}{\partial x} f(x, y), \text{ i.e. } \frac{\partial u}{\partial x},$$

and $\quad \dfrac{\partial}{\partial y} f(x, y + \theta_2 \Delta y) \quad$ becomes $\quad \dfrac{\partial}{\partial y} f(x, y), \text{ i.e. } \dfrac{\partial u}{\partial y}.$

$$\therefore \quad \frac{du}{dz} = \frac{\partial u}{\partial x} \frac{dx}{dz} + \frac{\partial u}{\partial y} \frac{dy}{dz}.$$

Corollary. If $z = x$, so that y is a function of x, and u, although expressed in terms of x and y, is a function of the single variable x,

then $\quad \dfrac{du}{dx} = \dfrac{\partial u}{\partial x} + \dfrac{\partial u}{\partial y} \dfrac{dy}{dx}, \text{ since } \dfrac{dx}{dx} = 1.$

Suppose now that $u = f(x, y) = 0$; then

$$0 = \frac{\partial u}{\partial x} + \frac{\partial u}{\partial y} \frac{dy}{dx},$$

or $\quad \dfrac{dy}{dx} = - \dfrac{\partial u}{\partial x} \bigg/ \dfrac{\partial u}{\partial y}.$

This is a convenient formula for obtaining $\dfrac{dy}{dx}$ when y is an implicit function of x.

For example, if $\quad x^2 + xy + y^2 = 0,$

$$0 = (2x + y) + (x + 2y) \frac{dy}{dx}.$$

$$\therefore \quad \frac{dy}{dx} = - \frac{2x + y}{x + 2y} \quad \text{as before.}$$

6. A further investigation of the theory of partial differentiation involves detailed mathematical analysis. Two important theorems are, however, worthy of mention:

(i) Defining $\dfrac{\partial^2 u}{\partial x \partial y}$ as the operation $\dfrac{\partial}{\partial x}\left(\dfrac{\partial u}{\partial y}\right)$, i.e. the process of partial differentiation of $\dfrac{\partial u}{\partial y}$ with respect to x, keeping y constant, it can be shown that

$$\frac{\partial^2 u}{\partial x \partial y} = \frac{\partial^2 u}{\partial y \partial x}.$$

In other words, the operations of differentiating partially with respect to x and y are commutative.

(ii) If $u = f(x, y)$ is a homogeneous function of the nth degree in x and y, then

$$x \frac{\partial u}{\partial x} + y \frac{\partial u}{\partial y} = nu \quad \text{(Euler's Theorem)}.$$

The proofs of these theorems are difficult, and it will be sufficient to verify that they are true by simple examples.

Example 6.

If $u = y^x$, show that $\dfrac{\partial^2 u}{\partial x \partial y} = \dfrac{\partial^2 u}{\partial y \partial x}$.

$$\frac{\partial u}{\partial y} = xy^{x-1}; \quad \frac{\partial^2 u}{\partial x \partial y} = \frac{\partial}{\partial x}\left(\frac{\partial u}{\partial y}\right) = y^{x-1} + xy^{x-1} \log y,$$

$$\frac{\partial u}{\partial x} = y^x \log y; \quad \frac{\partial^2 u}{\partial y \partial x} = \frac{\partial}{\partial y}\left(\frac{\partial u}{\partial x}\right) = xy^{x-1} \log y + y^x \frac{1}{y}$$

$$= xy^{x-1} \log y + y^{x-1},$$

which proves the proposition.

Example 7.

Show that Euler's Theorem for a homogeneous function of x and y holds for

$$ax^3 + by^3 + cx^2 y + dxy^2.$$

It is required to prove that, if

$$u = ax^3 + by^3 + cx^2 y + dxy^2,$$

then

$$x \frac{\partial u}{\partial x} + y \frac{\partial u}{\partial y} = 3u.$$

$$\frac{\partial u}{\partial x} = 3ax^2 + 2cxy + dy^2,$$

$$\frac{\partial u}{\partial y} = 3by^2 + cx^2 + 2dxy.$$

$$\therefore\ x\frac{\partial u}{\partial x}+y\frac{\partial u}{\partial y}=3ax^3+2cx^2y+dxy^2+3by^3+cx^2y+2dxy^2=3u.$$

Euler's Theorem can be extended to any number of variables, so that, if u is a homogeneous function of x, y, z, ... of degree n,

$$x\frac{\partial u}{\partial x}+y\frac{\partial u}{\partial y}+z\frac{\partial u}{\partial z}+\ldots=nu.$$

EXAMPLES 6

1. Obtain the limit when $n\to\infty$ of $\dfrac{x^n}{n!}$, where x is finite.

2. Evaluate $\underset{x\to0}{\text{Lt}}\ x\log x$.

Find the following limits:

3. $\underset{x\to1}{\text{Lt}}\ \dfrac{2x^3-3x^2+1}{3x^5-5x^3+2}$.

4. $\underset{x\to0}{\text{Lt}}\ \dfrac{a^x-1}{b^x-1}$.

5. $\underset{x\to1}{\text{Lt}}\ \dfrac{x^m-1}{x^n-1}$.

6. $\underset{x\to a}{\text{Lt}}\ [x^{\frac{1}{2}}-a^{\frac{1}{2}}+(x-a)^{\frac{1}{2}}](x^2-a^2)^{-\frac{1}{2}}$.

7. $\underset{x\to1}{\text{Lt}}\ \dfrac{1-x+\log x}{1-(2x-x^2)^{\frac{1}{2}}}$.

8. $\underset{x\to a}{\text{Lt}}\ \dfrac{x-a+\sqrt{x^m-a^m}}{\sqrt{x^n-a^n}}$.

9. $\underset{x\to0}{\text{Lt}}\ \dfrac{xe^x-\log(1+x)}{x^2}$.

10. $\underset{x\to0}{\text{Lt}}\ (1+x^3)^{\frac{1}{x^3}}$.

11. $\underset{x\to0}{\text{Lt}}\ (\log x)^{\log(1-x)}$.

12. $\underset{x\to0}{\text{Lt}}\ \dfrac{(1+x)^{\frac{1}{n}}-1}{x}$.

13. $\underset{x\to\infty}{\text{Lt}}\ x(a^{\frac{1}{x}}-1)$.

14. $\underset{x\to0}{\text{Lt}}\ \dfrac{(1+x)^{\frac{1}{x}}-e+\frac{1}{2}ex}{x^2}$.

15. $\underset{x\to0}{\text{Lt}}\ (x\log x)^x$.

16. $\underset{x\to0}{\text{Lt}}\ \dfrac{e^x-e^{-x}+2\sin x-4x}{x^5}$.

17. $\underset{x\to0}{\text{Lt}}\ \dfrac{\sin^{-1}x-x}{x^3\cos x}$.

18. An arithmetical and a geometrical progression have each the same first and last terms, a and b, and the same number of terms. If the sums of their terms are s_1 and s_2 respectively, find the limiting value of $\dfrac{s_1}{s_2}$ when the number of terms is indefinitely increased.

19. Prove that the limit of $\left(2 - \dfrac{x}{a}\right)^{\tan\frac{\pi x}{2a}}$ as x tends to a is $e^{\frac{2}{\pi}}$.

20. a and p are positive integers. Find
$$\underset{x \to 0}{\text{Lt}} \ \frac{(a + p)^x - a^x}{x^p}.$$

21. Determine a, b, c so that, as θ tends to zero, the function
$$\frac{\theta\,(a + b\cos\theta) - c\sin\theta}{\theta^5}$$
shall tend to the limit unity.

22. If $x = r\cos\theta$ and $y = r\sin\theta$, prove that
$$\frac{\partial x}{\partial r} = \frac{\partial r}{\partial x} = \cos\theta.$$

Find the value of $x\dfrac{\partial u}{\partial x} + y\dfrac{\partial u}{\partial y}$, given:

23. $u = \sin^{-1}\dfrac{\sqrt{x} - \sqrt{y}}{\sqrt{x} + \sqrt{y}}$.   **24.** $u = \sin^{-1}\dfrac{x}{y} + \tan^{-1}\dfrac{y}{x}$.

25. $u = x^3 \log \dfrac{\sqrt[3]{y} - \sqrt[3]{x}}{\sqrt[3]{y} + \sqrt[3]{x}}$.   **26.** $u = \dfrac{x^{\frac{1}{4}} + y^{\frac{1}{4}}}{x^{\frac{1}{5}} + y^{\frac{1}{5}}}$.

27. Show that $\dfrac{\partial^2 u}{\partial x\,\partial y} = \dfrac{\partial^2 u}{\partial y\,\partial x}$, where
$$u = \log(x^2 + y^2) - \log xy.$$

28. Find $\dfrac{dy}{dx}$, given $x^3 + y^3 + 3xy = 0$.

29. Prove that, if $x^3 + y^3 + 3xyz = u$, then
$$x\frac{\partial u}{\partial x} + y\frac{\partial u}{\partial y} + z\frac{\partial u}{\partial z} = 3u.$$

30. If $ue^v = x$, find the value of
$$x\frac{\partial u}{\partial x} + y\frac{\partial u}{\partial y}.$$

31. Prove that $\dfrac{du_x}{dx} = \dfrac{u_{x+m} - u_{x-m}}{2m}$ approximately.

Give a geometrical interpretation of this approximation.

CHAPTER VII

INTEGRAL CALCULUS

DEFINITIONS AND STANDARD FORMS

1. Let values of the continuous function $y = f(x)$ be given for equidistant intervals, and let $\phi(x)$ be a function such that

$$f(x+h) - f(x) = \phi(x).$$

Then
$$f(a+h) - f(a) = \phi(a),$$

$$f(a+2h) - f(a+h) = \phi(a+h),$$

$$\dots\dots\dots\dots\dots\dots$$

$$f(a+nh) - f(a+\overline{n-1}h) = \phi(a+\overline{n-1}h).$$

$\therefore$ by summation,

$$f(a+nh) - f(a) = \phi(a) + \phi(a+h) + \dots + \phi(a+\overline{n-1}h).$$

If $b = a + (n-1)h$ we may write this result in the form

$$\overset{b}{\underset{a}{\Sigma}} \, \phi(x) = f(a+nh) - f(a).$$

This gives an expression for the sum of the values of $\phi(x)$ for values of x differing by the constant finite difference h. We may obtain in a similar manner the limit of the sum of the values of $\phi(x)$ when the difference h tends to zero.

Let
$$\phi(x) = \frac{df(x)}{dx} = \underset{h \to 0}{\text{Lt}} \, \frac{f(x+h) - f(x)}{h}.$$

Then we may write

$$\phi(a) = \frac{f(a+h) - f(a)}{h} + \eta_1,$$

where η_1 tends to zero as h tends to zero.

$$\therefore \ h \, \phi \, (a) = f(a+h) - f(a) + h\eta_1.$$

Similarly,

$$h \, \phi \, (a+h) = f(a+2h) - f(a+h) + h\eta_2,$$

$$h \, \phi \, (a+2h) = f(a+3h) - f(a+2h) + h\eta_3,$$

$$\dotfill$$

$$h \, \phi \, (a + \overline{n-1}h) = f(a+nh) - f(a + \overline{n-1}h) + h\eta_n.$$

On summing:

$$h \, [\phi \, (a) + \phi \, (a+h) + \phi \, (a+2h) + \ldots + \phi \, (a + \overline{n-1}h)]$$

$$= f(a+nh) - f(a) + h \, (\eta_1 + \eta_2 + \eta_3 + \ldots + \eta_n).$$

If the n small quantities are all numerically less than η, then

$$h \, (\eta_1 + \eta_2 + \eta_3 + \ldots + \eta_n) < hn\eta.$$

If now $b - a = nh$, so that the product of n and h is always finite, then the limit of $hn\eta$ as $h \to 0$ is zero.

$$\therefore \ \text{Lt} \ h \, (\eta_1 + \eta_2 + \eta_3 + \ldots + \eta_n) = 0, \quad \text{when } h \to 0.$$

I.e. $\displaystyle \lim_{h \to 0} h \, [\phi \, (a) + \phi \, (a+h) + \phi \, (a+2h) + \ldots + \phi \, (a + \overline{n-1}h)]$

$$= f(a+nh) - f(a)$$

$$= f(b) - f(a).$$

The limit

$$\lim_{h \to 0} h \, [\phi \, (a) + \phi \, (a+h) + \phi \, (a+2h) + \ldots + \phi \, (a + \overline{n-1}h)]$$

is denoted by the symbol $\displaystyle \int_a^b \phi \, (x) \, dx$ and is called the *definite integral* of $\phi \, (x)$ with respect to x, between the limits $x = a$ and $x = b$.

Corresponding to the symbol D for the operation of differentiation, the symbol I is sometimes used to denote integration with respect to a variable.

2. The primary consideration when obtaining the value of the integral $\int_a^b \phi(x)\,dx$ is the finding of a function $f(x)$ such that $\dfrac{df(x)}{dx} = \phi(x)$. Where we are not concerned with the summation, but only with the initial problem of determining this inverse function, we are said to integrate $\phi(x)$ with respect to x. In that event we find the *indefinite integral* and write the integral function as $\int \phi(x)\,dx$. In the same way as $\dfrac{d}{dx}$ represents the operation of finding the differential coefficient of a function of x with respect to x, so $\int dx$ represents the operation of finding the integral. The symbol $\int$ is meaningless by itself, and we must be careful always to associate with this symbol the dx which renders it intelligible.

Every function of x is not integrable, and it is only by application of the known properties of the differential calculus that it is possible to evaluate $\int \phi(x)\,dx$.

3. Geometrical Interpretation of an integral.

Before proceeding to investigate methods of integrating functions of x it is helpful to illustrate the meaning of definite integration by reference to geometry.

Let AB represent the continuous function $y = f(x)$, and let P_0, P_n be two points on the curve whose coordinates are $\{a, f(a)\}$ and $\{b, f(b)\}$ respectively, so that $OM_0 = a$ and $OM_n = b$. Divide $M_0 M_n$ into n equal parts each equal to h. Then $nh = b - a$. If we complete the set of inner rectangles $P_0K_1M_1M_0$, $P_1K_2M_2M_1$,... $P_{n-1}K_nM_nM_{n-1}$ it is evident that the sum of these rectangles is slightly less than the area cut off by the curve, the ordinates P_0M_0, P_nM_n and the x-axis.

Again, if we complete the set of outer rectangles of which $Q_0P_1M_1M_0$ is the first and $Q_{n-1}P_nM_nM_{n-1}$ is the last, the sum of

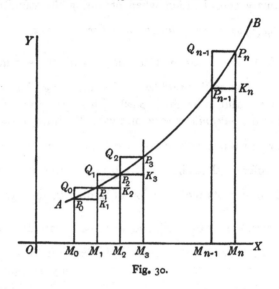

Fig. 30.

these outer rectangles will be slightly greater than the area of the curve $P_0P_nM_nM_0$.

Now the difference between the set of outer and of inner rectangles is evidently the sum of the small rectangles $Q_0P_0K_1P_1$, etc., and this sum is $h\,(P_nM_n - P_0M_0)$, since the rectangles are all of base h. Since $P_nM_n - P_0M_0$ is finite, the limit of $h\,(P_nM_n - P_0M_0)$ as n tends to infinity is zero. In other words, as $h \to 0$ the difference between the area $P_0P_nM_nM_0$ and the sum of the rectangles $P_0K_1M_1M_0$, $P_1K_2M_2M_1$, ... $P_{n-1}K_nM_nM_{n-1}$ tends to zero.

But $P_0K_1M_1M_0 = M_0M_1 . P_0M_0 = hf(a)$

         $P_1K_2M_2M_1 = M_1M_2 . P_1M_1 = hf(a+h)$

         ....

     $P_{n-1}K_nM_nM_{n-1} = M_{n-1}M_n . P_{n-1}M_{n-1} = hf(a + \overline{n-1}h)$.

$$\therefore \text{ Area } P_0 P_n M_n M_0 = \underset{h \to 0}{\text{Lt}} \ h \overset{a+(n-1)h}{\underset{a}{\Sigma}} f(x) = \int_a^b f(x)\, dx$$

where
$$b = a + nh.$$

We may therefore define the definite integral as the area of the curve $y = f(x)$ between the curve, the ordinates $x = a$, $x = b$ and the x-axis.

4. Alternatively we may proceed as follows:

Let PQ be the curve $y = f(x)$ and let the area $PHML$ be z. If H be the point (x, y), so that a small increase in the length OM,

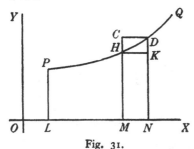

Fig. 31.

namely MN, may be denoted by Δx, then $DN = y + \Delta y$ and the area $PDNL = z + \Delta z$.

It is evident from Fig. 31 that the rectangle
$$CDNM = DN.MN = (y + \Delta y)\,\Delta x;$$

the area
$$HDNM = \Delta z;$$

and the rectangle
$$HKNM = y\Delta x.$$

$$\therefore \ (y + \Delta y)\,\Delta x > \Delta z > y\Delta x,$$

or
$$y + \Delta y > \Delta z/\Delta x > y,$$

when $\Delta x \to 0$, $y + \Delta y \to y$, since Δy tends to zero as Δx tends to zero.

Also
$$\underset{\Delta x \to 0}{\text{Lt}} \frac{\Delta z}{\Delta x} = \frac{dz}{dx},$$

$$\therefore \ y = \frac{dz}{dx},$$

and the area $z = \int y\, dx.$

The arguments in this paragraph and in para. 3 postulate a concave curve. Similar arguments apply to a convex curve. An ordinary curve having points of inflexion can be broken up into portions concave or convex as the case may be.

5. The definition of a definite integral enables us to represent in a convenient form the limits of the sums of certain series when the number of terms tends to infinity.

Example 1.

Obtain as a definite integral

$$\underset{n\to\infty}{\text{Lt}} \left[\frac{1}{\sqrt{n^2 - 1^2}} + \frac{1}{\sqrt{n^2 - 2^2}} + \ldots + \frac{1}{\sqrt{n^2 - (n-1)^2}} \right].$$

The expression in brackets may be written as

$$E = \frac{1}{n}\frac{1}{\sqrt{1 - (1/n)^2}} + \frac{1}{n}\frac{1}{\sqrt{1 - (2/n)^2}} + \ldots + \frac{1}{n}\frac{1}{\sqrt{1 - \{(n-1)/n\}^2}},$$

which is of the form

$$h\left[f(a) + f(a+h) + f(a+2h) + \ldots + f(a + \overline{n-1}h)\right],$$

where $h = \dfrac{1}{n}$, $a = 0$ and $f(x)$ is $\dfrac{1}{\sqrt{1 - x^2}}$.

$$\therefore \quad \underset{n\to\infty}{\text{Lt}}\, E = \underset{h\to 0}{\text{Lt}}\, E = \int_0^1 \frac{1}{\sqrt{1 - x^2}}\, dx.$$

6. Standard forms.

The two following theorems are almost self-evident:

(i) $\displaystyle\int a\,\phi(x)\,dx = a\int \phi(x)\,dx$, where a is independent of x.

(ii) $\displaystyle\int (u \pm v \pm w \pm \ldots)\,dx = \int u\,dx \pm \int v\,dx \pm \int w\,dx \pm \ldots,$

where u, v, w, ... are functions of x.

(i) follows directly from the fact that if $\phi(x) = \dfrac{df(x)}{dx}$,

then $\qquad \dfrac{d\,af(x)}{dx} = a\dfrac{df(x)}{dx} = a\,\phi(x),$

$$\therefore \quad \int a\,\phi(x)\,dx = af(x) = a\int \phi(x)\,dx.$$

(ii) $\quad \dfrac{d}{dx}\left(\displaystyle\int u\,dx \pm \int v\,dx \pm \int w\,dx \pm \ldots\right) = u \pm v \pm w \pm \ldots,$

$\therefore \displaystyle\int u\,dx \pm \int v\,dx \pm \int w\,dx \pm \ldots = \int (u \pm v \pm w \pm \ldots)\,dx.$

By the use of these theorems and the simpler standard results that have been obtained by direct differentiation of well-known forms, various integrals can be written down at once.

For example,

$$\frac{dx^{n+1}}{dx} = (n+1)\,x^n \quad \text{or} \quad \frac{d}{dx}\frac{x^{n+1}}{n+1} = x^n,$$

$$\therefore \int x^n\,dx = \frac{x^{n+1}}{n+1} \qquad \ldots\ldots\text{(i)}.$$

Since $\dfrac{d}{dx}\left\{\dfrac{x^{n+1}}{n+1} + c\right\} = x^n$, where c is any constant, the indefinite integral $\displaystyle\int x^n\,dx$ is $\dfrac{x^{n+1}}{n+1} + c$. Strictly speaking, in evaluating indefinite integrals the arbitrary constant should always be added to the result. The constant of integration will be omitted in the following examples, but wherever there is an indefinite integral the presence of the constant is to be inferred.

$$\frac{d}{dx}\log x = \frac{1}{x},$$

$$\therefore \int \frac{dx}{x} = \log x \qquad \ldots\ldots\text{(ii)}.$$

From the two theorems above it is evident that

$$\int (ax^n + b)\,dx = a\int x^n\,dx + b\int dx$$

$$= a\frac{x^{n+1}}{n+1} + bx \qquad \ldots\ldots\text{(iii)},$$

unless n is -1,

and $\qquad \displaystyle\int\left(\frac{a}{x} + b\right)dx = a\int \frac{dx}{x} + b\int dx$

$$= a\log x + bx \qquad \ldots\ldots\text{(iv)}.$$

$$\frac{de^x}{dx} = e^x,$$

$$\therefore \quad \int e^x dx = e^x \qquad\qquad \text{......(v)}.$$

$$\frac{d}{dx} \sin x = \cos x \quad \text{and} \quad \frac{d}{dx} \cos x = -\sin x,$$

$$\therefore \quad \left. \begin{array}{l} \int \cos x \, dx = \sin x \\[2ex] \int \sin x \, dx = -\cos x \end{array} \right\} \qquad \text{......(vi)}.$$

$$\frac{d}{dx} \tan x = \sec^2 x \quad \text{and} \quad \frac{d}{dx} \cot x = -\operatorname{cosec}^2 x,$$

$$\therefore \quad \left. \begin{array}{l} \int \sec^2 x \, dx = \tan x \\[2ex] \int \operatorname{cosec}^2 x \, dx = -\cot x \end{array} \right\} \qquad \text{......(vii)}.$$

$$\frac{d}{dx} \sin^{-1} x = \frac{1}{\sqrt{1-x^2}} \quad \text{and} \quad \frac{d}{dx} \cos^{-1} x = -\frac{1}{\sqrt{1-x^2}},$$

$$\therefore \quad \int \frac{dx}{\sqrt{1-x^2}} = \sin^{-1} x \quad \text{or} \quad -\cos^{-1} x \quad \text{......(viii)}.$$

These two apparently different results are the same, the difference being in the constant of integration. Let $\cos^{-1} x = \alpha$ so that $\cos \alpha = x$; then $\sin\left(n\frac{\pi}{2} - \alpha\right) = x$.

$$\therefore \quad \sin^{-1} x = n\frac{\pi}{2} - \alpha$$

$$= n\frac{\pi}{2} - \cos^{-1} x$$

$$= \text{constant} - \cos^{-1} x.$$

The above are the principal standard forms, and by the use of these forms in conjunction with methods which will be outlined later a large number of different forms of functions can be integrated (see Chapter VIII).

7. Some simple functions that can be integrated directly from the standard forms are given below.

Example 2.

Find $\int \dfrac{dx}{x^2 + a^2}$.

If we differentiate $\tan^{-1} x$ we obtain $\dfrac{1}{x^2 + 1}$. Let us see the effect of differentiating $\tan^{-1} kx$.

$$\frac{d}{dx} \tan^{-1} kx = \frac{d}{d(kx)} \tan^{-1} kx \frac{d(kx)}{dx}$$

$$= \frac{1}{1 + k^2 x^2} k.$$

This is almost in the form required if we replace k by $\dfrac{1}{a}$. Then

$$\frac{d}{dx} \tan^{-1} \frac{x}{a} = \frac{1}{1 + \dfrac{x^2}{a^2}} \frac{1}{a} = a \frac{1}{x^2 + a^2},$$

$$\therefore \ \tan^{-1} \frac{x}{a} = \int a \frac{1}{x^2 + a^2} dx,$$

or

$$\int \frac{dx}{x^2 + a^2} = \frac{1}{a} \tan^{-1} \frac{x}{a}.$$

Example 3.

Find $\int \dfrac{dx}{x^2 - a^2}$.

We cannot immediately recognize $\dfrac{1}{x^2 - a^2}$ as the differential coefficient of a known function. If, however, we express $\dfrac{1}{x^2 - a^2}$ as

$$\frac{1}{2a} \left[\frac{1}{x - a} - \frac{1}{x + a} \right],$$

we see at once that each of the component fractions is the derivative of a logarithmic function of x.

$$\int \frac{dx}{x - a} = \log (x - a),$$

$$\int \frac{dx}{x + a} = \log (x + a);$$

$$\therefore \int \frac{dx}{x^2 - a^2} = \frac{1}{2a} \int \left(\frac{1}{x - a} - \frac{1}{x + a} \right) dx$$

$$= \frac{1}{2a} \left[\log (x - a) - \log (x + a) \right]$$

$$= \frac{1}{2a} \log \frac{x - a}{x + a}.$$

Similarly

$$\int \frac{dx}{a^2 - x^2} = \frac{1}{2a} \int \left(\frac{1}{a - x} + \frac{1}{a + x} \right) dx$$

$$= \frac{1}{2a} \left[- \log (a - x) + \log (a + x) \right]$$

$$= \frac{1}{2a} \log \frac{a + x}{a - x}.$$

Example 4.

Find $\int \sin n\theta \, d\theta$ and $\int \cos n\theta \, d\theta$.

$$\frac{d}{d\theta} \sin n\theta = \frac{d}{d(n\theta)} \sin n\theta \frac{d(n\theta)}{d\theta}$$

$$= \cos n\theta . n$$

$$= n \cos n\theta,$$

$$\therefore \int \cos n\theta \, d\theta = \frac{1}{n} \sin n\theta.$$

Similarly

$$\int \sin n\theta \, d\theta = - \frac{1}{n} \cos n\theta.$$

Note: $\sin^n \theta$ and $\cos^n \theta$ are not immediately integrable. If, however, we express these functions in terms of multiple angles we can at once write down their integrals.

E.g.
$$\sin^2 \theta = \tfrac{1}{2} (1 - \cos 2\theta).$$

$$\therefore \int \sin^2 \theta \, d\theta = \int (\tfrac{1}{2} - \tfrac{1}{2} \cos 2\theta) \, d\theta$$

$$= \tfrac{1}{2}\theta - \tfrac{1}{2}.\tfrac{1}{2} \sin 2\theta$$

$$= \tfrac{1}{2}\theta - \tfrac{1}{4} \sin 2\theta.$$

Again
$$\sin 3\theta = 3 \sin \theta - 4 \sin^3 \theta,$$

$$\therefore \sin^3 \theta = \tfrac{3}{4} \sin \theta - \tfrac{1}{4} \sin 3\theta.$$

$$\therefore \int \sin^3 \theta \, d\theta = \int (\tfrac{3}{4} \sin \theta - \tfrac{1}{4} \sin 3\theta) \, d\theta$$

$$= - \tfrac{3}{4} \cos \theta + \tfrac{1}{12} \cos 3\theta,$$

and so on.

EXAMPLES 7

1. Prove that $\int_a^b f(x)\,dx = \underset{h \to 0}{\mathrm{Lt}}\ h \sum_{r=a}^{r=a+\overline{n-1}h} \phi(r)$, where $b = a + nh$, and find from the definition the value of $\int_0^4 x\,dx$.

Integrate the following expressions with respect to x:

2. $3x^n$; $\tfrac{1}{3}x^{-n}$; e^{2x}.

3. $(x^2 + a^2)^2$; $a + bx + cx^2$; $(x+1)^{-3}$.

4. $\sin x$; $\cos x$; $\mathrm{cosec}^2 x$.

5. a^x; $a^x + b$; $a^x + bx + c$.

6. $\sin 2x$; $\cos 3x$; $\sec^2 4x$.

7. $\dfrac{1}{x+1}$; $\dfrac{1}{(1-x)^{\frac{3}{2}}}$; $\dfrac{1}{(a+3x)^5}$.

8. $\dfrac{3x-2}{x^2}$; $\dfrac{ax^2 + bx + c}{x^n}$.

9. $\dfrac{1}{(x+1)(x-1)}$; $\dfrac{x^2 - x + 1}{x(x^2 + 1)}$.

10. $\dfrac{a}{\sqrt{1-x^2}}$; $\dfrac{1}{\sqrt{1-a^2x^2}}$.

11. Express $\cos 3x$ in terms of powers of $\cos x$ and hence integrate $\cos^3 x$.

12. Integrate $\dfrac{(y-1)^2}{y^n}$ with respect to y and deduce $\int \dfrac{x^2\,dx}{(1+x)^n}$.

13. Express as a definite integral the limit when x is increased indefinitely of

$$\frac{1}{x} + \frac{1}{x+m} + \frac{1}{x+2m} + \dots + \frac{1}{x+xm}.$$

14. Represent the sum of the series

$$\frac{n}{n^2 + 1^2} + \frac{n}{n^2 + 2^2} + \frac{n}{n^2 + 3^2} + \dots + \frac{n}{2n^2},$$

when n is increased indefinitely, as a definite integral.

15. Express $\dfrac{1}{x(x-1)(x-2)}$ in partial fractions and hence integrate the function with respect to x.

16. Evaluate $\int \dfrac{(x^2 + x)\,dx}{(1-x)(1+x^2)}$.

17. Integrate $(1 + x)^{-1}(1 - x^2)^{-1}$ with respect to x.

18. Prove from first principles that

(a) $\int_a^b e^{-x}\,dx = e^{-a} - e^{-b}$;   (b) $\int_a^b x^2\,dx = \tfrac{1}{3}(b^3 - a^3)$.

19. Prove by differentiation that $\log \left\{ \dfrac{(x + \sqrt{x^2 - a^2})}{a} \right\}$ is the integral of $\dfrac{1}{\sqrt{x^2 - a^2}}$.

20. Integrate

$$\text{(i) } 2\sqrt{x} - \frac{1}{2x^2}; \quad \text{(ii) } \sqrt{x}\left(x^5 + \frac{3}{x}\right),$$

and verify the result by differentiation.

21. $v = \dfrac{ds}{dt}$; $f = \dfrac{dv}{dt}$ and $s = 0$ when $t = 0$.

Prove that   (i) $v = u + ft$, where u is constant;
             (ii) $s = ut + \frac{1}{2}ft^2 +$ a constant;
             (iii) $2fs = v^2 - u^2$.

22. If $\dfrac{d^2 y}{dx^2}$ is constant, show that y is of the form $ax^2 + bx + c$.

23. $\dfrac{d^3 u_x}{dx^3} = e^x$. Find the form of u_x.

24. u and v are functions of t, viz. $\dfrac{du}{dt} = \sin t$; $\dfrac{dv}{dt} = \cos t$. Prove that a relation of the form $u^2 + v^2 - 2au - 2\beta v = \gamma$ exists, where a, β, γ are constants independent of t.

25. If $a^2 \dfrac{d^2 y}{dx^2} = a - x$, find y when $x = 2a$, any necessary constants being determined by the condition that when $x = a$, $\dfrac{dy}{dx} = 1$ and $y = a$.

26. If $u_x = A + Bc^x$ where A, B and c are constants and

$$u_x = -\frac{1}{l_x} \frac{dl_x}{dx},$$

find l_x in terms of x.

27. Find the value of $\displaystyle\int \left(\frac{du}{dt}\right)^2 dt$, where $u = \sin^{-1} t + k$.

28. Integrate

$$\frac{1}{2} \frac{d}{dx} \{\tan^{-1} x + \log \sqrt{1 + x} - \log \sqrt{1 - x}\}$$

with respect to x^4.

CHAPTER VIII

MORE DIFFICULT INTEGRALS:
INTEGRATION BY PARTS

1. Differentiation can be applied to any continuous function of x by the application of simple and straightforward principles. The inverse process of integration is at the best a tentative process and depends very largely on whether the function to be integrated can be recognized as the derivative of another function. It may happen that, although the function as it stands is not familiar as the differential coefficient of another function of the variable, it can be so transformed as to be immediately integrable. A simple example has been given in the previous chapter, where, knowing the standard form $\int (1 + x^2)^{-1}\,dx$, we can derive at once the integral of $(a^2 + x^2)^{-1}$ with respect to x.

The integration of more complicated functions is largely a matter of practice. There are, however, certain standard methods of attack, which, although they may not invariably produce the required result, can often be applied with success to the solution of the problems of integration.

2. The method of substitution.

Let us consider the problem that is denoted by $\int y\,dx$. In the first place, the dx shows that the independent variable is x. Secondly, y is a function of x such that if we know, or can find, z, another function of x, whose derivative with regard to x is y, then z is the required value.

Put shortly, if

$$\frac{dz}{dx} = y, \quad \text{then} \quad \int y\,dx = z.$$

A familiar example is

$$\frac{dx^{n+1}}{dx} = (n + 1)\,x^n,$$

or
$$\frac{d}{dx}\left\{\frac{1}{n+1}x^{n+1}\right\} = x^n,$$

so that if $y = x^n$, then

$$\int y\,dx = \frac{1}{n+1}x^{n+1}.$$

Suppose that y is a more complicated function of x, say $(a + bx)^n$. We do not immediately recognize $\int y\,dx$, and it is necessary to proceed further.

Let
$$z = a + bx.$$

Then
$$\frac{dz}{dx} = b,$$

and
$$\frac{dy}{dz} = \frac{dy}{dx}\frac{dx}{dz} = \frac{dy}{dx}\frac{1}{b}.$$

If therefore we replace the independent variable x by the new variable z, any differentiation with respect to x becomes a differentiation with respect to z by the simple process of dividing by the constant b.

The integral $\int y\,dx$ may therefore be written as $\int y\left[\frac{1}{b}\,dz\right]$, and, since $y = (a + bx)^n = z^n$,

$$\int y\,dx = \int (a + bx)^n\,dx = \int z^n\,dx$$

$$= \int z^n\left[\frac{1}{b}\,dz\right]$$

$$= \int \frac{1}{b}z^n\,dz$$

$$= \frac{1}{b}\frac{1}{n+1}z^{n+1}$$

$$= \frac{1}{b}\frac{1}{n+1}(a + bx)^{n+1}.$$

This is an example of the method of substitution.

Again, to evaluate $\int y\,dx$ where y is the function $\dfrac{\sin x}{1 + \cos x}$,

let
$$z = \cos x.$$

Then $\dfrac{dz}{dx} = -\sin x,$

$$\therefore \frac{dy}{dz} = \frac{dy}{dx}\frac{dx}{dz} = \frac{dy}{dx}\left[-\frac{1}{\sin x}\right].$$

Therefore, as above, $\int y\,dx$ becomes

$$\int\left[-\frac{1}{\sin x}\right]y\,dz;$$

i.e. $\displaystyle\int \frac{\sin x}{1 + \cos x}\,dx = \int \frac{\sin x}{1 + \cos x}\left[-\frac{1}{\sin x}\right]dz$

$$= \int\left[-\frac{1}{1 + \cos x}\right]dz$$

$$= \int -\frac{1}{1 + z}\,dz$$

$$= -\log(1 + z)$$

$$= -\log(1 + \cos x).$$

When applying the method of substitution it is customary to shorten the initial process. If the substitution is $z = \cos x$, we write, instead of

$$\frac{dz}{dx} = -\sin x,$$

the relation $\qquad dz = -\sin x\,dx,$

so that in the integral we may immediately replace dx by

$$\left[-\frac{1}{\sin x}\right]dz.$$

In general, if the substitution is $f(x) = \phi(y)$, instead of writing $f'(x) = \phi'(y)\dfrac{dy}{dx}$ we write immediately $f'(x)\,dx = \phi'(y)\,dy$. It will be observed that the process is to differentiate each function with regard to the variable in which it is expressed, x, y or z for example, and then to multiply by dx, dy or dz as the case may be. The expressions $f'(x)\,dx$, $\phi'(y)\,dy$, ... are termed *differentials* of $f(x)$, $\phi(y)$, ... respectively.

For the purpose of integration this procedure should be looked upon simply as a convenient means of passing from one variable to another, and not necessarily as a splitting up of the $\dfrac{dz}{dx}$ into two parts dz and dx.

We may consider the problem from another point of view. The definition of a definite integral is the limit of $h\Sigma\phi(x)$ between $x = a$ and $x = b - h$, as h tends to zero. Since h denotes a small increase in the value of the variable, we may equally well write the integral as

$$\underset{\Delta x \to 0}{\text{Lt}} \overset{x=b-\Delta x}{\underset{x=a}{\Sigma}} \phi(x).\Delta x = \underset{\Delta x \to 0}{\text{Lt}} \left[\phi(a)\Delta x + \phi(a + \Delta x)\Delta x + \ldots \right.$$
$$\left. + \phi(b - \Delta x)\,\Delta x\right],$$

or $\displaystyle\int_a^b \phi(x)\,dx$, where the Δx is the small increase in the value of x which tends to zero.

The method of substitution is then as follows. If, as in the second example above,

$$z = \cos x,$$

then

$$\Delta z = \cos(x + \Delta x) - \cos x$$
$$= -2\sin(x + \tfrac{1}{2}\Delta x)\sin\tfrac{1}{2}\Delta x.$$

Now

$$\underset{\Delta x \to 0}{\text{Lt}} -\sin(x + \tfrac{1}{2}\Delta x) = -\sin x,$$

and

$$\underset{\Delta x \to 0}{\text{Lt}} \frac{\sin\tfrac{1}{2}\Delta x}{\tfrac{1}{2}\Delta x} = 1,$$

$$\therefore \underset{\Delta z \to 0}{\text{Lt}} \phi(x)\Delta z = \underset{\Delta x \to 0}{\text{Lt}} \left\{-2\sin(x + \tfrac{1}{2}\Delta x)\sin\tfrac{1}{2}\Delta x.\phi(x)\right\}$$
$$= -2\sin x \underset{\Delta x \to 0}{\text{Lt}} \phi(x)\tfrac{1}{2}\Delta x$$
$$= -\sin x \underset{\Delta x \to 0}{\text{Lt}} \phi(x)\Delta x.$$

$$\therefore \underset{\Delta x \to 0}{\text{Lt}} \phi(x)\Delta x = \left[-\frac{1}{\sin x}\right]\underset{\Delta \to 0}{\text{Lt}} \phi(x)\Delta z,$$

which gives the same result as that found above.

3. If $y = f(x)$, then $\phi(y) = \phi\{f(x)\}$, and if $f'(x)$ denote, as usual, the differential coefficient of $f(x)$ with respect to x, then

$$\phi(y)\frac{dy}{dx} = \phi\{f(x)\}f'(x);$$

i.e.

$$\phi(y)\,dy = \phi\{f(x)\}f'(x)\,dx,$$

so that

$$\int\phi(y)\,dy = \int\phi\{f(x)\}f'(x)\,dx.$$

Now on the right-hand side the integrand is the product of two functions, $\phi\{f(x)\}$ and $f'(x)$. If we associate $f'(x)$ with dx we have (i) a function of x, namely $\phi\{f(x)\}$, and (ii) $f'(x)\,dx$, which is a differential. It is evident therefore that if it is required to integrate an expression consisting of the product of two functions, one the differential of a known function $f(x)$ and the other a function of $f(x)$, the substitution $f(x) = y$ will reduce the integral to the simpler form $\int \phi(y)\,dy$.

It must be noted, however, that if the product is to be simplified in this manner, both conditions must be satisfied. The form of substitution is frequently determined by the recognition that the expression to be integrated contains $f'(x)\,dx$, the differential of $f(x)$.

For example, consider the integrals

$$\int \frac{x\,dx}{\sqrt{1+x^2}}; \quad \int \frac{x^3\,dx}{\sqrt{1+x^2}}; \quad \int \frac{\sqrt{1+x^2}}{x}\,dx.$$

These may be written

$$\int \frac{1}{\sqrt{1+x^2}}\,x\,dx; \quad \int \frac{x^2}{\sqrt{1+x^2}}\,x\,dx; \quad \int \frac{\sqrt{1+x^2}}{x^2}\,x\,dx,$$

and it is evident that each of the expressions consists of $x\,dx$ (the differential of $\frac{1}{2}x^2$) and a function of $\frac{1}{2}x^2$. The substitution of y for x^2 will therefore simplify the process of integration for all three examples. It will be observed that this substitution is suggested partly, if not wholly, by the presence of $x\,dx$.

Again, consider

$$\int \frac{dx}{\sqrt{1+x^2}}; \quad \int \frac{x^2\,dx}{\sqrt{1+x^2}}; \quad \int \frac{\sqrt{1+x^2}}{x^2}\,dx.$$

It will not help to write these in the form $\int \phi(x^2)\,dx$, as the required $x\,dx$ is absent. The substitution $y = x^2$ will not therefore simplify the integrals.

4. Further examples of substitution.

It does not follow that any integral can be evaluated by a simple substitution nor indeed that the simplest substitution is the best.

The examples given below are merely indicative of the methods to be employed: they are not necessarily of universal application.

Example 1.

$$\int \frac{x^2}{(a + bx)^n}\, dx. \quad (n \neq 1.)$$

The substitution is $z = a + bx.$

We have $dz = b\, dx$ and $x = \dfrac{z - a}{b}.$

$$I = \int \left(\frac{z - a}{b}\right)^2 \frac{1}{z^n}\frac{1}{b}\, dz$$

$$= \int \frac{z^2 - 2az + a^2}{z^n} \frac{1}{b^3}\, dz$$

$$= \frac{1}{b^3} \int (z^{2-n} - 2az^{1-n} + a^2 z^{-n})\, dz$$

$$= \frac{1}{b^3} \left[\int z^{2-n}\, dz - 2a \int z^{1-n}\, dz + a^2 \int z^{-n}\, dz \right]$$

$$= \frac{1}{b^3} \left[\frac{1}{3 - n} z^{3-n} - 2a \frac{1}{2 - n} z^{2-n} + a^2 \frac{1}{1 - n} z^{1-n} \right].$$

If n is a positive integer greater than 3, this result is more conveniently written as

$$-\frac{1}{b^3} \left[\frac{1}{(n - 3)\, z^{n-3}} - \frac{2a}{(n - 2)\, z^{n-2}} + \frac{a^2}{(n - 1)\, z^{n-1}} \right],$$

where $z \equiv a + bx.$

The above method can be applied to any function of the form $\dfrac{x^m}{(a + bx)^n}$, where m is a positive integer. It is easily seen that the integral will be $\dfrac{1}{b^{m+1}} \int \dfrac{(z - a)^m}{z^n} dz$. By expanding the expression in brackets by the binomial theorem and integrating each term separately, the result follows.

Example 2.

$$\int \frac{2x\, dx}{1 + x^2}.$$

The facts that $2x\, dx$ is the differential of x^2 and that the remainder of the integrand is a function of x^2 suggest the substitution $x^2 = y$, or, better, $1 + x^2 = y$.

Put, therefore, $z = 1 + x^2$, so that $dz = 2x\,dx$.
Then

$$I = \int \frac{2x\,dx}{1 + x^2} = \int \frac{dz}{1 + x^2} = \int \frac{dz}{z} = \log z = \log (1 + x^2).$$

This is an example of a general proposition. Where the numerator of a fraction is the derivative of the denominator, the required integral is the logarithm of the denominator.

In other words:

$$\int \frac{\frac{dy}{dx}}{y}\,dx = \log y.$$

For example,

$$\int \frac{-\sin x}{1 + \cos x}\,dx = \int \frac{\frac{d\,(1 + \cos x)}{dx}}{1 + \cos x}\,dx = \log (1 + \cos x).$$

(Cf. para. 2 above.)

Again, $\displaystyle\int \cot x\,dx = \int \frac{\cos x}{\sin x}\,dx = \int \frac{\frac{d \sin x}{dx}}{\sin x}\,dx = \log \sin x.$

Example 3.

$$\int \frac{d\theta}{\sin \theta}.$$

Now $\displaystyle\qquad\qquad \sin \theta = \frac{2 \tan \tfrac{1}{2}\theta}{1 + \tan^2 \tfrac{1}{2}\theta}.$ (Chap. I, para. 16.)

$$\therefore\ I = \int \frac{1 + \tan^2 \tfrac{1}{2}\theta}{2 \tan \tfrac{1}{2}\theta}\,d\theta.$$

Put $\qquad\qquad t = \tan \tfrac{1}{2}\theta,$

$$dt = \tfrac{1}{2} \sec^2 \tfrac{1}{2}\theta\,d\theta = \tfrac{1}{2} (1 + \tan^2 \tfrac{1}{2}\theta)\,d\theta.$$

$$\therefore\ d\theta = \frac{2dt}{1 + \tan^2 \tfrac{1}{2}\theta}.$$

$$\therefore\ I = \int \frac{1 + \tan^2 \tfrac{1}{2}\theta}{2 \tan \tfrac{1}{2}\theta}\,\frac{2dt}{1 + \tan^2 \tfrac{1}{2}\theta} = \int \frac{dt}{\tan \tfrac{1}{2}\theta} = \int \frac{dt}{t}$$

$$= \log t$$

$$= \log \tan \tfrac{1}{2}\theta.$$

Corollary:

$$\int \frac{d\theta}{\cos \theta} = \int \frac{d\theta}{\sin (\frac{1}{2}\pi - \theta)}$$

$$= - \log \tan \tfrac{1}{2} (\tfrac{1}{2}\pi - \theta)$$

$$= - \log \tan (\tfrac{1}{4}\pi - \tfrac{1}{2}\theta)$$

$$= - \log \frac{\tan \tfrac{1}{4}\pi - \tan \tfrac{1}{2}\theta}{1 + \tan \tfrac{1}{4}\pi \tan \tfrac{1}{2}\theta}$$

$$= - \log \frac{1 - \tan \tfrac{1}{2}\theta}{1 + \tan \tfrac{1}{2}\theta} \qquad (\text{since } \tan \tfrac{1}{4}\pi = 1)$$

$$= \log \frac{1 + \tan \tfrac{1}{2}\theta}{1 - \tan \tfrac{1}{2}\theta}.$$

Example 4.

$$\int \frac{dx}{\sqrt{x^2 + a^2}}.$$

Method (i). Put $x = a \tan a$, so that $dx = a \sec^2 a\, da$.

$$I = \int \frac{1}{\sqrt{x^2 + a^2}} a \sec^2 a\, da$$

$$= \int \frac{1}{\sqrt{a^2 \tan^2 a + a^2}} a \sec^2 a\, da$$

$$= \int \frac{1}{a \sqrt{\tan^2 a + 1}} a \sec^2 a\, da$$

$$= \int \sec a\, da \qquad (\text{since } \tan^2 a + 1 = \sec^2 a)$$

$$= \int \frac{da}{\cos a}$$

$$= \log \frac{1 + \tan \tfrac{1}{2}a}{1 - \tan \tfrac{1}{2}a} \qquad (\text{from Example 3 above}),$$

where $\qquad\qquad \tan a = x/a$.

Method (ii). Put $\sqrt{x^2 + a^2} = z - x$.

Then $\qquad\qquad x^2 + a^2 = z^2 - 2zx + x^2,$

or $\qquad\qquad\qquad a^2 = z^2 - 2zx.$

$$\therefore \; 0 = 2z\, dz - 2z\, dx - 2x\, dz:$$

i.e. $\qquad\qquad dx = \frac{z - x}{z}\, dz.$

$$\therefore \; I = \int \frac{dx}{\sqrt{x^2 + a^2}} = \int \frac{1}{z - x} \frac{z - x}{z} \, dz = \int \frac{dz}{z}$$

$$= \log z$$

$$= \log (x + \sqrt{x^2 + a^2}).$$

This result is the same as that produced by the first method. For, if

$$x/a = \tan a,$$

$$\log (x + \sqrt{x^2 + a^2}) = \log (a \tan a + \sqrt{a^2 \tan^2 a + a^2})$$

$$= \log a (\tan a + \sec a)$$

$$= \log a + \log \left\{ \frac{\sin a}{\cos a} + \frac{1}{\cos a} \right\}$$

$$= \log a + \log \frac{\sin a + 1}{\cos a}$$

$$= \log a + \log \left\{ \frac{\dfrac{2 \tan \frac{1}{2}a}{1 + \tan^2 \frac{1}{2}a} + 1}{\dfrac{1 - \tan^2 \frac{1}{2}a}{1 + \tan^2 \frac{1}{2}a}} \right\}$$

$$= \log a + \log \frac{(1 + \tan \frac{1}{2}a)^2}{1 - \tan^2 \frac{1}{2}a}$$

$$= \log a + \log \frac{1 + \tan \frac{1}{2}a}{1 - \tan \frac{1}{2}a},$$

which is the solution given by Method (i), since $\log a$ is a constant, and the result of differentiating

$$\log \frac{1 + \tan \frac{1}{2}a}{1 - \tan \frac{1}{2}a} + \log a$$

is the same as that of differentiating

$$\log \frac{1 + \tan \frac{1}{2}a}{1 - \tan \frac{1}{2}a} + \text{any arbitrary constant.}$$

Method (iii). Put $x = 1/y$ in order to obtain an odd power of y outside the square root.

Then

$$dx = - (1/y^2) \, dy,$$

$$x^2 + a^2 = 1/y^2 + a^2 = (1 + a^2 y^2)/y^2.$$

$$\therefore \; \int \frac{dx}{\sqrt{x^2 + a^2}} = \int \frac{y}{\sqrt{1 + a^2 y^2}} \left(-\frac{1}{y^2} \right) dy$$

$$= \int \frac{- \, dy}{y \sqrt{1 + a^2 y^2}}.$$

To eliminate the square root, put $1 + a^2 y^2 = z^2$.

$$\therefore \ 2a^2 y \, dy = 2z \, dz,$$

and

$$I = \int \frac{-z \, dz}{a^2 y^2 z} = \int \frac{-dz}{z^2 - 1},$$

since

$$y^2 = \frac{(z^2 - 1)}{a^2}.$$

On integrating and substituting, first for z in terms of y, and then for y in terms of x, we have

$$I = \tfrac{1}{2} \log \frac{\sqrt{x^2 + a^2} + x}{\sqrt{x^2 + a^2} - x},$$

which is easily seen to be $\log (\sqrt{x^2 + a^2} + x) - \log a$ on multiplying numerator and denominator of the fraction by $\sqrt{x^2 + a^2} + x$.

Corollaries:

(i) $\displaystyle \int \frac{dx}{\sqrt{x^2 - a^2}} = \log (x + \sqrt{x^2 - a^2});$

(ii) $\displaystyle \int \frac{dx}{\sqrt{(x - a)(x - b)}} = \int \frac{dx}{\sqrt{x^2 - (a + b) x + ab}}$

$$= \int \frac{dx}{\sqrt{\{x - \tfrac{1}{2}(a + b)\}^2 - \{\tfrac{1}{2}(a - b)\}^2}}$$

$$= \log \{x - \tfrac{1}{2}(a + b) + \sqrt{(x - a)(x - b)}\}$$

$$= \log \tfrac{1}{2} \{(x - a) + (x - b) + 2\sqrt{(x - a)(x - b)}\}$$

$$= \log (\sqrt{x - a} + \sqrt{x - b})^2 - \log 2$$

$$= 2 \log (\sqrt{x - a} + \sqrt{x - b}),$$

disregarding the constant of integration.

Example 5.

$$\int \frac{dx}{1 + x^3}.$$

$\dfrac{1}{1 + x^3}$ is not recognizable as the derivative of another function of x.

We proceed therefore to express it in partial fractions.

$$\frac{1}{1 + x^3} = \frac{1}{3} \frac{1}{1 + x} + \frac{1}{3} \frac{2 - x}{1 - x + x^2}.$$

$$\int \frac{dx}{1 + x} = \log (1 + x) \qquad \text{at once.}$$

$$\int \frac{2 - x}{1 - x + x^2} \, dx \qquad \text{needs further investigation.}$$

Now if the fraction were of the form

$$\frac{\frac{df(x)}{dx}}{f(x)},$$

the integral would be $\log f(x)$. Here

$$f(x) = 1 - x + x^2 \quad \text{and} \quad \frac{df(x)}{dx} = -1 + 2x,$$

which is not the numerator in the given integral. If, however, we express the numerator thus:

$$2 - x = -\tfrac{1}{2}(-1 + 2x) + \tfrac{3}{2},$$

the integral becomes

$$\int -\frac{1}{2}\left\{\frac{-1+2x}{1-x+x^2}\right\} dx + \int \frac{3}{2}\frac{1}{1-x+x^2} dx.$$

The first of these is $-\tfrac{1}{2}\log(1 - x + x^2)$, and the second may be written in the form

$$\int \frac{3}{2} \frac{1}{(x-\tfrac{1}{2})^2 + (\sqrt{3}/2)^2} dx.$$

This is of the form

$$\int \frac{3}{2} \frac{1}{x^2 + a^2} dx,$$

the integral of which is

$$\frac{3}{2}\left\{\frac{1}{a}\tan^{-1}\frac{x}{a}\right\}.$$

$$\therefore \int \frac{3}{2} \frac{1}{(x-\tfrac{1}{2})^2 + (\sqrt{3}/2)^2} dx = \frac{3}{2} \frac{1}{\sqrt{3}/2} \tan^{-1} \frac{x - \tfrac{1}{2}}{\sqrt{3}/2},$$

or

$$\sqrt{3}\tan^{-1}\frac{2x-1}{\sqrt{3}}.$$

The complete integral is, therefore,

$$\int \frac{dx}{1+x^3} = \frac{1}{3}\int \frac{dx}{1+x} - \frac{1}{3}\int \frac{1}{2}\frac{-1+2x}{1-x+x^2} dx + \frac{1}{3}\int \frac{3}{2}\frac{1}{(x-\tfrac{1}{2})^2 + (\sqrt{3}/2)^2} dx$$

$$= \frac{1}{3}\log(1+x) - \frac{1}{6}\log(1-x+x^2) + \frac{1}{\sqrt{3}}\tan^{-1}\frac{2x-1}{\sqrt{3}}.$$

Example 6.

$$\int \frac{x^n}{\sqrt{x^2+a^2}} dx, \text{ where } n \text{ is an integer.}$$

From a consideration of the illustrative examples in para. 3 (p. 117), it will be seen that if n is a positive or negative odd integer, the integral can be simplified at once.

Let n be $2m + 1$. Then the integral becomes

$$\int \frac{(x^2)^m}{\sqrt{x^2 + a^2}} x\, dx,$$

and consists of the differential of $\frac{1}{2}x^2$, namely $x\, dx$, and a function of $\frac{1}{2}x^2$.

The substitution $\frac{1}{2}x^2 = y$, or, better, $x^2 + a^2 = y$, will therefore simplify the integral.

When n is even it will be found that, in expressions containing $\sqrt{x^2 \pm a^2}$, the substitution $x = 1/y$ has the effect of changing the index of the term outside the radical from an even number to an odd number.

Let n be $2m$. The integral becomes

$$\int \frac{x^{2m}}{\sqrt{x^2 + a^2}}\, dx.$$

Put $x = 1/y$, so that $dx = (- 1/y^2)\, dy$.

$$I = \int - \frac{1}{y^{2m} \sqrt{(1/y^2) + a^2}} \frac{1}{y^2}\, dy$$

$$= \int - \frac{1}{y^{2m+1} \sqrt{1 + a^2 y^2}}\, dy,$$

and the index of y^{2m+1} being an odd integer, the substitution $1 + a^2 y^2 = z^2$ will now be effective.

Corollary. Since

$$ax^2 + bx + c = a\left(x^2 + \frac{b}{a}x + \frac{c}{a}\right)$$

$$= a\left[\left(x + \frac{b}{2a}\right)^2 + \left(\frac{c}{a} - \frac{b^2}{4a^2}\right)\right],$$

which is of the form $a(x^2 + k^2)$, we may integrate by the above methods functions of the form

$$\frac{x^n}{\sqrt{ax^2 + bx + c}}.$$

5. Forms of integral which can be evaluated by the application of general methods are those involving irrational expressions of a simple linear or quadratic type.

Type (i).

$$\int \frac{dx}{(x + a) \sqrt{x + b}}.$$

Since the only consideration is the elimination of the radical, put $\sqrt{x + b} = z$, so that $x = z^2 - b$.

Then $$dx = 2z\,dz,$$

i.e. $$\frac{dx}{2\sqrt{x + b}} = \frac{dx}{2z} = dz,$$

and the integral becomes

$$\int \frac{2dz}{x + a} = \int \frac{2dz}{z^2 + a - b},$$

which is immediately integrable.

Corollary. The form

$$\int \frac{(x + a)\,dx}{(x + c)\,\sqrt{x + b}}$$

is evaluated by writing the integral as

$$\int \left[\frac{1}{\sqrt{x + b}} + \frac{a - c}{(x + c)\,\sqrt{x + b}} \right] dx.$$

The first integral is a standard form and the second is of Type (i) above.

Type (ii).

$$\int \frac{dx}{(x - k)\,\sqrt{a + 2bx + cx^2}} \qquad (c \text{ positive}).$$

Several methods are available here, the procedure depending upon the particular substitution adopted. We may consider either the quadratic function or the linear function as suitable for the substitution, but in neither case is the process immediately obvious.

(a) Let $$\sqrt{a + 2bx + cx^2} = z - x\sqrt{c}.$$

Then $$a + 2bx + cx^2 = z^2 - 2zx\sqrt{c} + cx^2,$$

or $$a + 2bx = z^2 - 2zx\sqrt{c}.$$

$$\therefore \quad 2b\,dx = 2z\,dz - 2\sqrt{c}\,(z\,dx + x\,dz),$$

and $$dx = \frac{z - x\sqrt{c}}{b + z\sqrt{c}}\,dz.$$

The integral is therefore

$$\int \frac{1}{(x-k)\,(z - x\,\sqrt{c})} \frac{z - x\,\sqrt{c}}{b + z\,\sqrt{c}}\,dz$$

$$= \int \frac{dz}{(b + z\,\sqrt{c})\,(x - k)},$$

and, since

$$a + 2bx = z^2 - 2zx\,\sqrt{c},$$

$$x = \frac{z^2 - a}{2\,(z\,\sqrt{c} + b)},$$

so that the integral takes the form

$$\int \frac{dz}{(b + z\,\sqrt{c})\left[\dfrac{z^2 - a}{2\,(z\,\sqrt{c} + b)} - k\right]}$$

$$= \int \frac{2dz}{z^2 - a - 2k\,(z\,\sqrt{c} + b)},$$

which is of the simple rational form

$$\int \frac{dz}{z^2 + Cz + D}.$$

(b) Let $x - k = \dfrac{1}{z},$ or $x = k + \dfrac{1}{z};$

then $dx = -\dfrac{1}{z^2}\,dz.$

$$\int \frac{dx}{(x-k)\,\sqrt{a + 2bx + cx^2}}$$

$$= \int -\frac{1}{z^2}\frac{1}{\dfrac{1}{z}\sqrt{\left\{a + 2b\left(k + \dfrac{1}{z}\right) + c\left(k + \dfrac{1}{z}\right)^2\right\}}}\,dz$$

$$= \int -\frac{1}{z^2}\,z\,\frac{1}{\dfrac{1}{z}\,\sqrt{Az^2 + Bz + C}}\,dz,$$

where $Az^2 + Bz + C \equiv (a + 2bk + ck^2)\,z^2 + 2k\,(b + c)\,z + c.$

$$\therefore \quad I = -\int \frac{dz}{\sqrt{Az^2 + Bz + C}},$$

which is immediately integrable.

For further information on the subject of these integrals the student is advised to read Williamson, *Integral Calculus*, Chapter IV. Another general method will be found in Henry, *Calculus and Probability*, where the required substitution is obtained by putting one of the constituent functions of the expression equal to y^r. The index r is then determined so that the integral can be evaluated by known processes.

6. Integration by parts.

Since
$$\frac{d}{dx}(uv) = u\frac{dv}{dx} + v\frac{du}{dx}$$

we may derive an expression for the integration of the product of two functions of x.

For, integrating both sides, we have

$$uv = \int u\frac{dv}{dx}\,dx + \int v\frac{du}{dx}\,dx,$$

or
$$\int u\frac{dv}{dx}\,dx = uv - \int v\frac{du}{dx}\,dx.$$

Replace u by U and let $\frac{dv}{dx} = V$, so that $v = \int V dx$.

Then
$$\int UV dx = U\int V dx - \int\left(\frac{dU}{dx}\int V dx\right)dx.$$

If therefore $\left[\frac{dU}{dx}\int V dx\right]$ is integrable we can at once find the value of $\int UV dx$.

In words the formula may be written thus:

The integral of the product of two functions of x = (the first function × integral of the second) − the integral of (the differential coefficient of the first × integral of the second).

A few simple examples will show the application of this process.

Example 7.

$$\int x e^x\,dx.$$

The point to consider at the outset is which of the two functions should be taken as "the first function" and which "the second." Take x as the first function; we are to differentiate the first function and the differentiation of x will produce a constant.

$$\int xe^x dx = x \int e^x dx - \int \left(\frac{dx}{dx} \int e^x dx \right) dx$$

$$= xe^x - \int e^x dx = xe^x - e^x.$$

Example 8.

$$\int x \log x \, dx.$$

We must choose $\log x$ as the function to be differentiated, for if we take x as the first function we shall have to find the integral of $\log x$—which is not apparent.

$$\int x \log x \, dx = \log x \int x \, dx - \int \left\{ \frac{d \log x}{dx} \left(\int x \, dx \right) \right\} dx$$

$$= \log x \frac{x^2}{2} - \int \frac{1}{x} \frac{x^2}{2} dx$$

$$= \frac{x^2}{2} \log x - \int \frac{x}{2} dx$$

$$= \frac{x^2}{2} \log x - \frac{x^2}{4}.$$

7. The method of integration by parts is useful even where we have to integrate a *single* function of x. We may treat $f(x)$ as the product of two functions, one function being $f(x)$ and the other unity.

Example 9.

$$\int \tan^{-1} x \, dx.$$

Let the first function be $\tan^{-1} x$ and the second function 1.
Then

$$\int \tan^{-1} x \, dx = \int \tan^{-1} x \cdot 1 \, dx$$

$$= \tan^{-1} x \int 1 \, dx - \int \left\{ \frac{d}{dx} (\tan^{-1} x) \int 1 \, dx \right\} dx$$

$$= \tan^{-1} x \cdot x - \int \frac{1}{1 + x^2} x \, dx$$

$$= x \tan^{-1} x - \tfrac{1}{2} \log (1 + x^2).$$

Example 10.

$$\int \sqrt{x^2 + a^2}\, dx.$$

As above

$$\int \sqrt{x^2 + a^2}\, dx = \int \sqrt{x^2 + a^2}\,.\,\mathrm{1}\, dx$$

$$= \sqrt{x^2 + a^2} \int \mathrm{1}\, dx - \int \left\{ \frac{d}{dx} \sqrt{x^2 + a^2} \int \mathrm{1}\, dx \right\} dx$$

$$= \sqrt{x^2 + a^2}\,.\,x - \int \frac{x}{\sqrt{x^2 + a^2}}\, x\, dx$$

$$= \sqrt{x^2 + a^2}\,.\,x - \int \frac{x^2}{\sqrt{x^2 + a^2}}\, dx$$

$$= \sqrt{x^2 + a^2}\,.\,x - \int \left\{ \frac{x^2 + a^2}{\sqrt{x^2 + a^2}} - \frac{a^2}{\sqrt{x^2 + a^2}} \right\} dx$$

$$= \sqrt{x^2 + a^2}\,.\,x - \int \sqrt{x^2 + a^2}\, dx + \int \frac{a^2 dx}{\sqrt{x^2 + a^2}}\,.$$

$$\therefore\ 2 \int \sqrt{x^2 + a^2}\, dx = x \sqrt{x^2 + a^2} + a^2 \int \frac{dx}{\sqrt{x^2 + a^2}}$$

$$= x \sqrt{x^2 + a^2} + a^2 \log (x + \sqrt{x^2 + a^2}).$$

$$\therefore\ \int \sqrt{x^2 + a^2}\, dx = \tfrac{1}{2} \{ x \sqrt{x^2 + a^2} + a^2 \log (x + \sqrt{x^2 + a^2}) \}.$$

This example is instructive in that the process of integration by parts does not immediately give the required result. When we have performed the necessary operations we are left with $\int \sqrt{x^2 + a^2}\, dx$ on both sides of the identity, and we have to clear the right-hand side of this integral before the answer is obtained.

A somewhat similar process is necessary in the evaluation of the following important integral involving trigonometrical functions.

Example 11.

$$\int e^x \sin x\, dx.$$

Here it is immaterial which function is chosen as the first function. Take e^x as the first function: then

$$\int e^x \sin x\, dx = e^x \int \sin x\, dx - \int \left\{ \frac{de^x}{dx} \int \sin x\, dx \right\}\, dx$$

$$= -e^x \cos x + \int e^x \cos x\, dx.$$

This does not immediately give the required result. If, however, we consider $\int e^x \cos x\, dx$ and integrate by parts, we obtain a further equality which enables the integral to be evaluated.

$$\int e^x \cos x\, dx = e^x \int \cos x\, dx - \int \left\{ \frac{de^x}{dx} \int \cos x\, dx \right\}\, dx$$

$$= e^x \sin x - \int e^x \sin x\, dx.$$

Let

$$\int e^x \sin x\, dx = S,$$

and

$$\int e^x \cos x\, dx = C.$$

Then

$$S = -e^x \cos x + C,$$

and

$$C = e^x \sin x - S,$$

or

$$S - C = -e^x \cos x,$$

$$S + C = e^x \sin x.$$

Hence

$$\int e^x \sin x\, dx = S = \tfrac{1}{2} e^x (\sin x - \cos x),$$

and

$$\int e^x \cos x\, dx = C = \tfrac{1}{2} e^x (\sin x + \cos x).$$

8. Reduction formulae.

It has been shown in the preceding paragraph that, in certain instances, integration by parts may not produce the required result immediately; another stage must be reached before the integration can be effected. It is often possible, however, to relate an integral to one or more integrals of similar form, so that by proceeding successively the original integral can eventually be obtained. If, for example, we are required to integrate u_n, where u_n is a function of x involving x^n and lower powers (n being a positive integer), it may be possible to relate the integral of the function to the integral of u_{n-1}. The formula connecting these integrals is called a "reduction formula." Reduction formulae are of importance in the integral calculus, and their use often leads to the evaluation of integrals which could not otherwise be obtained. For the purpose of illustration it is unnecessary to give more than a few elementary examples of the application of these formulae to indefinite integrals. It will be seen later (Chapter IX) that the process may be adopted to greater advantage in considering problems involving definite integrals.

Example 12.

$$\int e^x x^n \, dx.$$

$$u_n = \int e^x x^n \, dx = x^n e^x - \int n x^{n-1} e^x \, dx$$

$$= x^n e^x - n u_{n-1}.$$

Similarly

$$u_{n-1} = x^{n-1} e^x - (n-1) u_{n-2},$$

and so on.

The integral can therefore be made to depend upon the value of u_0, i.e. on $\int e^x \, dx$.

Thus

$$\int e^x x^3 \, dx = x^3 e^x - 3 \int e^x x^2 \, dx,$$

$$\int e^x x^2 \, dx = x^2 e^x - 2 \int e^x x \, dx,$$

$$\int e^x x \, dx = x e^x - \int e^x \, dx$$

$$= x e^x - e^x.$$

$$\therefore \int e^x x^3 \, dx = x^3 e^x - 3 \left[x^2 e^x - 2 \left(x e^x - e^x \right) \right]$$

$$= e^x \left(x^3 - 3x^2 + 6x - 6 \right).$$

Example 13.

$$\int \tan^n \theta \, d\theta,$$

where n is odd.

$$\tan^n \theta = \tan^{n-2} \theta \tan^2 \theta = \tan^{n-2} \theta \left(\sec^2 \theta - 1 \right).$$

$$\therefore \int \tan^n \theta \, d\theta = \int \tan^{n-2} \theta \sec^2 \theta \, d\theta - \int \tan^{n-2} \theta \, d\theta.$$

To evaluate

$$\int \tan^{n-2} \theta \sec^2 \theta \, d\theta,$$

put

$$\tan \theta = z.$$

Then $$\sec^2\theta\, d\theta = dz,$$

and $$\int \tan^{n-2}\theta \sec^2\theta\, d\theta = \int z^{n-2} dz = \frac{z^{n-1}}{n-1} = \frac{\tan^{n-1}\theta}{n-1}.$$

$$\therefore\ u_n = \frac{1}{n-1}\tan^{n-1}\theta - u_{n-2}$$

$$= \frac{1}{n-1}\tan^{n-1}\theta - \frac{1}{n-3}\tan^{n-3}\theta + \frac{1}{n-5}\tan^{n-5}\theta - \ldots,$$

where the last term is $(-1)^m \int \tan\theta\, d\theta$, since n is odd $(= 2m+1)$, or

$$(-1)^{m+1}\log\cos\theta.$$

Many reduction formulae result from the differentiation of simple functions of the variable. It will be sufficient to give one example of the process.

Example 14.

Find a reduction formula for the evaluation of the integral

$$\int \frac{x^n}{\sqrt{1+x^2}}\, dx,$$

where n is a positive integer.

We have identically

$$\frac{d}{dx} x^{n-1}\sqrt{1+x^2} = (n-1)x^{n-2}\sqrt{1+x^2} + \frac{x}{\sqrt{1+x^2}}x^{n-1}$$

$$= \frac{(n-1)x^{n-2}(1+x^2) + x^n}{\sqrt{1+x^2}}$$

$$= \frac{(n-1)x^{n-2} + (n-1)x^n + x^n}{\sqrt{1+x^2}}$$

$$= (n-1)\frac{x^{n-2}}{\sqrt{1+x^2}} + \frac{nx^n}{\sqrt{1+x^2}}.$$

By integration

$$x^{n-1}\sqrt{1+x^2} = (n-1)\int\frac{x^{n-2} dx}{\sqrt{1+x^2}} + n\int\frac{x^n dx}{\sqrt{1+x^2}},$$

i.e. $$u_n = \frac{1}{n} x^{n-1}\sqrt{1+x^2} - \frac{n-1}{n} u_{n-2}.$$

By continuing the process we arrive at the forms

$$\int \frac{dx}{\sqrt{1 + x^2}} \; (n \text{ even}), \text{ or } \int \frac{x\,dx}{\sqrt{1 + x^2}} \; (n \text{ odd}),$$

which are immediately integrable.

9. It is evident from the explanations above that the evaluation of an integral may depend on one or more of a number of different artifices. For complicated functions it may be necessary to resort to several alternatives before the solution can be found. Indeed, in many instances the integral may be no known function.

The following example is of a different type from those hitherto examined, and is given in order to show that certain obvious substitutions must be rejected as being unsuitable for the evaluation of the integral.

Example 15.

$$\int \frac{dy}{(1 - y^3)^{\frac{1}{3}}}.$$

Let

$$I = \int \frac{dy}{(1 - y^3)^{\frac{1}{3}}}.$$

(i) Put $1 - y^3 = z$, so that $y = (1 - z)^{\frac{1}{3}}$.

Then

$$- 3y^2\,dy = dz.$$

$$I = \int - \frac{1}{3y^2} \frac{1}{z^{\frac{1}{3}}}\,dz = - \frac{1}{3} \int \frac{dz}{z^{\frac{1}{3}}(1 - z)^{\frac{2}{3}}},$$

which has produced a more complicated form.

(ii) Put $(1 - y^3)^{\frac{1}{3}} = z$, so that $y^3 = 1 - z^3$.

Then

$$\tfrac{1}{3}(1 - y^3)^{-\frac{2}{3}}(- 3y^2)\,dy = dz;$$

i.e.

$$- y^2(1 - y^3)^{-\frac{2}{3}}\,dy = dz.$$

$$I = \int \frac{1}{z} \frac{- dz}{y^2(1 - y^3)^{-\frac{2}{3}}} = \int \frac{- z\,dz}{(1 - z^3)^{\frac{2}{3}}},$$

which is not immediately integrable.

(iii) Trials (i) and (ii) fail because the integrand does not contain a term $y^2\,dy$ which is the differential of $\tfrac{1}{3}y^3$. In dealing with functions of the form $\sqrt{a^2 + x^2}$ we have found that the substitution $x = 1/y$ changes the index of the term outside the radical, and this suggests that the above integral might be simplified by the substitution $y = 1/z$, so that

$$dy = (- 1/z^2)\, dz.$$

Carrying out this substitution, we obtain

$$I = - \int \frac{1}{z^2} \frac{dz}{(1 - 1/z^3)^{\frac{1}{3}}} = - \int \frac{dz}{z (z^3 - 1)^{\frac{1}{3}}} = - \int \frac{z^2\, dz}{z^3 (z^3 - 1)^{\frac{1}{3}}}.$$

Since the integrand now consists of the two parts (i) $z^2\, dz$, the differential of $\frac{1}{3}z^3$, and (ii) $z^3 (z^3 - 1)^{\frac{1}{3}}$, a function of $\frac{1}{3}z^3$, the required conditions are satisfied. The substitution $z^3 = x$ will therefore simplify the integral.

A better substitution, which will rationalize the denominator of the integrand, is $z^3 - 1 = x^3$: this substitution will not affect the above conditions.

Putting $z^3 - 1 = x^3$, we have $3z^2\, dz = 3x^2\, dx$, and

$$I = - \int \frac{x^2\, dx}{(x^3 + 1)\, x} = - \int \frac{x\, dx}{x^3 + 1}.$$

By expressing this in partial fractions, and employing the usual processes, the integral becomes

$$- \tfrac{1}{6} \log (1 - x + x^2) - \frac{1}{\sqrt 3} \tan^{-1} \frac{(2x - 1)}{\sqrt 3} + \tfrac{1}{3} \log (1 + x),$$

where

$$x = (z^3 - 1)^{\frac{1}{3}}$$
$$= \frac{(1 - y^3)^{\frac{1}{3}}}{y}.$$

EXAMPLES 8

Integrate the following functions with respect to x

1. $\dfrac{x^2}{(1 + x)^n}$; $\dfrac{x - 2}{x \sqrt x}$; $\dfrac{x + 1}{\sqrt{x + 2}}$.

2. $\dfrac{x + 1}{x^2 - 4x + 3}$; $\dfrac{3x^2 - 1}{x^2 - 3x + 2}$; $\dfrac{x^3}{\sqrt{x - 1}}$.

3. $\dfrac{x}{x^4 - a^4}$; $\dfrac{3x + 1}{(x - 1)^2 (x + 3)}$.

4. $\dfrac{\cos x}{3 + 4 \sin x}$; $\dfrac{8x}{4x^2 + 3}$; $\dfrac{e^x - \sin x}{e^x + \cos x}$.

5. $\dfrac{1}{\sqrt{2-x-x^2}}$; $\dfrac{1}{\sqrt{2+x+x^2}}$.

6. $\dfrac{\sin x}{\frac{1}{2}+\frac{1}{3}\cos x}$; $\dfrac{1}{1-x^3}$.

7. $\dfrac{x^2-1}{x^4+x^2+1}$; $\dfrac{x^2}{x^6-a^6}$.

8. $\dfrac{x}{\sqrt{1+x^2}}$; $\dfrac{3x+4}{4x^2+3}$.

9. $\sin 2x \cos 3x$; $\cos x \cos \frac{1}{2}x$.

10. $\dfrac{x^3}{\sqrt{a^2+x^2}}$; $\dfrac{1}{x\sqrt{1+x^n}}$.

11. Find the value of the integral of $\dfrac{1}{a+2bx+cx^2}$ according as $ac-b^2$ is of the form $-k^2$ or $+k^2$.

12. Evaluate $\displaystyle\int\dfrac{dx}{x^2\sqrt{2+x^2}}$.

13. Integrate with respect to x:

(i) $\dfrac{x}{y}$;   (ii) $\dfrac{x^2}{y}$;   (iii) $\dfrac{x^3}{y}$, where $y \equiv \sqrt{x^2-1}$.

14. Resolve $\dfrac{3x^2+x-2}{(x-1)^3(x^2+1)}$ into partial fractions and integrate it.

15. By using the known relations connecting $\sin x$ and $\cos x$ with t, where $t = \tan \frac{1}{2}x$, evaluate

$$\int\dfrac{dx}{\sin x};\quad \int\dfrac{dx}{1+\cos x};\quad \int\sec x \operatorname{cosec} x\,dx,$$

expressing the results in terms of t.

By using the formula for integration by parts, evaluate

16. $\displaystyle\int x \log x\,dx$; $\displaystyle\int e^{ax} x^2\,dx$.   17. $\displaystyle\int x^2 e^x\,dx$; $\displaystyle\int x^2 \log x\,dx$.

18. $\displaystyle\int x \sin x\,dx$; $\displaystyle\int x^3 \cos x\,dx$.   19. $\displaystyle\int x \tan^{-1} x\,dx$; $\displaystyle\int \dfrac{x e^x}{(1+x)^2}\,dx$.

20. $\displaystyle\int e^{ax} \cos bx\,dx$.

Integrate the following functions with respect to x:

21. $\dfrac{1}{\sqrt{4x^2 - 7}}$.

22. $\sec x$.

23. $\dfrac{\log (1 - x)}{(1 - x)}$.

24. $\dfrac{\log (\log x)}{x}$.

25. $(a^2 + x^2)^{-\frac{3}{2}}$.

26. $(x + b)(x^2 + 2bx + c)^n$.

27. $\dfrac{1}{\sqrt{3x^2 + x + 8}}$.

28. $\dfrac{1}{1 + c^x}$.

29. $\dfrac{x + 1}{x^2 + x + 1}$.

30. $\dfrac{x}{\sqrt{5 + 2x + x^2}}$.

31. $\dfrac{1}{x(1 + x^3)}$.

32. $\dfrac{1}{41 + 9 \cos x}$.

33. $\dfrac{1}{(1 + x)\sqrt{1 + x^2}}$.

34. $\dfrac{1}{x\sqrt{x^2 + 2x - 3}}$.

35. $\dfrac{1}{x\sqrt{2 + x - x^2}}$.

36. $\dfrac{\tan x}{a + b \tan^2 x}$.

37. $\sqrt{\dfrac{a + x}{a - x}}$.

38. $\dfrac{1}{\sqrt{x} + \sqrt{x + a}}$.

39. $\dfrac{\sin x}{4 \cos x + 3 \sin x}$.

40. $\dfrac{1}{a + b \cos^2 x}$.

41. Prove that

$$\int u \frac{d^2 v}{dx^2}\, dx = u \frac{dv}{dx} - v \frac{du}{dx} + \int v \frac{d^2 u}{dx^2}\, dx.$$

42. If y is a function of x whose integral is known show that the inverse function where x is regarded as a function of y can always be integrated. Apply this method to find:

(a) $\displaystyle\int \log y\, dy$, given that $\displaystyle\int e^x\, dx = e^x$;

(b) $\displaystyle\int \cos^{-1} y\, dy$, given that $\displaystyle\int \cos x\, dx = \sin x$.

43. Integrate $\dfrac{x^3}{(x^2 + 1)^3}$,

(i) by the substitution $u = x^2 + 1$;

(ii) by the substitution $x = \tan \theta$.

Explain the difference between the results.

44. If $\mu_x = -\dfrac{1}{l_x}\dfrac{dl_x}{dx}$ and is of the form $a + bx + mc^x$, show that l_x is of the form $ks^x w^{x^2} g^{c^x}$.

45. Integrate $\dfrac{x}{1 + x^4}$ with respect to x.

46. Evaluate $\displaystyle\int\dfrac{(x-1)^{\frac{1}{2}}\,dx}{x\,(x+1)^{\frac{1}{2}}}$.

47. If $a > b$, integrate $(a + b\cos x)^{-1}$ with respect to x.

48. Obtain by successive reduction
$$\int x^3\,(a^2 + x^2)^{-\frac{5}{2}}\,dx.$$

49. Find a formula of reduction for $\displaystyle\int e^{px}\,x^q\,dx$ and hence evaluate $\displaystyle\int x\,e^{ax}\,dx$.

50. By differentiating $\dfrac{x}{(x^2 - a^2)^{m-1}}$, find a formula of reduction for
$$\int\dfrac{dx}{(x^2 - a^2)^m}.$$
Hence or otherwise evaluate $\displaystyle\int\dfrac{dx}{(x^2 - a^2)^2}$.

51. Evaluate $\displaystyle\int x^3\,(\log x)^2\,dx$.

52. Prove that
$$\int\cos^m x\,\sin nx\,dx = \dfrac{m}{m + n}\int\cos^{m-1} x\,\sin(n-1)\,x\,dx - \dfrac{\cos^m x\,\cos nx}{m + n}.$$

53. If
$$u_n = \int x^n\,\sqrt{2ax - x^2}\,dx,$$
show that
$$(n + 2)\,u_n = (2n + 1)\,au_{n-1} - x^{n-1}\,(2ax - x^2)^{\frac{3}{2}}.$$
Hence obtain
$$\int x\,\sqrt{2ax - x^2}\,dx.$$

54. Integrate $\dfrac{1}{\sin(x - a)\,\sin(x - b)}$ with respect to x.

55. Use the method of integration by parts to find $\displaystyle\int x^2\,\sin^{-1} x\,dx$.

56. Find $\displaystyle\int\dfrac{\sin 2\phi}{\sin^4\phi + \cos^4\phi}\,d\phi$.

57. Show that the substitution $u^2 = \dfrac{x-a}{\beta-x}$ renders the integral $\int \sqrt{(x-a)(\beta-x)}\, dx$ integrable. ($\beta > a$.)

Hence evaluate $\int \sqrt{(3-x)(x-2)}\, dx$.

58. If μ_x is in the form of

$$A + Bc^x \left(\log_e x + \frac{1}{\log_e c}\frac{1}{x} \right),$$

find an expression for l_x, where

$$\mu_x = -\frac{1}{l_x}\frac{dl_x}{dx}.$$

59. Show that the integral

$$\int \frac{dx}{x\sqrt{3x^2 + 2x + 1}}$$

is rationalized by the substitution

$$x = \frac{2(y+1)}{y^2 - 3}.$$

By means of this substitution evaluate the integral.

60. Integrate $\operatorname{cosec}^3 x$ with respect to x.

61. Find $\int \dfrac{15 - \cos 2x}{3 + \cos 2x}\, dx$.

By means of the substitutions indicated, evaluate the following integrals:

62. $\int \dfrac{x^3\, dx}{(x^2+1)^3}$.   Substitution $x = \tan \phi$

63. $\int \dfrac{(x^4-1)\, dx}{x^2\sqrt{x^4+x^2+1}}$.   ,, $z = (x^4+1)/x^2$.

64. $\int \dfrac{(x^4-1)\, dx}{x^2\sqrt{x^4+x^2+1}}$.   ,, $z = x + 1/x$.

65. $\int \dfrac{dx}{x^5(2-x^3)^{\frac{1}{4}}}$.   ,, $z = (2-x^3)/x^3$.

66. $\int \dfrac{(1+2x^{\frac{3}{4}})^{\frac{2}{3}}\, dx}{x^3}$.   ,, $2 + x^{-\frac{3}{4}} = z$.

67. $\int \dfrac{x\,dx}{\sqrt{1+x}+\sqrt[3]{1+x}}$. Substitution $x + 1 = z^6$.

68. $\int \dfrac{dx}{\sqrt{x+a}+\sqrt{x+b}}$.   ,, $2x + a + b = \tfrac{1}{2}(a-b)(t^2+1/t^2)$.

(Express the result as a function of t.)

69. $\int \dfrac{dx}{x\,(a+bx^n)^4}$.   Substitution $a + bx^n = zx^n$.

70. $\int \dfrac{x^7\,dx}{x^{12}-1}$.   ,, $z = x^4$.

71. $\int \dfrac{d\phi}{2+\cos\phi}$.   ,, $x = (1 + 2\cos\phi)/(2+\cos\phi)$.

CHAPTER IX

DEFINITE INTEGRALS: AREAS: MISCELLANEOUS THEOREMS

1. The definite integral $\int_a^b \phi(x)\, dx$ has been defined thus: if $\frac{d}{dx} f(x) = \phi(x)$, then $\int_a^b \phi(x)\, dx = f(b) - f(a)$. In dealing with indefinite integrals the sole consideration is to obtain the function $f(x)$ which when differentiated will give $\phi(x)$. For definite integrals a further process is necessary, namely that of finding the values of $f(b)$ and $f(a)$. It should be noted that a definite integral will always be a function of a and b (the limits of the integration) and will not be a function of x, the independent variable.

The ordinary procedure follows similar lines to those adopted for summation in finite differences and the work is carried on thus:

Example 1.

Evaluate
$$\int_4^5 (x-3)^2\, dx.$$

$$\int_4^5 (x-3)^2\, dx = \left[\frac{(x-3)^3}{3}\right]_4^5$$
$$= \frac{(5-3)^3}{3} - \frac{(4-3)^3}{3}$$
$$= \frac{2^3}{3} - \frac{1^3}{3} = \frac{8}{3} - \frac{1}{3} = \frac{7}{3}.$$

2. Before proceeding to a detailed investigation of the methods for the solution of problems involving definite integration there are certain simple theorems to be proved. These are of general application.

(i)
$$\int_a^b \phi(x)\, dx = -\int_b^a \phi(x)\, dx.$$

If
$$\frac{d}{dx} f(x) = \phi(x), \quad \text{then} \quad \int \phi(x)\, dx = f(x).$$

$$\therefore \int_a^b \phi(x)\,dx = f(b) - f(a)$$
$$= -[f(a) - f(b)]$$
$$= -\int_b^a \phi(x)\,dx.$$

(ii) $\qquad \int_a^c \phi(x)\,dx = \int_a^b \phi(x)\,dx + \int_b^c \phi(x)\,dx.$

As before, if

$$\frac{d}{dx}f(x) = \phi(x), \quad \text{then} \quad \int \phi(x)\,dx = f(x).$$

$$\therefore \int_a^c \phi(x)\,dx = f(c) - f(a)$$
$$= f(c) - f(b) + f(b) - f(a)$$
$$= \int_b^c \phi(x)\,dx + \int_a^b \phi(x)\,dx.$$

(iii) $\qquad \int_0^a \phi(x)\,dx = \int_0^a \phi(a-x)\,dx.$

This is an example of the change of limits brought about by the substitution of a different variable for the original variable x.

If $\qquad\qquad (a-x) = y \quad \text{so that} \quad -dx = dy,$

then $\qquad\qquad \phi(a-x)\,dx = -\phi(y)\,dy.$

Also when $\qquad\qquad x = 0, \quad y = a,$

and when $\qquad\qquad x = a, \quad y = 0.$

$$\therefore \int_0^a \phi(x)\,dx = \int_0^a \phi(y)\,dy = \int_a^0 \phi(a-x).-dx$$
$$= -\int_a^0 \phi(a-x)\,dx = \int_0^a \phi(a-x)\,dx.$$

It should be noted that if the upper limit is the independent variable, the integral is not a definite integral, but simply another form of the indefinite integral.

For example,

$$\int_a^x \phi(x)\,dx = f(x) - f(a)$$
$$= f(x) + \text{a constant}$$
$$= \int \phi(x)\,dx.$$

3. There is no new principle involved in the evaluation of definite integrals. Care must be taken, however, that if a substitution be made for the independent variable, the limits of integration are changed accordingly. This is particularly to be noted when the substitution turns an algebraic expression into a trigonometrical expression, or vice versa.

The following illustrative examples show the procedure to be employed.

Example 2.

$$\int_0^1 \frac{x^2}{(3x+2)^2}\,dx.$$

Put $3x + 2 = y$: then when $x = 0$, $y = 2$; and when $x = 1$, $y = 5$. Also $3dx = dy$.

The integral becomes

$$\int_2^5 \frac{\left(\frac{y-2}{3}\right)^2}{y^2}\frac{dy}{3}$$

$$= \frac{1}{27}\cdot\int_2^5 \frac{y^2 - 4y + 4}{y^2}\,dy$$

$$= \frac{1}{27}\int_2^5 \left(1 - \frac{4}{y} + \frac{4}{y^2}\right)dy$$

$$= \frac{1}{27}\left[y - 4\log y - \frac{4}{y}\right]_2^5$$

$$= \frac{1}{27}\left[\left(5 - 4\log 5 - \frac{4}{5}\right) - \left(2 - 4\log 2 - \frac{4}{2}\right)\right]$$

$$= \frac{1}{27}\left(3 - 4\log\frac{5}{2} + \frac{6}{5}\right) = \frac{1}{27}\left(\frac{21}{5} - 4\log\frac{5}{2}\right).$$

Example 3.

$$\int_0^a \frac{dx}{a^2 + x^2}.$$

$\int \frac{dx}{a^2 + x^2}$ is a standard form and its value is $\frac{1}{a}\tan^{-1}\frac{x}{a}$.

Therefore the definite integral

$$= \left[\frac{1}{a}\tan^{-1}\frac{x}{a}\right]_0^a$$

$$= \frac{1}{a}\tan^{-1} 1 - \frac{1}{a}\tan^{-1} 0$$

$$= \frac{1}{a}\cdot\frac{\pi}{4} - \frac{1}{a}\cdot 0 = \frac{\pi}{4a}.$$

There are two points to be noted when evaluating a definite integral for which the indefinite integral is an inverse trigonometrical function. They are

(1) In no circumstances can the result be expressed in degrees, since the ordinary rules for the differentiation and integration of trigonometrical functions hold only when the angles are measured in radians.

(2) The value of the definite integral is usually the smallest positive angle. If, for example, $\tan x$ is made to vary continuously from 0 to 1 and x commences at the value 0, it will end at the value $\dfrac{\pi}{4}$: similarly if it commences at the value $n\pi$ it will end at the value $n\pi + \dfrac{\pi}{4}$.

The reasons for these restrictions will be more apparent when geometrical applications of definite integrals are considered. (See para. 6, later.)

Example 4.

$$\int_0^a \frac{dx}{(a^2 + x^2)^{\frac{3}{2}}}.$$

Let $x = a \tan \phi$; then $dx = a \sec^2 \phi \, d\phi$.

When $x = 0$, $\qquad \tan \phi = 0$ and $\phi = 0$;

and when $x = a$, $\qquad \tan \phi = 1$ and $\phi = \dfrac{\pi}{4}$.

Therefore the integral becomes

$$\int_0^{\frac{\pi}{4}} \frac{a \sec^2 \phi \, d\phi}{(a^2 \tan^2 \phi + a^2)^{\frac{3}{2}}}.$$

$$\int_0^{\frac{\pi}{4}} \frac{a \sec^2 \phi \, d\phi}{a^3 \sec^3 \phi} = \int_0^{\frac{\pi}{4}} \frac{1}{a^2} \cos \phi \, d\phi$$

$$= \left[\frac{1}{a^2} \sin \phi \right]_0^{\frac{\pi}{4}} \quad = \frac{1}{a^2} \left[\sin \frac{\pi}{4} - \sin 0 \right]$$

$$= \frac{1}{a^2} \left[\frac{1}{\sqrt{2}} - 0 \right]$$

$$= \frac{1}{a^2 \sqrt{2}}.$$

Note. The substitution $x = \dfrac{1}{y}$ will also simplify this integral.

Example 5.

$$\int_0^\pi \sin^2 x\,dx.$$

$$\int_0^\pi \sin^2 x\,dx = \int_0^\pi \tfrac{1}{2}.2 \sin^2 x\,dx = \int_0^\pi \tfrac{1}{2}(1 - \cos 2x)\,dx$$

$$= \left[\tfrac{1}{2}(x - \tfrac{1}{2}\sin 2x)\right]_0^\pi = \tfrac{1}{2}[\pi - \tfrac{1}{2}\sin 2\pi - 0] = \tfrac{1}{2}\pi,$$

since $\sin 2\pi = 0.$

Example 6.

Prove that $\displaystyle\int_0^{\frac{\pi}{2}} \sin^n x\,dx = \int_0^{\frac{\pi}{2}} \cos^n x\,dx.$

From (iii) above (para. 2),

$$\int_0^a f(x)\,dx = \int_0^a f(a - x)\,dx$$

and $\sin x = \cos\left(\dfrac{\pi}{2} - x\right).$

$$\therefore \int_0^{\frac{\pi}{2}} \sin^n x\,dx = \int_0^{\frac{\pi}{2}} \sin^n\left(\frac{\pi}{2} - x\right) dx = \int_0^{\frac{\pi}{2}} \cos^n x\,dx.$$

Example 7.

Evaluate $\displaystyle\int_0^{\frac{\pi}{2}} x \sin x\,dx.$

The function $x \sin x$ is the product of two functions of x and we must integrate the expression by parts. We may obtain the indefinite integral by this method and insert the limits after the integration has been performed.

$$\int x \sin x\,dx = -x \cos x - \int(-\cos x)\,dx$$

$$= -x \cos x + \sin x.$$

$$\therefore \int_0^{\frac{\pi}{2}} x \sin x\,dx = \left[-x \cos x + \sin x\right]_0^{\frac{\pi}{2}}$$

$$= -\frac{\pi}{2}\cos\frac{\pi}{2} + \sin\frac{\pi}{2} - 0\cos 0 + \sin 0$$

$$= 0 + 1 - 0 + 0$$

$$= 1.$$

4. When the function whose definite integral is required is the product of two functions of the variable, we may proceed as above, or we may adopt a more specific formula for definite integration.

Let u_t and v_t be two functions of a variable t, and let a and b be two constants independent of t.

Then

$$\int u_t v_t \, dt = u_t \int v_t \, dt - \int \frac{du_t}{dt} \left(\int v_t dt \right) dt.$$

We may write $\int v_t dt$ as $\int_a^t v_k dk$; for if $\int v_t dt = V_t$ then

$$\int_a^t v_k dk = \left[V_k \right]_a^t = V_t - V_a$$

$$= \int v_t dt - \text{constant}$$

$$= \int v_t dt,$$

the constant being simply the constant of integration. (See para. 2.)

$$\therefore \quad \int u_t v_t dt = u_t \int_a^t v_k dk - \int \frac{du_t}{dt} \left(\int_a^t v_k dk \right) dt.$$

$$\therefore \quad \int_a^b u_t v_t dt = \left[u_t \int_a^t v_k dk - \int \frac{du_t}{dt} \left(\int_a^t v_k dk \right) dt \right]_a^b$$

$$= u_b \int_a^b v_k dk - u_a \int_a^a v_k dk - \int_a^b \frac{du_t}{dt} \left(\int_a^t v_k dk \right) dt$$

$$= u_b \int_a^b v_k dk - \int_a^b \frac{du_t}{dt} \left(\int_a^t v_k dk \right) dt,$$

since

$$\int_a^a v_k dk = V_a - V_a = 0.$$

Alternatively, since

$$-\int_t^b v_k dk = -(V_b - V_t) = V_t - \text{constant} = \int v_t dt,$$

we may obtain

$$\int_a^b u_t v_t dt = u_a \int_a^b v_k dk + \int_a^b \frac{du_t}{dt} \left(\int_t^b v_k dk \right) dt.$$

(See Actuarial Note, *J.I.A.* vol. XLIV, pp. 403-5.)

Applying the first of these formulae to the evaluation of the integral in Ex. 7, we have

$$\int_0^{\frac{\pi}{2}} x \sin x \, dx = \frac{\pi}{2} \int_0^{\frac{\pi}{2}} \sin x \, dx - \int_0^{\frac{\pi}{2}} \frac{dx}{dx} \left(\int_0^x \sin k \, dk \right) dx,$$

where the "u" function is x, and the "v" function is $\sin x$.

Now

$$\int_0^x \sin k \, dk = \left[- \cos k \right]_0^x = - \cos x + \cos 0 = - \cos x + 1.$$

$$\therefore \quad \int_0^{\frac{\pi}{2}} x \sin x \, dx = \frac{\pi}{2} \left[- \cos x \right]_0^{\frac{\pi}{2}} - \int_0^{\frac{\pi}{2}} (- \cos x + 1) \, dx$$

$$= \frac{\pi}{2} \left[- \cos \frac{\pi}{2} + \cos 0 \right] - \left[- \sin x + x \right]_0^{\frac{\pi}{2}}$$

$$= \frac{\pi}{2} \left[0 + 1 \right] - \left[- \sin \frac{\pi}{2} + \frac{\pi}{2} \right]$$

$$= \frac{\pi}{2} + \sin \frac{\pi}{2} - \frac{\pi}{2}$$

$$= \sin \frac{\pi}{2}$$

$$= 1, \text{ as before.}$$

5. The following examples are illustrative of the methods employed in the evaluation of certain types of integrals.

The value of the function $\dfrac{x^n}{e^x}$ when $x = 0$ is evidently zero (since $e^0 = 1$), and the limit of the function when $x \to \infty$ is also zero (see Ex. 3, Chapter VI). These properties of the function enable the definite integral $\displaystyle\int_0^\infty x^n e^{-x} dx$ to be readily evaluated when n is a positive integer.

Thus

$$\int x^n e^{-x} dx = x^n (- e^{-x}) - \int \frac{dx^n}{dx} (- e^{-x}) \, dx$$

$$= - x^n e^{-x} + n \int x^{n-1} e^{-x} dx.$$

$$\therefore \int_0^\infty x^n e^{-x} dx = \left[-x^n e^{-x} \right]_0^\infty + n \int_0^\infty x^{n-1} e^{-x} dx$$

$$= n \int_0^\infty x^{n-1} e^{-x} dx \text{ since } \left[-x^n e^{-x} \right]_0^\infty \text{ is zero.}$$

Similarly

$$\int_0^\infty x^{n-1} e^{-x} dx = (n-1) \int_0^\infty x^{n-2} e^{-x} dx,$$

and so on.

$$\therefore \int_0^\infty x^n e^{-x} dx = n(n-1)(n-2) .. \int_0^\infty e^{-x} dx$$

$$= n(n-1)(n-2) ... \left[-e^{-x} \right]_0^\infty$$

$$\begin{cases} \underset{x \to \infty}{\text{Lt}} \ e^{-x} = \underset{x \to \infty}{\text{Lt}} \ \dfrac{1}{e^x} = 0 \\ \text{and } e^{-x} = 1 \quad \text{when} \quad x = 0. \end{cases}$$

$$\therefore \int_0^\infty x^n e^{-x} dx = n(n-1)(n-2) ... 1.$$

Again, consider the integral $\int_0^1 x^{n-1} (1-x)^{m-1} dx$, where m and n are positive and m is an integer. If we put $1 - x = z$, then $-dx = dz$. The new variable z takes the values 1 and 0 when x has the values 0 and 1 respectively, and the form of the integral is now $\int_1^0 - (1-z)^{n-1} z^{m-1} dz$.

This is the same as $\int_0^1 z^{m-1} (1-z)^{n-1} dz$.

Changing the variable to x—which does not alter the value of the integral—the integral becomes $\int_0^1 x^{m-1} (1-x)^{n-1} dx$.

To evaluate the integral we proceed in the usual manner.

$$\int x^{n-1} (1-x)^{m-1} dx = \frac{x^n}{n} (1-x)^{m-1} - \int \frac{d}{dx} (1-x)^{m-1} \frac{x^n}{n} dx$$

$$= \frac{x^n}{n} (1-x)^{m-1} + \int \frac{m-1}{n} x^n (1-x)^{m-2} dx$$

$$= \frac{x^n}{n} (1-x)^{m-1} + \frac{m-1}{n} \int x^n (1-x)^{m-2} dx.$$

The term $\dfrac{x^n}{n}\,(1 - x)^{m-1}$ vanishes for limits $x = 0$ and $x = 1$.

$$\therefore \int_0^1 x^{n-1}\,(1 - x)^{m-1}\,dx = \frac{m - 1}{n} \int_0^1 x^n\,(1 - x)^{m-2}\,dx$$

$$= \frac{m - 1}{n}\,\frac{m - 2}{n + 1} \int_0^1 x^{n+1}\,(1 - x)^{m-3}\,dx,$$

similarly.

....

$$= \frac{(m - 1)\,(m - 2)\dots 2 \cdot 1}{n\,(n + 1)\dots(n + m - 2)} \int_0^1 x^{m+n-2}\,dx$$

$$= \frac{(m - 1)\,(m - 2)\dots 2 \cdot 1}{n\,(n + 1)\dots(n + m - 1)}.$$

The above integrals are of the utmost importance in the higher branches of mathematics. They are called Eulerian Integrals,

$$\int_0^1 x^{m-1}\,(1 - x)^{n-1}\,dx$$

being the First Eulerian Integral and

$$\int_0^\infty x^n e^{-x}\,dx$$

the Second Eulerian Integral. The proofs above have been based on the assumption that the indices have particular values (e.g. in $\int_0^1 x^{m-1}\,(1 - x)^{n-1}\,dx$, m is an integer). It can be proved, however, that the properties of the integrals are the same if certain of these restrictions are removed. The First Eulerian Integral $\int_0^1 x^{m-1}\,(1 - x)^{n-1}\,dx$ is a function of the positive quantities m and n and is written as $\beta\,(m, n)$; the Second Eulerian Integral is a function of n alone and is written as $\Gamma\,(n + 1)$. These functions are called Beta and Gamma functions respectively.

We have $\qquad \beta\,(m, n) = \displaystyle\int_0^1 x^{m-1}\,(1 - x)^{n-1}\,dx$

$$= \frac{(m - 1)\,(m - 2)\dots 2 \cdot 1}{n\,(n + 1)\dots(n + m - 1)}$$

$$= \frac{(m - 1)!\,(n - 1)!}{(n + m - 1)!},$$

if m and n are positive integers.

Also $\quad \Gamma(n+1) = \int_0^\infty x^n e^{-x} dx = n(n-1) \ldots 3.2.1,$

which is $n!$ when n is a positive integer.

Hence $\quad \beta(m, n) = \Gamma(m)\,\Gamma(n)/\Gamma(m+n) = \beta(n, m).$

6. Areas of curves.

It has been shown that the integral $\int_a^b \phi(x)\,dx$ represents the area of the curve $y = \phi(x)$ between the curve, the x-axis and the two ordinates $x = a$ and $x = b$. Every definite integral denotes an area, and provided that the function in question is integrable we can find areas of those parts of curves cut off by different straight lines and, in many instances, by other curves. In solving problems connected with areas it is always advisable to draw a rough graph of the curve: otherwise the true area required may not be apparent.

Example 8.

Find the area cut off by the curve $y^2 = 4x$, the x-axis and the ordinates $x = 0$ and $x = 4$.

The curve is the parabola LOK in the diagram, and the area required is that bounded by the curve OL and the straight lines OX, LM, i.e. the part OLM.

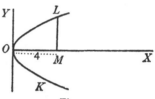

Fig. 32.

$$\text{Area} = \int_0^4 y\,dx$$

$$= \int_0^4 2\sqrt{x}\,dx, \qquad \text{since } y^2 = 4x$$

$$= 2\int_0^4 x^{\frac{1}{2}}\,dx$$

$$= 2\left[\frac{x^{\frac{3}{2}}}{\frac{3}{2}}\right]_0^4$$

$$= \tfrac{4}{3}[4^{\frac{3}{2}}] = 10\tfrac{2}{3}.$$

Note. Since the result represents an area, we should write $10\tfrac{2}{3}$ *square units* as our answer. In practice, the words " square units " are omitted, but it should not be forgotten that this qualification always exists. If, for example, squared paper were used and we chose an inch as our unit for x (along OX) and for y (along OY), the area OML would be 10⅔ square inches.

Similarly, if the integral to be evaluated were

$$\int_0^1 \frac{dx}{\sqrt{1-x^2}},$$

the area required would be

$$\left[\sin^{-1}x\right]_0^1 \quad \text{or} \quad (\sin^{-1}1 - \sin^{-1}0),$$

the value of which is $\frac{\pi}{2}$. The full result would be "$\frac{\pi}{2}$ square units" or "$\frac{1}{2}(3\cdot14159\ldots)$ square units," so that if our units were inches the area would be $1\cdot571$ square inches, correct to three decimal places.

Example 9.

Find the area of the loop of the curve $y^2 = x^4(x+2)$.

For real values of the variables x cannot be less than -2. Also when $y = 0$, $x = 0$ or -2. Again for every value of x between 0 and -2

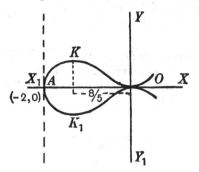

Fig. 33.

there will be two values of y, equal in magnitude and opposite in sign.

Also

$$\frac{dy}{dx} = \frac{d}{dx}\left(x^2\sqrt{x+2}\right)$$

$$= \frac{x^2}{2\sqrt{x+2}} + 2x\sqrt{x+2}.$$

If this be equated to zero,

$$x^2 + 4x(x+2) = 0;$$

i.e.

$$5x^2 + 8x = 0,$$

$$\therefore \ x = 0 \text{ or } -8/5.$$

Of these $x = -8/5$ gives a maximum value to y, and K will be the highest point of the loop.

If we integrate y between the limits -2 and 0 we shall obtain the area cut off by the curve between the axes and the ordinate $x = -2$, i.e. the area OKA. The area of the whole loop $OKAK_1$ will be twice this area.

Therefore the area of the loop

$$= 2 \int_{-2}^{0} y \, dx = 2 \int_{-2}^{0} x^2 (x + 2)^{\frac{1}{2}} \, dx.$$

To evaluate the integral, let $(x + 2)^{\frac{1}{2}} = z$.

Then when $x = -2$, $z = 0$, and when $x = 0$, $z = \sqrt{2}$.

Also

$$\frac{dx}{2 (x + 2)^{\frac{1}{2}}} = dz.$$

The required area is therefore

$$2 \int_{0}^{\sqrt{2}} (z^2 - 2)^2 z \cdot 2z \, dz$$

$$= 2 \int_{0}^{\sqrt{2}} (z^4 - 4z^2 + 4) 2z^2 \, dz$$

$$= 2 \int_{0}^{\sqrt{2}} (2z^6 - 8z^4 + 8z^2) \, dz$$

$$= 2 \left[\frac{2z^7}{7} - \frac{8z^5}{5} + \frac{8z^3}{3} \right]_{0}^{\sqrt{2}}$$

$$= 2 \left[\frac{2 \cdot 2^{\frac{7}{2}}}{7} - \frac{8 \cdot 2^{\frac{5}{2}}}{5} + \frac{8 \cdot 2^{\frac{3}{2}}}{3} \right],$$

which simplifies to

$$\frac{256 \sqrt{2}}{105}.$$

Note. In the above figure the area AKO corresponds to the positive value of $\sqrt{x + 2}$, and the area $AK_1 O$ to the negative value. The area $= 2 \int_{-2}^{0} x^2 \sqrt{x + 2} \, dx$, where the $\sqrt{x + 2}$ means the positive value of the square root; there is therefore no ambiguity of sign when z is substituted for $\sqrt{x + 2}$.

Example 10.

Find the area between the curve $y^2 (1 - x) = x^3$ and its asymptote.

The straight line $x = 1$ is an asymptote to the curve. x cannot exceed 1 for real values of y, and the curve gradually approaches the straight line $x = 1$, meeting it only at an infinite distance from the origin.

We require therefore

$$2 \int_0^1 y\, dx = 2 \int_0^1 x^{\frac{3}{2}}/(1 - x)^{\frac{1}{2}}\, dx.$$

The substitution is $x = \sin^2 \theta$ and the integral becomes

$$2 \int_0^{\frac{\pi}{2}} 2 \sin^4 \theta\, d\theta.$$

Expressing $\sin^4 \theta$ in terms of multiple angles, we have for the area required

$$2 \int_0^{\frac{\pi}{2}} 2 \left(\tfrac{3}{8} - \tfrac{1}{2} \cos 2\theta + \tfrac{1}{8} \cos 4\theta\right) d\theta$$

$$= 4 \left[\tfrac{3}{8}\theta - \tfrac{1}{4} \sin 2\theta + \tfrac{1}{32} \sin 4\theta\right]_0^{\frac{\pi}{2}}$$

$$= 4 \left[\frac{3}{8} \cdot \frac{\pi}{2}\right]$$

$$= \tfrac{3}{4}\pi.$$

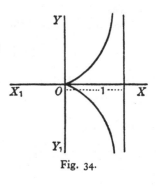

Fig. 34.

7. Differentiation under the integral sign.

There are various devices for evaluating definite integrals where the function to be integrated is of the form $f(x, k)$, k being independent of x. A method that can often be used to advantage depends upon the process of differentiating under the integral sign.

Let $u = \int_a^b f(x, k)\, dx$ where a and b are constants independent of k. Suppose that k be changed to $k + \Delta k$, so that u becomes $u + \Delta u$, x remaining unaltered.

Then $\quad u + \Delta u = \int_a^b f(x, k + \Delta k)\, dx$

and $\qquad \Delta u = \int_a^b f(x, k + \Delta k)\, dx - \int_a^b f(x, k)\, dx$

$$= \int_a^b [f(x, k + \Delta k) - f(x, k)]\, dx,$$

$$\therefore \frac{\Delta u}{\Delta k} = \int_a^b \frac{f(x, k + \Delta k) - f(x, k)}{\Delta k}\, dx.$$

But $\qquad \dfrac{f(x, k + \Delta k) - f(x, k)}{\Delta k} = \dfrac{df(x, k)}{dk} + \alpha,$

where α is a small quantity which vanishes in the limit as $\Delta k \to 0$;

$$\therefore \frac{\Delta u}{\Delta k} = \int_a^b \frac{df(x, k)}{dk}\, dx + \int_a^b \alpha\, dx.$$

When $\Delta k \to 0$ the second integral vanishes, for it cannot be numerically greater than $(b - a)\, \alpha_1$ (where α_1 is the greatest value of α), and α_1 ultimately vanishes.

Therefore when $\Delta k \to 0$ we shall have

$$\frac{du}{dk} = \operatorname*{Lt}_{\Delta k \to 0} \frac{\Delta u}{\Delta k} = \int_a^b \frac{df(x, k)}{dk}\, dx.$$

By successive differentiation it follows that

$$\frac{d^n u}{dk^n} = \int_a^b \frac{d^n f(x, k)}{dk^n}\, dx.$$

If a or b be infinite this proof will not hold, for then we cannot say that, when $\Delta k \to 0$, $(b - a)\, \alpha_1$ vanishes. A complete proof involves higher mathematical analysis and it will be sufficient to assume that in the examples dealt with in this chapter we may differentiate under the integral sign, even if one of the limits be infinite.

The following example is a practical application of the method.

Example 11.

We have
$$\int_0^1 x^{n-1}\, dx = \left[\frac{x^n}{n}\right]_0^1 = \frac{1}{n}.$$

Let $x = \dfrac{z}{a + z}$, where a and z are independent; then when $x = 0$, $z = 0$.

We may write the expression for x as
$$\frac{1}{1 + a/z},$$

so that when $x = 1$, $a/z = 0$ and z is infinite.

$$dx = d\left(\frac{z}{a + z}\right) = d\left(1 - \frac{a}{a + z}\right)$$

$$= \frac{a}{(a + z)^2}\, dz.$$

$$\therefore \int_0^1 x^{n-1}\, dx = \int_0^\infty \left(\frac{z}{a + z}\right)^{n-1} \frac{a}{(a + z)^2}\, dz$$

$$= \int_0^\infty \frac{a z^{n-1}}{(a + z)^{n+1}}\, dz.$$

But
$$\int_0^1 x^{n-1}\,dx = 1/n;$$

$$\therefore \int_0^\infty \frac{z^{n-1}}{(a+z)^{n+1}}\,dz = 1/an.$$

Since a is independent of z, we have

$$\frac{d}{da}\int_0^\infty \frac{z^{n-1}}{(a+z)^{n+1}}\,dz = \int_0^\infty \left[\frac{d}{da}\frac{z^{n-1}}{(a+z)^{n+1}}\right]dz = \int_0^\infty \frac{-(n+1)\,z^{n-1}}{(a+z)^{n+2}}\,dz.$$

Since
$$\int_0^\infty \frac{z^{n-1}}{(a+z)^{n+1}}\,dz = 1/an,$$

$$\frac{d}{da}\int_0^\infty \frac{z^{n-1}}{(a+z)^{n+1}}\,dz = \frac{d}{da}\left(\frac{1}{an}\right) = \frac{1}{n}\left(\frac{-1}{a^2}\right).$$

Also
$$\frac{d}{da}\int_0^\infty \frac{z^{n-1}}{(a+z)^{n+1}}\,dz = \int_0^\infty \frac{-(n+1)\,z^{n-1}}{(a+z)^{n+2}}\,dz,$$

$$\therefore \int_0^\infty \frac{-(n+1)\,z^{n-1}}{(a+z)^{n+2}}\,dz = \frac{1}{n}\left(\frac{-1}{a^2}\right),$$

i.e.
$$\int_0^\infty \frac{z^{n-1}}{(a+z)^{n+2}}\,dz = \frac{1}{n(n+1)}\frac{1}{a^2}.$$

From the known integral $\int_0^\infty \dfrac{z^{n-1}}{(a+z)^{n+1}}\,dz$ we have therefore obtained the integral $\int_0^\infty \dfrac{z^{n-1}}{(a+z)^{n+2}}\,dz$.

This process may be repeated, and we shall have

$$\int_0^\infty \frac{z^{n-1}}{(a+z)^{n+3}}\,dz = \frac{1\cdot 2}{n(n+1)(n+2)}\frac{1}{a^3},$$

$$\int_0^\infty \frac{z^{n-1}}{(a+z)^{n+4}}\,dz = \frac{1\cdot 2\cdot 3}{n(n+1)(n+2)(n+3)}\frac{1}{a^4},$$

so that generally

$$\int_0^\infty \frac{z^{n-1}}{(a+z)^{n+r}}\,dz = \frac{1\cdot 2\cdot 3\ldots(r-1)}{n(n+1)(n+2)\ldots(n+r-1)}\frac{1}{a^r}$$

$$= \frac{(r-1)!\,(n-1)!}{(n+r-1)!}\frac{1}{a^r},$$

if r and n are positive integers.

8. Double integrals.

The formula for integration by parts is

$$\int uv\,dx = u\int v\,dx - \int\left(u'\int v\,dx\right)dx.$$

If x be the function u the second term on the right-hand side is

$$\int\left(x'\int v\,dx\right)dx, \quad \text{i.e.} \quad \int\left(\int v\,dx\right)dx.$$

Omitting the brackets the term is $\iint v\,dx\,dx$. This is a form of double integral, and its meaning is simply that we must integrate v with respect to x, and then integrate the result also with respect to x.

Thus, since $\qquad \int xe^x\,dx = xe^x - e^x,$

$$\iint xe^x\,dx\,dx = \int(xe^x - e^x)\,dx = (xe^x - e^x) - e^x = xe^x - 2e^x.$$

A more general form of double integral is the form in which there are two independent variables. If v be a function of x and y, $\iint v\,dx\,dy$ denotes the process of integrating v with respect to x and then integrating the new function with respect to y.

In performing the integration with respect to x, y must be assumed constant, and similarly when integrating the result with respect to y, x must be assumed constant.

Example 12.

Evaluate $\qquad \iint(4x + 3y^2)\,dx\,dy.$

Since this is an abbreviated form of $\int\left[\int(4x + 3y^2)\,dx\right]dy$, we must first find $\int(4x + 3y^2)\,dx$, where y is assumed to be independent of x.

$$\int(4x + 3y^2)\,dx = 4\frac{x^2}{2} + 3xy^2 + a.$$

Again, $\quad \int(2x^2 + 3xy^2 + a)\,dy = 2x^2y + xy^3 + ay + b;$

$$\therefore \iint (4x + 3y^2)\, dx\, dy = 2x^2 y + xy^3 + ay + b,$$

where a and b are arbitrary constants.

If we had been required to integrate $\iint (4x + 3y^2)\, dy\, dx$, we should have obtained, firstly,

$$\int (4x + 3y^2)\, dy = 4xy + y^3 + c,$$

and then

$$\int (4xy + y^3 + c)\, dx = 2x^2 y + xy^3 + cx + d,$$

where c and d are constants not necessarily the same as a and b above.

9. Suppose that, in the above example, we had had to evaluate the integral between limits, so that the problem read thus:

Find the value of $\displaystyle\int_1^2 \int_3^4 (4x + 3y^2)\, dx\, dy.$

Firstly,
$$\int_3^4 (4x + 3y^2)\, dx = \left[2x^2 + 3xy^2 \right]_3^4$$
$$= 2 \cdot 4^2 + 3 \cdot 4y^2 - 2 \cdot 3^2 - 3 \cdot 3y^2$$
$$= 14 + 3y^2.$$

Secondly,
$$\int_1^2 (14 + 3y^2)\, dy = \left[14y + y^3 \right]_1^2$$
$$= 14 \cdot 2 + 2^3 - 14 \cdot 1 - 1^3$$
$$= 21.$$

Now if the order of integration had been reversed, we should have had to evaluate $\displaystyle\int_3^4 \int_1^2 (4x + 3y^2)\, dy\, dx.$

In the usual manner,

$$\int_1^2 (4x + 3y^2)\, dy = \left[4xy + y^3 \right]_1^2$$
$$= 4 \cdot 2x + 2^3 - 4 \cdot 1x - 1^3$$
$$= 4x + 7.$$

$$\int_3^4 (4x + 7)\, dx = \left[2x^2 + 7x \right]_3^4$$
$$= 2 \cdot 4^2 + 7 \cdot 4 - 2 \cdot 3^2 - 7 \cdot 3$$
$$= 21, \text{ as before.}$$

This leads to the general proposition:
If x and y be independent, then

$$\int_a^\beta \int_a^b f(x, y)\, dx\, dy = \int_a^b \int_a^\beta f(x, y)\, dy\, dx,$$

provided that the limits of x and y are independent of each other, and that neither $f(x, y)$ nor its integrals become infinite for any values of x and y between the limits of integration.

The proof of this theorem is difficult, the most satisfactory demonstration depending on a double summation. It will be therefore taken for granted that the proposition holds within the limitations imposed. For a rigid proof of the proposition the student should consult any recognized textbook on more advanced Integral Calculus.

10. It should be noted that where one or more of the limits of a double integral is a function of either variable, we may not take the order of integration indifferently. A common form of double integral that occurs in mean value and probability problems is one in which one of the limits for integration involves one of the variables. The integral is of the type

$$\int_0^a \int_0^{a-x} f(x, y)\, dy\, dx,$$

where the result of integrating $f(x, y)$ with respect to y and inserting the limits produces a function of x. In these problems it is necessary to adhere strictly to the order of the integration.

Example 13.
Show that

$$\int_0^a \int_0^{a-x} (x^2 + y^2)\, dy\, dx \neq \int_0^{a-x} \int_0^a (x^2 + y^2)\, dx\, dy.$$

$$\int_0^a \int_0^{a-x} (x^2 + y^2)\, dy\, dx = \int_0^a \left[x^2 y + \tfrac{1}{3} y^3 \right]_0^{a-x} dx$$

$$= \int_0^a \left[x^2 (a - x) + \tfrac{1}{3} (a - x)^3 \right] dx$$

$$= \int_0^a \left(ax^2 - x^3 + \tfrac{1}{3} a^3 - a^2 x + ax^2 - \tfrac{1}{3} x^3 \right) dx$$

$$= \frac{1}{3} \int_0^a \left(a^3 - 3a^2 x + 6ax^2 - 4x^3 \right) dx$$

$$= \frac{1}{3} \left[a^3 x - \frac{3a^2 x^2}{2} + \frac{6ax^3}{3} - \frac{4x^4}{4} \right]_0^a$$

$$= \frac{1}{3} \left[a^4 - \frac{3a^4}{2} + \frac{6a^4}{3} - \frac{4a^4}{4} \right]$$

$$= \frac{a^4}{6}.$$

$$\int_0^{a-x} \int_0^a (x^2 + y^2) \, dx \, dy = \int_0^{a-x} \left[\tfrac{1}{3}x^3 + xy^2 \right]_0^a dy$$

$$= \int_0^{a-x} (\tfrac{1}{3}a^3 + ay^2) \, dy$$

$$= \left[\frac{a^3 y}{3} + \frac{ay^3}{3} \right]_0^{a-x}$$

$$= \frac{a}{3} [a^2 (a - x) + (a - x)^3],$$

which is a function of x and is obviously not equal to the constant quantity $\frac{a^4}{6}$.

EXAMPLES 9

1. Prove that

$$\int_a^b \phi (x) \, dx = h\phi \{a + \theta h\},$$

where $h = b - a$ and $0 < \theta < 1$.

Evaluate the following definite integrals:

2. $\displaystyle\int_0^n x^n \, dx; \quad \int_1^5 (ax + bx^2) \, dx.$

3. $\displaystyle\int_0^k e^{-a^2 x} \, dx; \quad \int_{-5}^5 \sqrt{x^{m+n}} \, dx.$

4. $\displaystyle\int_0^{\frac{\pi}{4}} \sin x \, dx; \quad \int_0^1 \tan^{-1} x \, dx.$

5. $\displaystyle\int_{3\frac{1}{2}}^4 \frac{dx}{1 + 3x + 2x^2}; \quad \int_0^1 \frac{1 - x + 2x^2}{1 + x + x^2} \, dx.$

6. $\displaystyle\int_1^2 \frac{dx}{x^3 (3 - x)}; \quad \int_0^\pi \frac{dx}{2 - \cos x}.$

7. $\int_0^a \dfrac{dx}{\sqrt{x+a}+\sqrt{x}}$; $\int_0^{\frac{\pi}{4}} \sin\theta \sec^2\theta\, d\theta$.

8. $\int_0^{\frac{\pi}{2}} \cos^4 x\, dx$; $\int_0^{\pi} \dfrac{dx}{17+8\cos x}$.

9. $\int_0^1 \dfrac{x^3}{(2x+1)^5}\, dx$; $\int_0^1 x^3(1-x)^{\frac{3}{2}}\, dx$.

10. $\int_a^b x\log x\, dx$; $\int_{-\frac{\pi}{2}}^{\frac{\pi}{2}} e^x\cos x\, dx$.

11. $\int_0^{\frac{\pi}{2}} x^2\sin x\, dx$; $\int_0^1 e^{-\frac{1}{2}x} x^2\, dx$.

12. Prove that
$$\int_0^{\frac{1}{2}} \dfrac{dx}{(1-2x^2)\sqrt{1-x^2}} = \tfrac{1}{2}\log(2+\sqrt{3}).$$

13. Use the substitution $x=\sec\theta$ to evaluate $\int_2^4 \dfrac{dx}{x(x^2-1)}$.

14. Prove that
$$\int_1^e x(\log x)^3\, dx = \dfrac{e^2+3}{8}.$$

15. If $b>(a+1)$, find the value of
$$\int_{a+1}^b (x-b)\log(x-a)\, dx.$$

16. Evaluate $\int_0^{\infty} \dfrac{dx}{(1+x^2)^3}$.

17. Prove that if a and b are positive and b is less than a
$$\int_0^{\pi} \dfrac{dx}{a+b\cos x} = \dfrac{\pi}{\sqrt{a^2-b^2}}.$$

18. Find $\int_0^{\frac{\pi}{4}} \tan^5 x\, dx$.

19. Integrate $\dfrac{e^x(1+x\log x)}{x}$ between the limits $x=1$ and $x=2$.

20. Prove that
$$\int_a^h u_t\left(\int_t^h v_t\, dt\right) dt = \int_a^h v_t\left(\int_a^t u_t\, dt\right) dt.$$

21. In the curve $y = x^2$ the abscissa from 0 to 2 is divided into n equal parts each of length $2/n$. Show that the area of the set of inner rectangles is

$$\frac{8}{3}\left[1 - \frac{3}{2n} + \frac{1}{2n^2}\right]$$

and that the area of the set of outer rectangles is

$$\frac{8}{3}\left[1 + \frac{3}{2n} + \frac{1}{2n^2}\right].$$

Putting $n = 10, 100, 1000, 10,000, \ldots$ etc. obtain two series between which there is only one number and deduce that this number must be the area contained between the curve, the axis of x and the ordinate corresponding to the abscissa $x = 2$.

22. Prove directly from the definition of a definite integral as the limit of the sum of a series that

$$\int_0^a \sin nx \, dx = \frac{1}{n} - \frac{\cos na}{n}.$$

23. By evaluating $\int_0^1 (1 - x^2)^n \, dx$ in two different ways (n being a positive integer), prove that

$$1 - \frac{n}{3 \cdot 1!} + \frac{n(n-1)}{5 \cdot 2!} - \frac{n(n-1)(n-2)}{7 \cdot 3!} + \ldots = \frac{2^n n!}{3 \cdot 5 \cdot 7 \ldots (2n+1)}.$$

24. Evaluate $\int_1^2 \frac{(2 - 3x)}{x^3(2 + x)} \, dx.$

25. Prove that $\int_1^5 \frac{(x + 1) \, dx}{(x^2 - 6x + 13)^2} = \frac{1}{8}(\pi + 2).$

26. Find $\int_0^1 \frac{x^2 + \frac{3}{4}}{2x^2 + x + \frac{5}{4}} \, dx.$

27. Prove that $\int_0^{\frac{\pi}{2}} \cos^3 x \sin 5x \, dx = \frac{1}{4}.$

28. Find the area enclosed between the curve $y^2 = 4ax$, the x-axis and the straight line $x = 9a$.

29. Find the area between the curve $y^2 = 4ax$, the x-axis and the ordinates $2ab$ and $2ac$.

30. Plot the curve $y^2 = x(x - 1)^2$ between $x = 0$ and $x = 3$ and find the area of the loop.

31. Find the area between the curve $y^2 = 4ax$ and the straight line $y = x$.

32. Draw a rough sketch of the curve $y^2 = x^4 (1 + x)$ between $x = 0$ and $x = -1$ and find the area of the loop.

33. Find the area between the axes of co-ordinates, the ordinate $y = 9$ and the curve $y = \frac{1}{2}(e^x + e^{-x})$.

34. Find the area of the loop of the curve $y^2 = x^3 + 3x^2$.

35. The equation of a curve is given by $y = \log x + \frac{1}{x}$. Find the area bounded by the axis of y, the curve, and the two abscissae whose lengths are 2 and 3.

36. Find the areas cut off between the axis of the co-ordinates, the ordinate $x = 3a$ and (1) the parabola $y^2 = ax$, (2) the circle $x^2 + y^2 = 4ax$. Hence find the area common to the two curves.

37. Trace the curve $xy^2 = 4(2 - x)$ and find the area which lies between it and the y-axis.

38. Prove that the area of the loop of the curve $y^2 (a + x) = x^2 (a - x)$ is $2a^2 \left(1 - \dfrac{\pi}{4}\right)$.

39. Find the area included between the curves $y^2 - 4ax = 0$ and $x^2 - 4ay = 0$.

40. Find separately the two finite areas each bounded by the three curves: (a) $xy = 1$, (b) $y^2 = x$, (c) $x = 2$.

41. Given that

$$\int \frac{dx}{\sqrt{x^2 + a^2}} = \log (x + \sqrt{x^2 + a^2}),$$

deduce $\qquad \displaystyle\int (x^2 + a^2)^{-\frac{3}{2}}\, dx$

by differentiation under the sign of integration.

42. Prove that

$$\frac{d}{dc}\left(\int_a^b f(x, c)\, dx\right) = \int_a^b \frac{df(x, c)}{dc}\, dx,$$

where the limits are independent of c.

Given $\qquad \displaystyle\int_0^\pi \frac{x\, dx}{1 + \cos a \sin x} = \frac{\pi a}{\sin a}$,

deduce the value of

$$\int_0^\pi \frac{x\, dx}{(1 + \cos a \sin x)^2}.$$

43. Prove that

$$\int_0^1 \frac{dx}{1 + 2x \cos \theta + x^2} = \frac{\theta}{2 \sin \theta},$$

where θ is independent of x.

44. Definite integrals may sometimes be obtained by differentiating under the sign of integration. Illustrate the process by finding the values of the definite integrals

$$\int_0^\infty x^n e^{-ax} \, dx; \quad \int_0^\infty \frac{\log (1 + a^2 x^2)}{1 + x^2} \, dx.$$

45. Given that the length of the arc of the curve $y = \phi(x)$ between the points whose abscissae are a and b is

$$\int_a^b \sqrt{1 + \left(\frac{dy}{dx}\right)^2} \, dx,$$

find the equation of the curve the arc of which beginning from $x = 0$ is always $\sqrt{2ax}$.

46. Show that a form of Maclaurin's series expressing $f(x)$ in terms of $f(0)$, $f'(0)$, $f''(0)$, ... can be obtained by repeatedly integrating by parts the integral

$$\frac{x^n}{(n-1)!} \int_0^1 (1 - t)^{n-1} f^{(n)}(xt) \, dt.$$

47. Evaluate $\quad \int_0^1 (x^4 + x^2 + 1)(x^2 + 1)^{-\frac{1}{2}} \, dx.$

48. Prove that, if $m > n$,

$$\int_0^1 \int_x^{\frac{1}{x}} x^{m-1} y^{n-1} \, dy \, dx = \frac{2}{m^2 - n^2}.$$

49. If x and y are independent variables, find $\int_0^x \sqrt{x^2 + y^2} \, dy$, and integrate the result with respect to x between the limits $x = 0$ and $x = 1$.

50. Evaluate $\quad \dfrac{\displaystyle\int_0^a \int_0^{a-x} \frac{1}{2} a (x + y) \, dy \, dx}{\displaystyle\int_0^a \int_0^{a-x} dy \, dx}.$

MISCELLANEOUS EXAMPLES

1. Make a rough sketch of the curve $y^2 = x^2(1-x^2)$. Find the maximum and minimum values of y and the area enclosed by the curve.

2. Differentiate   (i) $\left(x + \dfrac{a}{x}\right)^{\frac{2}{3}}$;   (ii) $\sin^{-1}(\sin^{-1}x)$.

3. Evaluate   (i) $\operatorname*{Lt}\limits_{x \to 1} \dfrac{x^4 - 2x^3 + 2x^2 - 2x + 1}{x^3 - x^2 - x + 1}$;

   (ii) $\operatorname*{Lt}\limits_{\theta \to 0} \dfrac{\operatorname{cosec}\theta - \cot\theta}{\theta}$.

4. Integrate $\displaystyle\int \dfrac{x^2 + 4}{x^2 + 2x + 3}\,dx$ and $\displaystyle\int \dfrac{a^2 + b^2\cos^2 x}{\cos x}\,dx.$

5. Differentiate

$$\tan^{-1}\frac{bx - a}{ax + b};\quad \sin^{-1}\frac{3 + 4x}{5\sqrt{1 + x^2}};\quad \cos^{-1}\frac{1 - x^2}{1 + x^2}.$$

6. Prove that $\displaystyle\int_0^{\frac{\pi}{2}} \dfrac{dx}{1 + 2\cos x} = \dfrac{1}{\sqrt{3}}\log(2 + \sqrt{3}).$

7. The area of a curve is given by $A = y\sqrt{(25 + 4y)(4 - y)}$. Plot A against y on squared paper and hence obtain the maximum value of A and the value of y for which A is a maximum. Verify your results by the methods of the calculus.

8. Define the following types of functions, giving examples: Inverse function; Rational Integral function; Multiple-valued function; Algebraic function.

$$\phi(x) = \frac{a^x - a^{-x}}{a^x + a^{-x}}. \quad \text{Prove that} \quad \frac{\phi(x) + \phi(y)}{1 + \phi(x)\,\phi(y)} = \phi(x + y).$$

9. Prove that $\log(1 - x) + x(1 - x)^{-\frac{1}{2}}$ is positive for all values of x between o and unity.

10. A horizontal trough with vertical ends is of V-shaped cross-section, the angle between the sides being 60°, and the length of the trough 6 feet. If water enters at the rate of 4 cu. ft. per min., find the rate at which the surface is rising when the depth is 1 foot.

11. If m and n are positive integers, find by successive integration by parts the value of $\int_0^1 (1 - x^{\frac{1}{n}})^m \, dx$.

By expanding the integrand and integrating each term, deduce the value of the sum of the series

$$\frac{1}{n} - \frac{m_{(1)}}{n+1} + \frac{m_{(2)}}{n+2} - \frac{m_{(3)}}{n+3} + \dots + (-1)^m \frac{m_{(m)}}{n+m},$$

where $m_{(r)} \equiv m!/r! \, (m-r)!$.

12. If $\log \theta = n \log t - \dfrac{x^2 + y^2}{4t}$, find what value of n will make

$$\frac{\partial^2 \theta}{\partial x^2} + \frac{\partial^2 \theta}{\partial y^2} = \frac{\partial \theta}{\partial t}.$$

13. Transform the integral $\int_0^a x^2 (a^2 - x^2)^{\frac{1}{2}} \, dx$ by the substitution $x = a \cos \phi$; and find its value, explaining by reference to a diagram what are the new limits of integration.

14. A reservoir has plane sloping sides and ends; its top and base are horizontal rectangles of sides 24 ft., 16 ft. and 12 ft., 8 ft. respectively, and its depth is 40 ft. If water flows into it at the uniform rate of 30 cu. ft. per minute, at what rate is the surface rising when the depth of the water is 10 ft.?

15. Define a differential coefficient. If Δx is a finite increment, is it ever true that $\dfrac{\Delta y}{\Delta x}$ is equal to $\dfrac{dy}{dx}$?

If V be the volume of a regular polyhedron, and x the length of an edge, what is the meaning of $\dfrac{dV}{dx}$, and of $\dfrac{d^2V}{dx^2}$? Illustrate with a regular tetrahedron.

16. $u_1 = 3$; $u_2 = 44$; $\left(\dfrac{du}{dx}\right)_{x=1} = 25$; $\int_0^1 u_x \, dx = -\frac{11}{12}$. Find u_0.

17. Evaluate $\int_0^1 x^2 \tan^{-1} x \, dx$ and $\int_0^{\frac{\pi}{2}} \sin^4 x \, dx$.

18. If $x = \tan \phi - \phi$ and $y = \sec \phi$, prove that $\left(\dfrac{dy}{dx}\right)^4 + y^3 \left(\dfrac{d^2y}{dx^2}\right) = 0$.

19. Prove that $\int \dfrac{dx}{x\sqrt{x+a}} = \dfrac{2}{\sqrt{a}} \log \dfrac{\sqrt{x}}{\sqrt{x+a}+\sqrt{a}} + K$.

Hence prove that

$$\int \frac{(1+x^2)\,dx}{(1-x^2)\sqrt{1+x^4}} = \frac{1}{\sqrt{2}}\log\frac{\sqrt{1+x^4}+x\sqrt{2}}{1-x^2}+K.$$

20. Show that $x^2-2x+4\log(x+2)$ increases with x from $x=-2$ to $x=-1$, then diminishes from $x=-1$ to $x=0$ and then increases.

21. If n be a positive integer find the limit when $n\to\infty$ of

$$\left[\left(1+\frac{1}{n}\right)\left(1+\frac{2}{n}\right)\left(1+\frac{3}{n}\right)\dots\left(1+\frac{n}{n}\right)\right]^{1/n}.$$

22. Two straight roads meet at X at an angle of $\sin^{-1}\frac{3}{5}$. A is travelling in the direction of X along one of the roads at 40 miles an hour, and B is walking along the other road, also towards X, at the rate of 4 miles an hour. When A is 62 miles from X, B is 81 miles from X. Find their minimum distance apart.

23. Given $u_{-2}=4$, $u_0=6{\cdot}5$, $u_2=6{\cdot}3$, and that u_x has a maximum value when $x=1$, find an approximate value for u_1.

24. Find the value of $\int\dfrac{P\,dx}{1+e^x}$, where P has the values

    (i) 1;   (ii) e^x;   (iii) e^{2x};   (iv) e^{-x}.

25. If $x=y^3+3a^2y$ for real values of y, find by means of Maclaurin's theorem the expansion of y in powers of x as far as the term involving x^3.

26. Find the value of $\dfrac{d}{dt}\displaystyle\int_0^{\log t}e^{tx}\,dx$, where t is independent of x.

27. If $A=x/(2x+z)$ and $B=-A^2y/x$, prove that

$$\frac{\partial^2 A}{\partial z^2}=\frac{\partial^2 B}{\partial z\,\partial y}.$$

28. A person X walks along the diagonal of a square field $ABCD$ from B to D at the uniform rate of 5 feet per second. A second person Y proceeds along the side of the field from B to C at such a rate that the positions of X and Y at any moment lie on a straight line which, when produced, would pass through A. At what speed is Y moving when X has walked one-fourth of the distance from B to D?

29. Show that the infinite series $1-\frac{1}{5}+\frac{1}{7}-\frac{1}{11}+\frac{1}{13}-\frac{1}{17}+\dots$ can be expressed in the form

$$\int_0^1 \frac{1-x^4}{1-x^6}\,dx,$$

and hence deduce its value.

30. Integrate

$$\text{(i)} \int x \, (1+x)^{-\frac{1}{2}} \, dx; \qquad \text{(ii)} \int \frac{3 \sin x - 5 \cos x}{4 \sin x + \cos x} \, dx.$$

31. A closed circular cylinder of height h is to be inscribed in a given sphere of radius R. If the whole surface of the cylinder, including the base and the lid, is to be a maximum, prove that

$$\frac{h^2}{R^2} = 2 \left(1 - \frac{1}{\sqrt{5}} \right).$$

32. Show that $\dfrac{d}{dx} \{(1 + 1/x)^x\} = e/2x^2$ approximately, if x is large.

33. Show that

$$\frac{d^n}{dx^n} \left\{ \frac{\log x}{x^m} \right\} = \frac{(-1)^n \, n!}{(m-1)! \, x^{m+n}} \left\{ \frac{(m+n-1)!}{n!} \log x - \sum_{r=0}^{r=n-1} \frac{(m+r-1)!}{r! \, (n-r)} \right\}.$$

34. (i) If $K/(y-u) = Kv/(t-x) = (1+v^2)^{\frac{1}{2}}$, where $v = du/dt$ and K is a constant, find the differential coefficient of y with respect to x.

(ii) Given that $be^{x/a} = \sin(y/a - c)$, find the value of

$$Dy \, [1 + (Dy)^2]/D^2y.$$

35. Evaluate $\displaystyle \int x^3 \, (\log x)^2 \, dx$ and $\displaystyle \int \sin^2 x \cos^3 x \, dx.$

36. A thin closed rectangular box is to have one edge n times the length of another edge and the volume is to be V. Prove that the least surface S is given by

$$nS^3 = 54 \, (n+1)^2 \, V^2.$$

37. Prove that if the polar coordinates of two points on the curve $r = f(\theta)$ be (r_1, θ_1) and (r_2, θ_2), the area contained by the curve and the two radii r_1 and r_2 is $\frac{1}{2} \displaystyle\int_{\theta_1}^{\theta_2} r^2 \, d\theta.$

Hence prove that the whole area of the curve $r^2 = a^2 \cos 2\theta$ is a^2.

38. Integrate $\displaystyle \int \frac{dx}{\sqrt{k} + \sqrt{x}}$ according as

(i) k is a constant;

(ii) $k = x - a$, where a is independent of x;

(iii) $1/k = x$.

39. Evaluate $\quad \underset{x \to 0}{\text{Lt}} \dfrac{\log (1 + e^x) - \log 2 - \frac{1}{2}x}{x \log (x + \sqrt{1 + x^2})}$,

and find the limit of

$$\frac{\log x + \log y}{x + y - 2} \quad \text{when } x \text{ and } y \text{ each} \to 1.$$

40. Differentiate with respect to x:

$$x \sin^{-1} x \log ae/x + \sqrt{1 - x^2} \log a/x + \log \{x/(1 + \sqrt{1 - x^2})\}.$$

41. Prove that, if $y = \cos (m \cos^{-1} nx)$, then

$$(1 - n^2 x^2) \frac{d^2y}{dx^2} - n^2 x \frac{dy}{dx} + m^2 n^2 y = 0.$$

42. Prove that the limit of the series

$$\frac{n}{(n + 1) \sqrt{2n + 1}} + \frac{n}{(n + 2) \sqrt{2 (2n + 2)}} + \frac{n}{(n + 3) \sqrt{3 (2n + 3)}} + \dots$$
$$+ \frac{n}{2n \sqrt{n (3n)}}$$

when $n \to \infty$ is $\frac{1}{3}\pi$.

43. If $y^{1/p} + y^{-1/p} = 2x$, prove that

$$(x^2 - 1) D^{n+2} y + (2n + 1) x D^{n+1} y + (n^2 - p^2) D^n y = 0.$$

44. Prove that

$$\frac{d}{dx} \{x^{m-2} (1 - 2x^2)^{p+1}\} = Ax^{m-3} (1 - 2x^2)^p + Bx^{m-1} (1 - 2x^2)^p,$$

where A and B are constants.

Find A and B and hence show that $\int x^6 (1 - 2x^2)^{\frac{5}{2}} dx$ can be expressed in the form $aI - \{f(x).(1 - 2x^2)^{\frac{7}{2}}\}$, where $I \equiv \int (1 - 2x^2)^{\frac{5}{2}} dx$ and a is a constant.

45. (i) Find $\dfrac{d}{dx} (\sin^{-1} x . \log \cos x)$; and $\dfrac{d}{dx} (a^x + x^a)$, where $ax = 1 + x$.

(ii) If x has any positive value, prove that $x (e^{2x} + 1) - e^{2x} + 1$ is always positive.

46. If $u_x = a + br^x$, and $v_x = v_0 - \displaystyle\int_0^x (u_x v_x) dx$, show that $\log v_x$ can be written in the form $Au_x + Bx + C$.

47. Draw a graph of $y = 6 \cos x - \cos 3x$ for values of x between 0 and 2π. Find all the maximum and minimum values of y within this range.

48. If a_r is the coefficient of x^r in the expansion of $\sin (m \tan^{-1} x)$ in ascending powers of x, prove that

$$(n^2 + 3n + 2) a_{n+2} + (2n^2 + m^2) a_n + (n^2 - 3n + 2) a_{n-2} = 0.$$

49. Prove that the area enclosed by the curve

$$y^2 (b - x) = c^2 (x - a) \qquad (b > a)$$

and its asymptote is $\pi c (b - a)$.

50. Prove that if $f(x)$, a rational integral function of the third degree in x, has a maximum value when $x = x_1$ and a minimum value when $x = x_2$, then

$$\int_{x_1}^{x_2} f(x) \, dx = \tfrac{1}{2} (x_2 - x_1) \{ f(x_2) + f(x_1) \}.$$

51. Evaluate

$$\int_{\frac{1}{4}}^{\frac{1}{2}} x^{-2} (1 - x^2)^{-1} \, dx \quad \text{and} \quad \int \frac{dx}{\sin x + \sin 3x}.$$

52. Find the limit of $(ax + 1)^x (ax - 1)^{-x}$ as $x \to \infty$ and the limit of $[x^{\frac{1}{2}} - a^{\frac{1}{2}} + (x - a)^{\frac{1}{2}}] (x^2 - a^2)^{-\frac{1}{2}}$ as $x \to a$.

53. Interpret by means of a diagram the following expressions relating to the curve $y = f(x)$:

(i) $f(a) - af'(a)$;   (ii) $\dfrac{\{f(a)\}^2}{2f'(a)}$;   (iii) $af(a) - \displaystyle\int_0^a f(x) \, dx$.

54. If $y = \cos (a \cos^{-1} bx)$ obtain a differential equation connecting

$$y, \quad \frac{dy}{dx} \quad \text{and} \quad \frac{d^2y}{dx^2}.$$

55. Prove that for positive integral values of n

$$\int_0^{\frac{\pi}{2}} \cos^n x \, dx = \frac{(n-1)(n-3)\ldots 3 \cdot 1}{n(n-2)\ldots 4 \cdot 2} \cdot \frac{\pi}{2} \text{ if } n \text{ is even}$$

and
$$= \frac{(n-1)(n-3)\ldots 4 \cdot 2}{n(n-2)\ldots 3 \cdot 1} \text{ if } n \text{ is odd.}$$

56. Give two methods for evaluating integrals of the type

$$\int \frac{dx}{(x - k) \sqrt{a + bx + cx^2}} \qquad (c \text{ positive}).$$

Evaluate $\displaystyle\int (x - 2)^{-1} (x^2 + 2x + 3)^{-\frac{1}{2}} \, dx$.

57. Use Maclaurin's theorem to expand $\log(1+z)$ in ascending powers of z when z is numerically less than 1, giving the coefficient of z^n.

Obtain the coefficients of x^{3n-1}, x^{3n}, x^{3n+1} in the expansion of

$$\log(1 - x + x^2)$$

in ascending powers of x.

58. If
$$u_n = \int_0^{\frac{\pi}{2}} x^n \sin x \, dx,$$

prove that
$$u_n + n(n-1)u_{n-2} = n\left(\frac{\pi}{2}\right)^{n-1},$$

and hence find $\int_0^{\frac{\pi}{2}} x^3 \sin x \, dx$.

59. Find $x\dfrac{\partial u}{\partial x} + y\dfrac{\partial u}{\partial y}$ in the following cases:

(i) $u = xe^{-y}$,

(ii) $u = \sin^{-1}\{(x^2+y^2)^{\frac{1}{2}}(x+y)^{-1}\}$,

(iii) $u = \sin^{-1}\{(x+y)(x^{\frac{1}{3}}+y^{\frac{1}{3}})^{-1}\}$.

60. Given that u is a rational integral function of t of the third degree which vanishes when $t = 0$, complete the following table of u and its differential coefficients:

t	-1	0.5	2
u	-2		
$\dfrac{du}{dt}$		15.25	
$\dfrac{d^2u}{dt^2}$			
$\dfrac{d^3u}{dt^3}$			18

61. (i) Evaluate $\int x \cos^{-1} ax\, dx.$

(ii) Obtain a relation between
$$u_{m:n} \quad \text{and} \quad u_{m-2:n-1},$$
where
$$u_{r:s} = \int x^r (1+x^2)^{-s}\, dx.$$

62. If $x = \theta - \sin \theta$ and $y = 1 - \cos \theta$, express
$$\frac{d^2y}{dx^2} \quad \text{and} \quad \int \left\{ 1 + \left(\frac{dy}{dx}\right)^2 \right\}^{\frac{1}{2}} dx$$
as functions of y only.

63. (i) Prove that the straight line $\dfrac{x}{a} + \dfrac{y}{b} = 1$ touches the curve $y = be^{-\frac{x}{a}}$ at the point where the curve crosses the axis of y.

(ii) Find the equations to the tangents at the origin to the curve
$$(x^2 + y^2)^2 = x^2 - y^2.$$

64. Evaluate $\displaystyle\int_e^{e^2} y\,(1 - 24y^4)\, dx$, where $y \log x = 1$.

65. Express $\sec 4\theta$ in terms of $\tan \theta$. Hence or otherwise evaluate $\dfrac{d \sec 4\theta}{dt}$ in terms of t, where $t \equiv \tan \theta$.

66. Prove that

(i) $\displaystyle\int_0^{\frac{\pi}{2}} \sin^2 x \cos^3 x\, dx = \int_0^{\frac{\pi}{2}} \sin^3 x \cos^2 x\, dx = \frac{2}{15}$,

(ii) $\displaystyle\int_a^b (x-a)^2 (b-x)^3\, dx = \int_a^b (x-a)^3 (b-x)^2\, dx = \frac{(b-a)^6}{60}.$

67. It is given that the total surface area S and the volume V of a closed vessel in the shape of a right circular cone are
$$S = \pi h^2 (\tan^2 \alpha + \sec \alpha \tan \alpha),$$
$$V = \tfrac{1}{3}\pi h^3 \tan^2 \alpha,$$
where h is the height and α is the semivertical angle of the cone. Prove that, if the volume is given, the surface area is least when $\sin \alpha = 1/3$.

68. Water escapes through a small hole in the horizontal base of a rectangular tank which is initially full. It is assumed that the rate of efflux at each instant is proportional to the square root of the depth of water at that instant. If the tank is half emptied in 2 hours, calculate after how long it will be completely empty.

69. Prove that the area common to the ellipse $x^2 + 2y^2 = 2$ and the parabola $y^2 = 4x$ is equal to

$$\tfrac{2}{3}(\sqrt{2} - 1)^3 \sqrt{2\sqrt{2}} + \sqrt{2} \cos^{-1}(\sqrt{2} - 1)^2.$$

70. Show that, if $m < 1$,

$$\int_0^{\frac{\pi}{2}} \frac{d\theta}{\sqrt{m - \cos^2\theta}} = \frac{p\pi}{\sqrt{2}}\left\{1 + \frac{3p^4}{16} + \frac{105p^8}{1024} + \dots\right\},$$

where

$$p = 1/\sqrt{2m - 1}.$$

A point moves in such a way that the sum of its distances from two fixed points two inches apart is always four inches. Find to the nearest hundredth of an inch the average distance of the moving point from the centre of the straight line joining the two fixed points.

ANSWERS TO THE EXAMPLES

Examples 1.

1. $\frac{1}{2}, -\frac{\sqrt{3}}{2}, -\frac{1}{\sqrt{3}}; \frac{1}{\sqrt{2}}, -\frac{1}{\sqrt{2}}, -1; \frac{1}{2}, \frac{\sqrt{3}}{2}, \frac{1}{\sqrt{3}}; -\frac{1}{2}, -\frac{\sqrt{3}}{2}, \frac{1}{\sqrt{3}}.$

2. $\frac{5\pi}{6}, \frac{3\pi}{4}, \frac{25\pi}{6}, \frac{7\pi}{6}.$

4. (a) $\frac{\pi}{6}$; (b) $\frac{2\pi}{3}$; (c) $\frac{\pi}{16}$; (d) $\frac{\pi}{4}$; (e) o.

5. (a) $1\cdot008$; (b) $1\cdot006$; (c) $2\cdot233$.

7. (i) $n\pi + (-1)^n \frac{\pi}{4}$; (ii) $2n\pi \pm \frac{\pi}{3}$; (iii) $n\pi + 5\frac{\pi}{6}$; (iv) $n\pi + \frac{\pi}{4}$;
   (v) $n\pi + \frac{\pi}{4}$.

8. (i) $\frac{\pi}{2}$; (ii) $\frac{\pi}{2}$; (iii) $\frac{\pi}{2}$; (iv) 2π; (v) $\frac{2\pi}{3}$; (vi) $\frac{\pi}{4}$; (vii) 4π;
   (viii) $\frac{8\pi}{3}$; (ix) 2π; (x) $\frac{19\pi}{6}$.

9. (i) $\frac{\pi}{18}$; (ii) $\frac{\pi}{22}$; (iii) $\frac{\pi}{8}$; (iv) $\frac{5\pi}{2}$; (v) $(3n - \frac{1}{2})\frac{\pi}{7}$.

10. $-\cos\theta$; $-\sin\theta$; $-\tan\theta$; $\tan\theta$; $\operatorname{cosec}\theta$; $\operatorname{cosec}\theta$; $-\cot\theta$;
    $\sin\theta$; $\sin\theta$.

12. $\frac{56}{65}$; $\frac{13}{85}$; $\frac{19}{13\sqrt{5}}$; $\frac{29}{13\sqrt{5}}$; $\frac{240}{289}$; $\frac{3}{5}$; $\frac{56}{33}$; $\frac{2}{11}$; $-2\cdot45\ldots$; $-2\cdot1\ldots$.

33. $(4n + 1)\frac{\pi}{2}$ or $(2n + 3)\frac{\pi}{2} + \tan^{-1}\frac{20}{21}$.

34. $(2n - \frac{1}{4})\pi - a.$

35. $\pm \cos^{-1}\frac{3}{\sqrt{10}}.$

36. $n\pi + (-1)^n \sin^{-1}\left\{\frac{-1 \pm \sqrt{5}}{4}\right\}.$

37. $\frac{n\pi}{8}.$

38. Solving in the ordinary way, $x = 2$. On substitution, however, $x = 2$ gives a positive value to the left-hand side of the equation, whereas the right-hand side is apparently negative. The smallest positive value of $\tan^{-1}(-7)$ must therefore be taken to check this value.

39. $2n\pi \pm \frac{\pi}{2}$, $4n\pi \pm \pi$ or $\frac{1}{3}(4n\pi \pm \pi).$

40. $x = \frac{\pi}{4}.$

46. $\{\frac{1}{2}n + \frac{1}{12}\}\pi$ or $\{n - \frac{1}{6}\}\pi.$

48. $\pm\frac{\sqrt{3}}{2}.$

49. $a = \frac{1}{2}n\pi + (-1)^n \frac{1}{4}\pi$; $\beta = \frac{1}{2}n\pi + (-1)^n \frac{1}{12}\pi.$

50. $\dfrac{\sin\{a + \frac{1}{2}(n-1)\beta\}\sin\frac{1}{2}n\beta}{\sin\frac{1}{2}\beta}.$

Examples 2.

1. $\dfrac{p}{q}\,a^{p-q}$.   3. $\frac{1}{2}(\log a)^2$.   5. $\frac{1}{2}(a-k)$.   7. 0.

8. $\frac{1}{2}a^2$.   9. $\dfrac{2\sqrt{3}}{9}$.   10. $\frac{1}{2}$.   11. $-\frac{3}{2}$.

2. $\dfrac{a-b}{e\,(\log a - \log b)}$.   13. $\dfrac{m}{n}$.   14. 1.   15. $\dfrac{1}{\sqrt{2a}}$.

6. ∞.   17. 0.   20. $\frac{3}{4}$.

Examples 3.

5. $\sqrt{a^2-x^2}-\dfrac{x^2}{\sqrt{a^2-x^2}}$; $e^{x\log x}(\log x + 1)$.

6. $5x^4$; $an(ax+b)^{n-1}$; $x^x(1+\log x)$.

7. $bn(a+bx)^{n-1}$; $na^{nx}\log a$; $2x/n\,(a^2+x^2)^{\frac{n-1}{n}}$; $\dfrac{1}{x}-\log a$.

8. $\dfrac{2(x^4-1)}{x^3}$; $x^{m-1}(1-x)^{n-1}(m-\overline{m+n}x)$; $x^{m-1}e^x(x+m)$;

   $x^{n-1}(1+n\log x)$.

9. $-\dfrac{\log_x a}{x\log_e x}$; $x(1+2\log x)$; $10^{10^x}(\log_e 10)^2\,10^x$; $\dfrac{1-\log x}{x^2}$.

10. $2\sin x\cos x$; $2\cos 2x$; $-3\cos^2 x\sin x$; $x\sec x(2+x\tan x)$.

11. $\dfrac{2x}{\sqrt{1-x^4}}$; $\dfrac{\sin x + x\cos x}{2\sqrt{x\sin x}}$; $\sec^2 x\tan 2x + 2\sec^2 2x\tan x$.

12. $\cos^{-1} x - \dfrac{x}{\sqrt{1-x^2}}$; $2x\tan^{-1} x + \dfrac{x^2}{1+x^2}$;

   $\cos x\,(\tan^{-1} x)^2 + \dfrac{2\sin x\tan^{-1} x}{1+x^2}$.

13. $(5+4x)^{\log x}\left\{\dfrac{1}{x}\log(5+4x)+\dfrac{4}{5+4x}\log x\right\}$;

   $\dfrac{-mx^{m-1}}{\sqrt{1-x^2}\{1-\sqrt{1-x^2}\}^m}$; $\dfrac{1}{x\log x}$.

14. $a^x\log a + ax^{a-1}$; $x^x(1+\log x)-2mx(1-x^2)^{m-1}$;

   $x^{x^n}x^{n-1}(n\log x + 1)$.

15. $\dfrac{3(1-4x^2)}{(1+x^2)(1+16x^2)}$; $\dfrac{3}{2}\sqrt{x}\,\sqrt{\cos^{-1} x}-\dfrac{1}{2}\dfrac{x\sqrt{x}}{\sqrt{1-x^2}\,\sqrt{\cos^{-1} x}}$.

18. $\dfrac{y^2}{x-xy\log x}$.   19. $\dfrac{1}{x}-\dfrac{1}{e^x-1}$.   20. $\frac{5}{8}$ feet per second.

21. (i) $\dfrac{x^4-2a^2x^2+4a^4}{(x^2-a^2)^{\frac{3}{2}}(x^2-4a^2)^{\frac{1}{2}}}$; (ii) $\dfrac{na^{\frac{1}{2}}}{2x(a+bx^n)^{\frac{1}{2}}}$.

23. $-\dfrac{4x}{4x^4 + 1}\left\{\tan^{-1}\left(\dfrac{2x^2 + a}{2ax^2 - 1}\right)\right\}^{-1}$.

24. (i) $e^x x^{e^x}\left\{\log x + \dfrac{1}{x}\right\}$; (ii) $\left\{\log\dfrac{y}{1 + x} - \dfrac{x}{1 + x}\right\}\Big/\left\{1 - \dfrac{x}{y}\right\}$.

26. $3(\log x)^2\, x^{(\log x)^2}$.   **27.** $\frac{1}{2}$.

28. $\dfrac{2(1 - t^2)}{(1 + t^2)^2}$; $\dfrac{-4t}{(1 + t^2)^2}$; $\dfrac{8t(1 + t^2)}{(1 - t^2)^3}$; $\dfrac{2}{(1 + t^2)}$.

29. $\dfrac{1}{3}\dfrac{3a^2x^2 + 2ax^3 + x^4}{(a + x)(a^2 + x^2)(a^2 + ax + x^2)}$.

30. $\dfrac{1}{2x^2\log_e 10}$; $\dfrac{1 + \sqrt{1 - x^4}}{x^6}$.   **32.** $\dfrac{2e^x}{\sqrt{e^{2x} - a^2}}$.

33. $\dfrac{1 - 2xy}{x^2 + 3y^2 - 1}$.   **34.** (i) $\cot x$; (ii) $\dfrac{4}{1 + x^2}$.

35. $a_r = -\dfrac{n!}{(n - r)!}$.   **36.** $\dfrac{a}{2x^2}\cdot\dfrac{\sin a/x - \cos a/x}{1 + \sin a/x \cos a/x}$.

37. (i) $\dfrac{a}{y}$; (ii) $2y - \dfrac{c}{y}$.   **38.** $\dfrac{2x^4 + y^2}{x^3}$.

39. (i) $e^{x^x} x^x (1 + \log x)$; (ii) $\dfrac{e^{x^x} x^x (1 + \log x)}{e^x}$; (iii) e^{x^x}.

41. (i) $6c^2\dfrac{(ad - bc)}{(cx + d)^4}$; (ii) $\dfrac{11 - 6\log x}{x^4}$.

44. $4x^2 - 4x$.   **46.** $\dfrac{2\log a}{a}$.   **50.** o.

51. $(-1)^n n!\left\{\dfrac{pa + q}{(a - b)(a - c)}\cdot\dfrac{1}{(x - a)^{n+1}} + \dfrac{pb + q}{(b - c)(b - a)}\cdot\dfrac{1}{(x - b)^{n+1}}\right.$
$\left. + \dfrac{pc + q}{(c - a)(c - b)}\cdot\dfrac{1}{(x - c)^{n+1}}\right\}$.

52. $(-1)^n n!\left\{\dfrac{6}{(x - 2)^{n+1}} - \dfrac{2}{(x - 1)^{n+1}}\right\}$.

53. $\dfrac{(-1)^n n!}{c - d}\left\{\dfrac{(c - a)(c - b)}{(x - c)^{n+1}} - \dfrac{(d - a)(d - b)}{(x - d)^{n+1}}\right\}$.

54. $\dfrac{8}{(1 - x)^5} + \dfrac{256}{(1 + 2x)^5}$.

57. (i) $(-1)^{n-1}\dfrac{2(n - 3)!}{x^{n-2}}$; (ii) $(-1)^n n!\left\{\dfrac{5\cdot 3^n}{(3x + 1)^{n+1}} + \dfrac{1}{(x - 1)^{n+1}}\right\}$.

59. $a^{n+2} x^2 e^{ax}$.

60. $(-1)^n\dfrac{n!}{(b - a)^2}\left\{\dfrac{1}{(x - b)^{n+1}} - \dfrac{1}{(x - a)^{n+1}}\right\} - (-1)^n\dfrac{(n + 1)!}{(b - a)}\dfrac{1}{(x - a)^{n+2}}$.

70. $p = (\log s)^2$; $q = \log c \log g (\log cs^2)$; $r = (\log g \log c)^2$.

71. (i) $\dfrac{-\cos\theta}{\sqrt{\cos 2\theta - \operatorname{cosec}^2\theta \cos^2 2\theta}}$; (ii) $\dfrac{1}{2(1 + x^2)}$.

73. 3. **74.** (0, 0) and $(2a, -4a^3/3b^2)$.

75. (i) $(-2, 3)(-2, -1)$; (ii) $(1, 1)(-5, 1)$.

Examples 4.

2. $\log 2 + \dfrac{x}{2} + \dfrac{x^2}{8} - \dfrac{x^4}{192}\ldots$

3. $1 + x^2 - \dfrac{x^3}{2} + \dfrac{5x^4}{6}\ldots$

6. $1 + \dfrac{x}{2} - \dfrac{x^2}{12} + \dfrac{x^3}{24}\ldots$

7. $1 + 2x + \dfrac{3x^2}{2} + \dfrac{x^3}{6} + \dfrac{x^4}{12} + \dfrac{x^5}{40} + \dfrac{x^6}{720}\ldots$

9. $x - \dfrac{x^3}{3} + \dfrac{x^5}{5} - \dfrac{x^7}{7}\ldots$

10. $\dfrac{\pi}{4} + \dfrac{x}{2} + \dfrac{x^2}{4} - \dfrac{5x^3}{12}\ldots$

12. $-\frac{1}{45}$.

13. $1 + \dfrac{x}{3a} - \dfrac{x^3}{81a^3}\ldots$

14. $x - \frac{1}{6}x^3 + \frac{27}{40}x^5\ldots$

17. $-\frac{11}{24}$.

18. $1 + \frac{3}{2}x + \frac{11}{8}x^2 + \frac{23}{16}x^3\ldots$

20. $\dfrac{1}{e^x + 1} = \dfrac{1}{2} - \dfrac{x}{4} + \dfrac{x^3}{48} - \dfrac{x^5}{480}\ldots$

22. $px - \frac{1}{6}p(p^2 + 6)x^3 + \frac{1}{120}p(p^4 + 20p^2 + 60)x^5\ldots$

Examples 5.

1. Max. 1; Min. $-\frac{1}{11}$.

2. Max. $9a^3$; Min. $-\dfrac{5a^3}{3}$.

3. Max. 3; Min. $\frac{1}{3}$.

4. Max. $\frac{4}{27}, \frac{4}{27}$; Min. 0.

5. Max. 73; Min. $69, 69$.

6. Max. $\dfrac{2}{6^3}, \dfrac{2}{6^3}$; Min. $-\frac{1}{27}$.

7. Max. 13; Min. -10; Point of inflexion where $x = 0$.

8. Max. $\dfrac{2\sqrt{ab} + a + b}{2\sqrt{ab} - a - b}$; Min. $\dfrac{2\sqrt{ab} - a - b}{2\sqrt{ab} + a + b}$.

9. Max. $\frac{4}{27}$; Min. 0.

10. Max. $-2c\sqrt{ab}$; Min. $2c\sqrt{ab}$.

11. $\dfrac{a}{n}$.

12. Max. $4\frac{1}{3}$; Min. 3.

13. $207\cdot8$.

14. $e^{\frac{1}{e}}$.

16. $3 - 3\log_e 3$.

17. $a = -6$; $\beta = 9$.

18. 125 yards from A along AB and then across the grass to C.

19. $\dfrac{c^3}{6\sqrt{3}}$.

20. n parts.

21. $\frac{1}{6}\{(a + b) - \sqrt{a^2 - ab + b^2}\}$.

22. $(a^{\frac{2}{3}} + b^{\frac{2}{3}})^{\frac{3}{2}}$.

23. 66 minutes.

24. Max. $\dfrac{-c}{\sqrt{ab} - h}$; Min. $\dfrac{-c}{\sqrt{ab} + h}$.

27. $\dfrac{a}{\sqrt{\lambda^2 - 1}}$.

30. $2\sqrt{ab}$.

31. $\frac{1}{2}(a + b)^2$.

32. 165 feet.   **33.** $y = 2x^3 + \dfrac{3}{x^2}$.   **34.** Max. 2; Min. $\frac{8}{9}$.

35. Max. -6; Min. 2.   **36.** Max. 12; Min. -100, 8.

38. $x = 0$.   **39.** $\pm \dfrac{1}{\sqrt{2}}$.   **40.** $\pm \dfrac{1}{\sqrt{3}}$.

43. Max. $\frac{8}{9}$; Min. 0.   **44.** Max. 4·317; Min. 4·183.

45. Max. $\frac{10}{9}$; Min. $\frac{12}{5}$.   **46.** -5.   **47.** $(a + b)^2$.

Examples 6.

1. 0.   **2.** 0.   **3.** $\frac{1}{6}$.   **4.** $\log_b a$.

5. $\dfrac{m}{n}$.   **6.** $\dfrac{1}{\sqrt{2a}}$.   **7.** -1.   **8.** $\sqrt{\dfrac{m}{n}}\, a^{\frac{1}{2}(m-n)}$.

9. $\frac{3}{2}$.   **10.** 1.   **11.** 1.   **12.** $\dfrac{1}{n}$.

13. $\log_e a$.   **14.** $\dfrac{11e}{24}$.   **15.** 1.   **16.** $\frac{1}{80}$.

17. $\frac{1}{6}$.   **18.** $\dfrac{1}{2}\dfrac{b+a}{b-a}\log\dfrac{b}{a}$.   **20.** ∞.

21. $a = 120$; $b = 60$; $c = 180$.   **23.** 0.   **24.** 0.

25. $3u$.   **26.** $\frac{1}{20}u$.   **28.** $-\dfrac{x^2 + y}{y^2 + x}$.   **30.** $u - uy$.

Examples 7.

Note. In the answers to questions on indefinite integrals, the presence of the constant of integration is to be inferred.

2. $\dfrac{3x^{n+1}}{n+1}$; $\dfrac{x^{-n+1}}{3(-n+1)}$; $\frac{1}{2}e^{2x}$.

3. $\frac{1}{5}x^5 + \frac{2}{3}x^3 a^2 + xa^4$; $ax + \frac{1}{2}bx^2 + \frac{1}{3}cx^3$; $-\frac{1}{2}(1+x)^{-2}$.

4. $-\cos x$; $\sin x$; $-\cot x$.   **5.** $\dfrac{a^x}{\log_e a}$; $\dfrac{a^x}{\log_e a} + bx$; $\dfrac{a^x}{\log_e a} + \frac{1}{2}bx^2 + cx$.

6. $-\frac{1}{2}\cos 2x$; $\frac{1}{3}\sin 3x$; $\frac{1}{4}\tan 4x$.

7. $\log(x+1)$; $\dfrac{1}{1-x}$; $-\dfrac{1}{12}\cdot\dfrac{1}{(a+3x)^4}$.

8. $3\log x + \dfrac{2}{x}$; $-\left[\dfrac{a}{(n-3)x^{n-3}} + \dfrac{b}{(n-2)x^{n-2}} + \dfrac{c}{(n-1)x^{n-1}}\right]$.

9. $\frac{1}{2}\log\dfrac{x-1}{x+1}$; $\log x - \tan^{-1}x$.

10. $a\sin^{-1}x$; $\dfrac{1}{a}\sin^{-1}ax$.   **11.** $\frac{1}{12}\sin 3x + \frac{1}{4}\sin x$.

12. $-\left[\dfrac{1}{(n-3)\,y^{n-3}} - \dfrac{2}{(n-2)\,y^{n-2}} + \dfrac{1}{(n-1)\,y^{n-1}}\right];$

$-\left[\dfrac{1}{(n-3)\,(1+x)^{n-3}} - \dfrac{2}{(n-2)\,(1+x)^{n-2}} + \dfrac{1}{(n-1)\,(1+x)^{n-1}}\right].$

13. $\dfrac{1}{m}\displaystyle\int_{1}^{1+m}\dfrac{dy}{y}.$ **14.** $\displaystyle\int_{0}^{1}\dfrac{dx}{1+x^2}.$ **15.** $\log\left\{\dfrac{\sqrt{x^2-2x}}{x-1}\right\}.$

16. $-\log(1-x) - \tan^{-1}x.$ **17.** $\tfrac{1}{4}\log\dfrac{1+x}{1-x} - \dfrac{1}{2\,(1+x)}.$

23. $e^x + ax^2 + bx + c.$ **25.** $\dfrac{11a}{6}.$

26. $l_x = ke^{-Ax-Bc^x/\log_e c}.$ **27.** $\tfrac{1}{2}\log\dfrac{1+t}{1-t}.$ **28.** $\log\dfrac{1}{1-x^4}.$

Examples 8.

Note. In the answers to questions on indefinite integrals, the presence of the constant of integration is to be inferred.

1. $\dfrac{1}{n-1}\cdot\dfrac{1}{(1+x)^{n-1}} + \dfrac{2}{n-2}\cdot\dfrac{1}{(1+x)^{n-2}} - \dfrac{1}{n-3}\cdot\dfrac{1}{(1+x)^{n-3}};\ 2\sqrt{x}+\dfrac{4}{\sqrt{x}};$

$\tfrac{2}{3}(x-1)(x+2)^{\frac{1}{2}}.$

2. $2\log(x-3) - \log(x-1);\ 3x + 11\log(x-2) - 2\log(x-1);$

$\dfrac{2\sqrt{x-1}}{35}(5x^3 + 6x^2 + 8x + 16).$

3. $\dfrac{1}{4a^2}\log\dfrac{x^2-a^2}{x^2+a^2};\ -\dfrac{1}{x-1} + \tfrac{1}{2}\log\dfrac{x-1}{x+3}.$

4. $\tfrac{1}{4}\log(3 + 4\sin x);\ \log(4x^2 + 3);\ \log(e^x + \cos x).$

5. $\sin^{-1}\dfrac{2x+1}{3};\ \log(x + \tfrac{1}{2} + \sqrt{2 + x + x^2}).$

6. $-3\log\{\tfrac{1}{2} + \tfrac{1}{3}\cos x\};\ \tfrac{1}{6}\log\dfrac{1 + x + x^2}{(1-x)^2} + \dfrac{1}{\sqrt{3}}\tan^{-1}\dfrac{2x+1}{\sqrt{3}}.$

7. $\log\sqrt{\dfrac{x^2 - x + 1}{x^2 + x + 1}};\ \dfrac{1}{6a^3}\log\dfrac{x^3 - a^3}{x^3 + a^3}.$

8. $\sqrt{1 + x^2};\ \tfrac{1}{8}\log(4x^2 + 3) + \dfrac{2}{\sqrt{3}}\tan^{-1}\dfrac{2x}{\sqrt{3}}.$

9. $\tfrac{1}{2}\{\cos x - \tfrac{1}{5}\cos 5x\};\ \sin\tfrac{1}{2}x + \tfrac{1}{3}\sin\tfrac{3}{2}x.$

10. $\tfrac{1}{3}(x^2 - 2a^2)\sqrt{a^2 + x^2};\ \dfrac{1}{n}\log\dfrac{\sqrt{1 + x^n} - 1}{\sqrt{1 + x^n} + 1}.$

11. $\dfrac{1}{2k}\log\dfrac{cx + b - k}{cx + b + k}$ or $\dfrac{1}{k}\tan^{-1}\dfrac{cx + b}{k}.$ **12.** $-\dfrac{1}{2}\sqrt{\dfrac{2 + x^2}{x^2}}.$

13. (i) $\sqrt{x^2-1}$;   (ii) $\frac{1}{2}\{x\sqrt{x^2-1}+\log(x+\sqrt{x^2-1})\}$;
(iii) $\frac{1}{3}(x^2-1)^{\frac{3}{2}}+\sqrt{x^2-1}$.

14. $-\frac{3}{2}\log(x-1)-\dfrac{5}{2(x-1)}-\dfrac{1}{2(x-1)^2}-\tan^{-1}x+\frac{1}{4}\log(1+x^2)$.

15. $\log t$; t; $\log\dfrac{t}{1-t^2}$.   **16.** $\frac{1}{2}x^2\log x-\frac{1}{4}x^2$; $\dfrac{e^{ax}}{a^3}(2-2ax+a^2x^2)$.

17. $e^x(x^2-2x+2)$; $\frac{1}{3}(x^3\log x-\frac{1}{3}x^3)$.

18. $\sin x-x\cos x$; $x^3\sin x+3x^2\cos x-6x\sin x-6\cos x$.

19. $\frac{1}{2}\{(x^2+1)\tan^{-1}x-x\}$; $e^x/(x+1)$.

20. $e^{ax}(a\cos bx+b\sin bx)/(a^2+b^2)$.

21. $\frac{1}{2}\log(2x+\sqrt{4x^2-7})$.   **22.** $\log\tan(\frac{1}{4}\pi+\frac{1}{2}x)$.

23. $-\frac{1}{2}\{\log(1-x)\}^2$.   **24.** $\log x\{\log(\log x)-1\}$.

25. $\dfrac{x(3a^2+2x^2)}{3a^4(a^2+x^2)^{\frac{3}{2}}}$.   **26.** $\dfrac{(x^2+2bx+c)^{n+1}}{2(n+1)}$.

27. $\dfrac{1}{\sqrt{3}}\{\log(6x+1)+2\sqrt{3}\sqrt{3x^2+x+8}\}$.

28. $x-\log_e(1+c^x)/\log_e c$.

29. $\log\sqrt{x^2+x+1}+\dfrac{1}{\sqrt{3}}\tan^{-1}\{(2x+1)/\sqrt{3}\}$.

30. $\sqrt{5+2x+x^2}-\log(1+x+\sqrt{5+2x+x^2})$.

31. $\log x-\frac{1}{3}\log(1+x^3)$.   **32.** $\frac{1}{20}\tan^{-1}(\frac{5}{4}\tan\frac{1}{2}x)$.

33. $\dfrac{1}{\sqrt{2}}\log\dfrac{x-\sqrt{2}+\sqrt{1+x^2}+1}{x+\sqrt{2}+\sqrt{1+x^2}+1}$.   **34.** $-\dfrac{1}{\sqrt{3}}\sin^{-1}\dfrac{3-x}{2x}$.

35. $-\dfrac{1}{\sqrt{2}}\log\{x+4+2\sqrt{2}\sqrt{2+x-x^2}\}+\dfrac{1}{\sqrt{2}}\log x$.

36. $\dfrac{1}{2(a-b)}\log\dfrac{\sec^2 x}{a+b\tan^2 x}$.   **37.** $a\sin^{-1}(x/a)-\sqrt{a^2-x^2}$.

38. $\dfrac{2}{3a}\{(x+a)^{\frac{3}{2}}-x^{\frac{3}{2}}\}$.   **39.** $\frac{1}{25}\{3x-4\log(4\cos x+3\sin x)\}$.

40. $\dfrac{1}{\sqrt{a^2+ab}}\tan^{-1}\left\{\dfrac{\sqrt{a}}{\sqrt{a+b}}\tan x\right\}$.

42. (a) $y(\log y-1)$;   (b) $y\cos^{-1}y-\sqrt{1-y^2}$.

43. $-\frac{1}{4}(2x^2+1)/(x^2+1)^2+$ a constant.   **45.** $\frac{1}{2}\tan^{-1}x^2$.

46. $\log(x+\sqrt{x^2-1})-\sec^{-1}x$.   **47.** $\dfrac{2}{\sqrt{a^2-b^2}}\tan^{-1}\left\{\dfrac{\sqrt{a-b}}{\sqrt{a+b}}\tan\frac{1}{2}x\right\}$.

48. $-\frac{1}{3}(a^2+x^2)^{-\frac{3}{2}}(2a^2+3x^2)$.   **49.** $e^{qx}(x/q-1/q^2)$.

50. $I_m = \dfrac{1}{(2 - 2m)\, a^2}\, \dfrac{x}{(x^2 - a^2)^{m-1}} - \dfrac{3 - 2m}{(2 - 2m)\, a^2}\, I_{m-1};$

$\quad - \dfrac{1}{2a^2}\, \dfrac{x}{x^2 - a^2} - \dfrac{1}{4a^3} \log \dfrac{x - a}{x + a}.$

51. $\frac{1}{4} x^4 (\log x)^2 - \frac{1}{8} x^4 \log x + \frac{1}{32} x^4.$

53. $- \frac{1}{2} \{a (a - x) \sqrt{2ax - x^2} + a^3 \sin^{-1} (a - x)/a\} - \frac{1}{3} (2ax - x^2)^{\frac{3}{2}}.$

54. $\dfrac{1}{\sin (a - b)} \log \dfrac{\sin (x - a)}{\sin (x - b)}.$

55. $\frac{1}{3} x^3 \sin^{-1} x + \frac{1}{9} (2 + x^2) \sqrt{1 - x^2}.$ **56.** $\tan^{-1} (- \cos 2\theta).$

57. $\dfrac{1}{4} \left\{ \tan^{-1} \sqrt{\dfrac{x - 2}{3 - x}} - (5 - 2x) \sqrt{(x - 2)(3 - x)} \right\}.$

58. $ke^{-Ax} x^{pc^x},$ where $p \equiv - B/\log c.$

59. $\log x - \log \{(x + 1) + \sqrt{3x^2 + 2x + 1}\}.$

60. $\frac{1}{2} \log \tan \frac{1}{2} x - \dfrac{\cos x}{2 \sin^2 x}.$ **61.** $\dfrac{9}{\sqrt{2}} \tan^{-1} \left(\dfrac{1}{\sqrt{2}} \tan x \right) - x.$

62. $- \dfrac{2x^2 + 1}{4 (x^2 + 1)^2}.$ **63.** $\dfrac{\sqrt{x^4 + x^2 + 1}}{x}.$

65. $\frac{1}{16} z^{-\frac{2}{3}} - \frac{1}{4} z^{\frac{1}{3}} - \frac{1}{32} z^{\frac{4}{3}},$ where $z \equiv (2 - x^3)/x^3.$

66. $\frac{2}{5} (2 + x^{-\frac{2}{4}})^{\frac{5}{2}} - \frac{1}{3} (2 + x^{-\frac{2}{4}})^{\frac{3}{2}}.$

67. $6 (\frac{1}{9} z^9 - \frac{1}{8} z^8 + \frac{1}{7} z^7 - \frac{1}{6} z^6 + \frac{1}{5} z^5 - \frac{1}{4} z^4),$ where $z \equiv (x + 1)^{\frac{1}{6}}.$

68. $\frac{1}{2} \sqrt{a - b} \left(t + \dfrac{1}{3t^3} \right).$

69. $- \dfrac{1}{a^4 n} (\log z + 3bz^{-1} - \frac{3}{2} b^2 z^{-2} + \frac{1}{3} b^3 z^{-3}).$

$\quad$ where $z \equiv ax^{-n} + b.$

70. $\frac{1}{24} \log \{(x^4 - 1)^2/(x^8 + x^4 + 1)\} + \dfrac{1}{4 \sqrt{3}} \tan^{-1} \{(2x^4 + 1)/\sqrt{3}\}.$

71. $\dfrac{1}{\sqrt{3}} \cos^{-1} \left(\dfrac{1 + 2 \cos \theta}{2 + \cos \theta} \right).$

Examples 9.

2. $n^{n+1}/(n + 1);$ $12a + 41\frac{1}{3} b.$

3. $(1 - e^{-a^2 k})/a^2;$ $2 [5^{\frac{1}{2}(m+n+2)} - (- 5)^{\frac{1}{2}(m+n+2)}]/(m + n + 2).$

4. $1 - \dfrac{1}{\sqrt{2}};$ $\frac{1}{4} \pi - \frac{1}{2} \log 2.$ **5.** $\log \frac{81}{80};$ $2 - \frac{3}{2} \log 3 + \pi/6 \sqrt{3}.$

6. $\frac{2}{27} \log 2 + \frac{13}{72};$ $\pi/\sqrt{3}.$ **7.** $\frac{4}{3} \sqrt{a} (\sqrt{2} - 1);$ $\sqrt{2} - 1.$

8. $3\pi/16;$ $\pi/15.$ **9.** $\frac{1}{324};$ $\frac{32}{3003}.$

10. $\frac{1}{2} (b^2 \log b - a^2 \log a) - \frac{1}{4} (b^2 - a^2);$ $\frac{1}{2} (e^{\frac{\pi}{2}} + e^{-\frac{\pi}{2}}).$

11. $\pi - 2$; $- 26e^{-\frac{1}{2}} + 16$. **13.** $\frac{1}{2}\log \frac{5}{4}$.

15. $\frac{1}{4}(b - a - 1)(3b - 3a - 1) - \frac{1}{2}(a - b)^2 \log (b - a)$. **16.** $3\pi/16$.

18. $\frac{1}{2}\log 2 - \frac{1}{4}$. **19.** $e^2 \log 2$. **24.** $\log \frac{3}{2} - \frac{5}{8}$.

26. $\frac{1}{2} + \frac{1}{8}\log \frac{5}{17} + \frac{1}{6}\tan^{-1}\frac{9}{7}$. **28.** $36a^2$.

29. $\frac{4}{3}a^2 (c^3 - b^3)$. **30.** $\frac{8}{15}$. **31.** $8a^2/3$. **32.** $\frac{32}{105}$.

33. $\frac{1}{2}(e^9 - e^{-9})$. **34.** $24\sqrt{3}/5$. **35.** $1 - \log \frac{3}{2}$.

36. $(8\pi/3 - 3\sqrt{3})\,a^2$; $(4\pi/3 + 3\sqrt{3})\,a^2$. **37.** 4π.

39. $16a^2/3$. **40.** $\frac{2}{3}(2^{\frac{3}{2}} - 1) - \log 2$; $\frac{2}{3}(2^{\frac{3}{2}} + 1) + \log 2$.

41. $- \dfrac{1}{\sqrt{x^2 + a^2}\,(x + \sqrt{x^2 + a^2})}$. **42.** $\dfrac{\pi (a - \sin a \cos a)}{\sin^3 a}$.

44. $n!/a^{n+1}$; $\pi \log (a + 1)$. **45.** $y = \frac{1}{2}a \sin^{-1}\sqrt{2x/a} + \frac{1}{2}\sqrt{2ax - 4x^2}$.

47. $3\sqrt{2}/8 + \frac{7}{8}\log (\sqrt{2} + 1)$.

49. $x^2\left\{\dfrac{1}{\sqrt{2}} + \frac{1}{2}\log (1 + \sqrt{2})\right\}$; $\dfrac{1}{3}\left\{\dfrac{1}{\sqrt{2}} + \frac{1}{2}\log (1 + \sqrt{2})\right\}$. **50.** $\frac{1}{3}a^2$.

Miscellaneous Examples.

1. Max. $\frac{1}{2}$; Min. $- \frac{1}{2}$; Area $\frac{4}{3}$.

2. (i) $\dfrac{2}{3}\left(1 - \dfrac{a}{x^2}\right)\left(x + \dfrac{a}{x}\right)^{-\frac{1}{3}}$; (ii) $\dfrac{1}{\sqrt{(1 - x^2)\{1 - (\sin^{-1} x)^2\}}}$.

3. (i) 1; (ii) $\frac{1}{2}$.

4. $x - \log(x^2 + 2x + 3) + \dfrac{3}{\sqrt{2}}\tan^{-1}\dfrac{x + 1}{\sqrt{2}}$; $a^2\log \tan(\frac{1}{4}\pi + \frac{1}{2}x) + b^2 \sin x$.

5. $\dfrac{1}{1 + x^2}$; $\dfrac{1}{1 + x^2}$; $\dfrac{2}{1 + x^2}$. **7.** $A = 18$, $y = 2\cdot8$.

10. $0\cdot577\ldots$ ft. per min. **11.** $\dfrac{m!\,n!}{(m + n)!}$; $\dfrac{m!\,(n - 1)!}{(m + n)!}$.

12. $- 1$. **13.** $\dfrac{\pi a^4}{16}$. **14.** $\frac{1}{8}$ ft. per min.

16. $- 12$. **17.** $\dfrac{\pi}{12} + \frac{1}{6}\log 2 - \frac{1}{4}$; $\dfrac{3\pi}{16}$.

21. $4e^{-1}$. **22.** $48\cdot68\ldots$ miles. **23.** $7\cdot04\ldots$

24. (i) $x - \log (1 + e^x)$; (ii) $\log (1 + e^x)$; (iii) $e^x - \log (1 + e^x)$;
(iv) $\log (1 + e^x) - x - e^{-x}$.

25. $\dfrac{x}{3a^2} - \dfrac{x^3}{81a^8} \ldots$ **26.** $\dfrac{1}{t^2}\{t^{t+1}(\log t + 1) - t^t + 1\}$.

28. $\dfrac{40\sqrt{2}}{9}$ ft. per sec.   **29.** $\dfrac{\pi}{2\sqrt{3}}$.

30. (i) $\tfrac{3}{10}(2x-3)(1+x)^{\frac{3}{2}}$;   (ii) $\tfrac{1}{17}[7x-23\log(4\sin x+\cos x)]$.

34. (i) v;   (ii) a.

35. $\dfrac{x^4}{4}\{\tfrac{1}{8}+(\log x)^2-\tfrac{1}{2}\log x\}$; $\tfrac{1}{3}\sin^3 x-\tfrac{1}{5}\sin^5 x$.

38. (i) $2\sqrt{x}-2\sqrt{k}\log\{\sqrt{k}+\sqrt{x}\}$;   (ii) $\dfrac{2}{3a}\{x^{\frac{3}{2}}-(x-a)^{\frac{3}{2}}\}$;

   (iii) $2\sqrt{x}-2\tan^{-1}\sqrt{x}$.

39. $\tfrac{1}{8}$; 1.   **40.** $\sin^{-1}x\log\left(\dfrac{a}{x}\right)+\dfrac{2x}{\sqrt{1-x^2}}$.

45. (i) $\dfrac{1}{\sqrt{1-x^2}}\log\cos x-\sin^{-1}x\tan x$;

   $a^{x-1}+a^x(\log a-1)+x^{a-2}(ax-\log x)$.

47. Max. $-5,\ 3\sqrt{3},\ 3\sqrt{3}$; Min. $-3\sqrt{3},\ 5,\ -3\sqrt{3},\ 5$.

51. $\tfrac{1}{2}\{1+\log\tfrac{5}{3}\}$; $\tfrac{1}{4}\left\{\sec x-\log\cot\dfrac{x}{2}\right\}$.

52. $e^{2/a}$; $(2a)^{-\frac{1}{4}}$.   **54.** $(1-b^2x^2)\dfrac{d^2y}{dx^2}-b^2x\dfrac{dy}{dx}+a^2b^2y=0$.

56. $-\dfrac{1}{\sqrt{11}}[\log\{(3x+5)+\sqrt{x^2+2x+3}\}-\log(x-2)]$.

57. $\dfrac{1}{3n-1}$; $\dfrac{1}{3n}[1-3(-1)^{n-1}]$; $\dfrac{1}{3n+1}$.   **58.** $\tfrac{3}{4}\pi^2-6$.

59. (i) $u-uy$;   (ii) 0;   (iii) $\tfrac{1}{2}\tan u$.

60. The missing values are: t, $5\cdot125$ and 64; $\dfrac{du}{dt}$, 1 and 70; $\dfrac{d^2u}{dt^2}$, -4, 23

   and 50; $\dfrac{d^3u}{dt^3}$, 18 and 18.

61. (i) $\dfrac{1}{4a^2}\{(2a^2x^2-1)\cos^{-1}ax-ax\sqrt{1-a^2x^2}\}$;

   (ii) $u_{m-2:n-1}=\dfrac{1}{m-1}\left\{\dfrac{x^{m-1}}{(1+x^2)^{n-1}}+2(n-1)u_{m:n}\right\}$.

62. $-\dfrac{1}{y^2}$; $-4\sqrt{1-\tfrac{1}{2}y}$.

63. (ii) $y=\pm x$.   **64.** $\dfrac{11e^2}{8}-10e$.

65. $\dfrac{1+2\tan^2\theta+\tan^4\theta}{1-6\tan^2\theta+\tan^4\theta}$; $\dfrac{16t(1-t^4)}{(1-6t^2+t^4)^2}$.

68. After another $4\cdot8$ hr. approx.   **70.** $1\cdot85$ in.

INDEX

The numbers refer to the pages

Printed in the United States
By Bookmasters